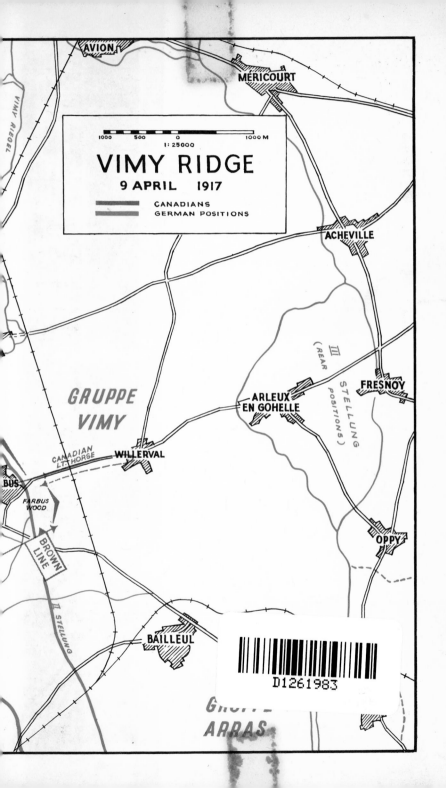

VIMY RIDGE

9 APRIL 1917

1000   500   0   1000 M
1 : 25000

CANADIANS
GERMAN POSITIONS

AVION

MERICOURT

ACHEVILLE

VIMY RIEGEL

GRUPPE

VIMY

FRESNOY

ARLEUX
EN GOHELLE

III
(REAR)

STELLUNG
(REAR POSITIONS)

CANADIAN
LT. HORSE

WILLERVAL

BUS

FARBUS
WOOD

BROWN
LINE

II STELLUNG

OPPY

BAILLEUL

GRUPPE
ARRAS

The Battle of Vimy Ridge

The Battle of

Vimy Ridge

ALEXANDER McKEE

5D STEIN AND DAY/*Publishers*/New York

Also by
Alexander McKee

THE COAL-SCUTTLE BRIGADE
BLACK SATURDAY
STRIKE FROM THE SKY
THE GOLDEN WRECK
THE FRIENDLESS SKY
FROM MERCILESS INVADERS
CAEN : ANVIL OF VICTORY

First published in the United States of America by
Stein and Day, *Publishers*, 1967

Printed in the United States of America

Stein and Day/*Publishers*/7 East 48 Street, New York, N.Y. 10017

CONTENTS

5

CONTENTS

6

ILLUSTRATIONS

7

ILLUSTRATIONS

FOREWORD

As the turbo-prop whispered in towards the Belgian coast, the water turned from green to blue. For many miles out from shore, the sandbanks stretched, barely covered. The dreaded ' banks of Dunkirk ', onto which the English Admirals had nearly driven the whole Armada in 1588; there would be some half-a-dozen Spanish wrecks down there still, off Nieuport, Blankenberg, Ostend. Here, in the ' cockpit of Europe ', history was compressed into a very small space. As the coast between La Panne and Dunkirk slid beneath the port engines, it was not hard to visualise the black smoke of the oil-fires and the stukas peeling off like shot birds towards the ships waiting out beyond the banks and the little, crowded boats going out to them from the beaches. Here, too, four years later, the firing sites of the first blind, ' push-button ' weapons had been over-run in the break-out from Normandy and it was the turn of the German garrison of Dunkirk to be beleaguered.

From the coast to Brussels was twenty minutes' flying time. In perhaps five minutes the dunes had given way to soggy, water-logged land intersected by a green, meandering river—was it the Lys? In that time we had passed from 1944 to 1914-18. These were the blood-soaked battlefields of the First World War, the network of trench-lines stretching right across Europe, in which Europe began to perish. Higher than Immelmann's Fokker or the red Albatros of Richthofen, we whispered swiftly across the same sky.

The rain-clouds began as we started the let-down into the Brussels circuit, masking with grey mist the century we had jumped in a quarter-of-an-hour. The village of Waterloo, and the six fields or so outside in which the battle had been fought, were indistinguishable from less momentous earth. And gone now, no doubt, the German S.P. gun which had been knocked out there in 1944. The time-clock jumped another century, from Wellington to Marlborough, as the train to Ypres roared without stopping through a minor country station called Oudenarde. That was nearer home, for the victory there had taken Marlborough's forces up to the outskirts of Arras, by Vimy Ridge, and that was my objective.

The final link fell into place when I walked up to the hotel in Ypres where I was to rendezvous with a party from the Canadian Veterans' Association of the United Kingdom in order to visit the Vimy battlefield next day, and be shown over it by men who had fought there in 1917. It turned out to be in the main street, almost directly opposite the rebuilt Cloth Hall, and a hundred yards from the Menin Gate, which is built into the massive ramparts raised by the Spaniards, in the time of Elizabeth the dominant military nation of Europe. I realised that I had passed through that street once before, in a Canadian Army vehicle at thirty miles an hour. Now, I asked the hotel keepers if they had been there in September, 1944, too. Indeed, they had. " We thought you'd never come! What a time that was! "

It was near Ypres, with the signposts beginning to read ZONNEBEKE, DIKKEBUSCH, KEMMEL, YPER, MEENEN, that we had woken up to the fact that this was not just one more foreign town on the long road from Normandy. The incongruity of simply driving across the trench lines which had held our fathers for four years, had brought the decisive, self-centred and selfish reaction, ' Thank God I wasn't in that one '. The experience of the two generations had been of a totally different order, almost beyond analysis.

The outward symbols were clear. They were older by twenty years, wore their medals, and frequently re-visited their old battlefields in large parties. We did not bother to relive, except occasionally and privately a war which was only twenty years old; but what they were remembering had taken place nearly half a century before. It seemed incredible, and certainly their wives were not taking them seriously. " They're just little boys at heart, really," I was told too many times to mention. At this, the old men would stiffen and explain carefully that the purpose of these yearly visits to the battlefields was to do honour to the dead.

And, clearly, none of this was really true; or, at least, not adequate. The only reason forceful enough to explain it was that these men must have undergone together an experience so appalling that the bonds linking them were indissoluble. Such a tiny area of Europe, after all; holding the same ground, day after day until the days became years; and the old faces became dead faces, the new faces were blown away also; until those few who were left had common ground only among themselves. They were survivors. And those who had not endured, and survived— or, as it may be, died—were strangers. In that sense, perhaps it was true after all that they came here yearly to honour the dead.

The first view of the Ridge was from what had been the Canadian side, near Neuville St. Vaast. It was not an impressive feature, the upward slope in front was green and gentle; but if someone was shooting at you from the top, it would be different. But, come to that, the German front line trenches, on the Canadian side of the Ridge, would have been vulnerable to observed fire, too. The visit was not as valuable as it might have been, for none of the villages (in 1917 they were heavily fortified strongpoints) were visible one from another; groves of young trees, including specially planted Canadian pines, obstructed the view in almost all directions. It had not been so then, for the Ridge had been a desolation; the various woods, such as Farbus, existed no longer in fact but merely as names for localities on the military maps. They, like the villages, had been tornadoed out of existence. Vimy Ridge, as one awed and shocked war correspondent had put it, was not to be described as desolated ground, but literally as a " compost heap." The soil over the entire area, to a depth of many feet, had been shaken up and redistributed, was merely loose earth—or deep mud—mixed with the debris of years of battle, rusting equipment and decaying men.

It was true. Even now, nearly half a century and another war afterwards, the fresh carpet of spring grass could not conceal the fact that there was no level ground anywhere, but a stumbly, jumbled surface, with here and there the hint of a crater or original trench, now more like a shallow ditch than an earthwork. And no doubt that was truer to the facts of the time than where now, on the Ridge, the front-line trenches had been permanently preserved, complete with long-life concrete ' sandbags '. But the shock, for me, was the close proximity of the front-lines.

The most urgent reason for my visit was to grasp the actual
conditions of the time; so that I should not confuse them with
those of 1944/1945, when ranges were in many hundreds of yards
and there was a lightly held 'Forward Area' rather than lines
of trenches containing masses of men. This defensive concept
had in fact been evolved by the Germans at the time of the
Canadian assault on the Ridge, but to their undoing they had
not used it there, relying instead on the deep tunnels and dugouts they had excavated in the chalk. But to stand in what had
been the Canadian front line trench, then walk up a short sap
leading into No-man's-land, and to see the head of the opposing
German sap no more than fifty feet away, was still a shock. Here,
the opposing armies had lived almost in each other's pockets.
No wonder there had been at times a certain fellow feeling for
the enemy soldier; and, equally, little wonder that turning a
hole in the ground into a near-permanent home had led to a
compensating comradeship among the men who had endured
on these slopes.

The importance of the Ridge, militarily, was less easy to
understand when actually on it. It was far from being the only
height in the area, and it was not even the dominating one. That
was a looming distant spur, of which I asked the name.
" Lorette," was the reply. " Who held it at the time?" " We did,"
was the answer. Admittedly, from the highest part of the Ridge,
Point 145, which is now ceded to Canada in perpetuity and
where the Canadian Memorial now stands, there was reasonable
observation for many miles out over the plain to Douai and
Lille.

But the Germans had never insisted, as we had done, on sitting
uncomfortably at the foot of a height held by the enemy; they
prepared rearward defences at leisure and then fell back to
them, like the cold professionals they were. However, it was when
I took a taxi out over the plain, through what had been their
back areas before the Canadians stormed the Ridge, that the
full significance of Vimy became immediately apparent. Crowned
white by the monument, it ran along the horizon like a wave;
like the first breaker rolling on a shore. All the land behind,
then in Allied hands, had the same wave formation; possession
of Vimy meant complete domination of the plain, and that plain,

with its industries and coal mines, had been of importance to the blockaded Germany of the First World War.

But why did it mean so much more to Canadians than to anyone else? For the full answer to that, I had to contact many witnesses. Slow work, for they were in their sixties and seventies, and although some were still spry and active, all too many were in poor health. Correspondence was interrupted by bouts in hospital, and sometimes, alas, more finally. This was certainly the last chance to get any new first-hand material at all. And in recreating the story I had to think of them as they had been nearly fifty years before—young fit men, the elite of Canada formed into four formidable divisions. Storming Vimy Ridge in a snowstorm, without greatcoats, struggling through the mud to the top of that long, sinister hogsback of a hill, when the sun shone out and the dazed German defenders saw the summit alive with ' teller helmets ' and knew that their three-year fortress had fallen to the arms of Canada. The ' Easter Battle ', they called it, except that in the German tongue the word for ' battle ' is direct and unambiguous. What the English call a battlefield they call a ' Schlachtfeld '—a field of slaughter. And so it was, on that Easter Monday, 1917. And in the three years of failure which had gone before.

CHAPTER ONE

THEY'RE MOVING THE
FURNITURE AGAIN AT VIMY

1914 - 1916

Michael Volkheimer came to Vimy Ridge with Bavarian Reserve Infantry Regiment No. 3 in October, 1914. The grey-green columns came flooding forward across the plain from the northeast, just as Marlborough's red coats had done in 1710, and with the same objective. In the long term—Paris. But in the short term—Arras. That fortified town was the hub of a radius of roads, waterways, and railways situated at a gap in the hills under the Vimy height. It had been militarily important since Roman times, and continued to be so. " We met very severe opposition from the enemy, especially on the road through Lille and Lens to Arras," recollected Volkeimer. " Indeed, we were only just able to get on to the heights of Thelus, a hill of which Vimy Ridge is an extension to the north. That was in November, 1914, and it gave us a wide field of observation over Roclincourt, Ecurie, and the other suburbs of Arras which were still in French hands. Repeated attacks on our positions at Vimy—by French, English, and Canadian troops in turn—were unsuccessful until the time of the Easter Battle in 1917." In that final battle, Volkeimer's unit was driven out of Thelus and back onto the plain. As a German soldier, he did not return to Thelus for more than twenty years. Then, in June, 1940, after Major-General Erwin Rommel's 7th Panzer Division had driven through Arras and beyond, he found himself once again at Thelus, this time listening to a car radio which was broadcasting a running commentary from Paris, then being entered by German troops in parade order, bands playing victoriously.

The position of Arras was always precarious, with Vimy in German hands; likewise the German position on the Lens-Lille-Douai plain would be precarious, if the French could take the heights. The doctrine that the aggressive attack, forcefully pushed home, must overwhelm the numerically weaker side, regardless of technical considerations, was still held. Therefore, in the spring of 1915, the French attacked. They knew now that more than a few field guns were needed to blast a way for the infantry through machine-gun posts; but, unlike the Germans, the French had few heavy guns and insufficient ammunition for what they did have. It was impossible to assault the Ridge along its whole six-mile length simultaneously. The attack had to go in on a narrow front, against which all the superior German gunpower could be concentrated. Paradoxically, the very lack of adequate artillery support, by lending surprise, led to initial success. The French stormed the Lorette spur, which butts on to Vimy, and fought up the long slopes to the Ridge between Neuville St. Vaast and the Souchez valley. They struggled with desperate gallantry all through May and June; and again in September, October, and November. They gained Lorette and a part of the Vimy slope; but they did not get the crest two hundred feet above. And they paid for their gains with 150,000 men dead, wounded, or missing, proof enough that bravery was not enough.

But, in the French Army, as in the British, the staff were out of touch both with their men and with reality, and still fiercely believed—it was easy to be ferocious some miles behind the lines—in bayonets, bravado, and what they assumed to be the lessons learned by the Japanese Army in Manchuria ten years before. These appeared to prove that infantry, if sufficiently suicidally inclined, could prevail over rifle and machine-gun fire, even if almost wiped out in the process. Therefore, any failure must be a failing in determination on the part of the infantry, and certainly not a flaw in the appreciations of the staff. But, if more Resolution (on the part of the infantry) equalled Victory, then, equally, a failure of Resolution equalled Defeat. And this must not be. In the winter of 1915, the French High Command took drastic measures against the growing reluctance of their soldiers to commit hara-kiri in vain.

In November, the Fifth Battalion of the 63rd Infantry Regiment refused to follow their officers over the top in an attack, and General Deletoile had the entire Battalion court-martialled.

As a result, six soldiers were ordered to be shot for cowardice, and five actually were shot. But the real story did not emerge until 1934, nearly twenty years later, when the mothers of four of the men brought an action against the French Army in order to clear their name. At the subsequent trial, there was the extraordinary spectacle of their former C.O., Major Dubosc, supporting the men's refusal to obey his orders. The Battalion, he explained, had had a great fighting reputation; it had been wiped out no less than three times. In November, 1915, they had come out of battle shattered once more, and then, because a strongpoint had been lost, their exhausted and demoralised remnants had immediately been ordered back into the line to retake it. "It was a veritable charnel house," he testified. "There was not a yard of ground without the body of one of my heroes. When we were ordered to attack again, the officers left the trenches and advanced a few yards into No-man's-land under tremendous machine-gun fire. The men did not follow, and I cannot blame them, it would have been a hecatomb. I protested against this butchery at the time. Finally, I received the order to select one man per company. There were six companies, but only five men chosen by lot were shot, because Lieutenant Voulant, commanding the Fourth Company, with great courage refused point blank to carry out his orders."

A surviving company commander, Lieutenant Meinieux, then gave evidence. "I had nothing to reproach any one of my men more than another. My corporal gave me a hat with forty numbers. I drew out number seventeen. That was my poor Fontanaud." The five condemned men had refused unanimously to plead for mercy, because, they said, "It would only mean one of our comrades instead of us. It may as well be us as anyone else."

On the strategic as well as the tactical level there was a fatal flaw in the French and British staff appreciations. The battle of attrition they were waging, with superior Allied forces against inferior German forces, could be won quickly and decisively only if the losses of both sides were approximately equal; if that were so, then undoubtedly the Germans would crack first. But it was not so; the German losses were much less, and an important contributory factor in this was the tactical incompetence and conservatism of the Allied generals themselves. The results were very quickly seen. Instead of bleeding the German Army to death, the French were so weakened by their losses, which had brought them no gains in ground worth mentioning, that they were unable even to hold their front; and had to ask the British to take over part of their line, which included Arras and Vimy. This the British could still do, because, like the Americans later on, they had discovered that it took a long time to build up a great continental-scale army; in 1916, they still had man-power to spare.

When they took over that March, they found what had happened to the manpower of France: there were more dead Frenchmen in and around the trenches than there were live soldiers. The 5th Division took over the sector from Arras to the south-west slope of Vimy, overlooked by Thelus, and an officer of 15th Royal Warwickshire Regiment, Major C. A. Bill, has described the scene: " My company front was about 250 yards. The French, who had held this part until our Division came in, had evidently been through some severe fighting. In the rough grass just behind our front line I came across a long line of Zouaves who had been mown down like a swathe of corn while advancing in the open, and from the condition of the bodies they must have been lying out there for twelve months. It was no uncommon thing while repairing our trenches to find the re-mains of French troops buried in the parapet. I remember a small hole in the wall of one of the fire bays which actually was formed by the collar bones of a body, and one could look into the inside of the trunk. I went out one night to make a thorough inspection of the wire, and while crawling up to No-man's-land I saw a round whitish object which, by reason of something peculiar about its shape, piqued my curiosity. I stretched out my hand and with mixed feelings found I was grasping the bleached skull of some African soldier (presumably a Zouave) with the curly black hair adhering to it. I brought it in with me and piling some filled sandbags up in a corner of an unoccupied fire bay stuck the skull on top of them. It was a childish thing to do, and I received my punishment later when Anderson came bursting with indignation against the perpetrator of a low-down trick which had nearly startled his platoon sergeant out of his wits. Anyway, together we went down and hurled the offending relic back into the night."[1]

Mr. R. B. Raisin came to Vimy Ridge in March, 1916, as a soldier of the 5th Sherwood Foresters. As they marched along the Rue de Bethune they were halted for the hourly rest by a small tomb-like monument which marked the spot where the Count of Luxembourg had died of the wounds he had received from the English at the Battle of Agincourt in 1415, and some esprit-de-corps-conscious wag remarked, " So we've been here before, then!" (The affair came fuller circle in the Second World War, when Mr. Raisin, as War Office RQMS, issued the current Count of Luxembourg with his equipment!) As the British entered the rearward defence lines after dark they were greeted by French poilus waving bottles of wine and calling out, " Bon sante!" In daylight, they looked around them with interest.

The French rear dugouts were deep, sound, and luxurious compared to the miserable affairs the British had been used to on their own front; but the dugouts in the front line were just shelters with a few sandbags on top. This was because the French had more up-to-date ideas than the British. The historian of the Foresters wrote: " Their system of holding the front was very different from our own; they seemed to rely on the protection of their 75 mm guns, and only had sentries in the front line. Company commanders were empowered to requisition artillery direct, up to sixty rounds, which gave us the idea that their stock of shells was considerably greater than ours."[2] The idea of a lightly held forward area acting as a cushion between the enemy and the main ' Battle Zone', where the bulk of the troops were stationed, was being pondered by the Germans also, and, being sound policy, was virtually standard in the Second World War. In the First, however, the British insisted on packing the vulnerable forward area with men to act as targets for the enemy's superior artillery power, as part of a policy of ' aggression'.

" Vimy was a dirty place," recollected Mr. Raisin, " with the Germans overlooking our positions and running all their drain-

[1] *The 15th Battalion Royal Warwickshire Regiment in the Great War*, by Major C. A. Bill (Cornish Brothers Ltd., 1932).
[2] *The War History of the Fifth Battalion the Sherwood Foresters 1914-1918*, by L. W. de Grave (Bemrose, 1930).

age down onto us. In front of us was rising ground, with the shattered, tattered remnants of La Folie Wood. The earth above the chalk formation was heavy loam which made very sticky mud; it was difficult to keep dry, even in gum boots, and an ailment known as 'trench feet', needing hospital treatment, was a regular cause of casualties. Chloride of lime was used extensively to keep down the stench of decayed, rotting flesh. Bodies lay about here and there, very exposed from the poor, hasty burial. One rear trench was cut across the spot where a dead German lay about two feet below the parapet. He, or *it*, was jack-booted, with one jack-boot sticking out into the fairway, as it were; we always lingered there, shook the leg, and made comments such as 'Ta, ta, Jerry.' At another place, quite close to our dugout, lay another German almost fully exposed, and on his back. I remember the ghoulish battalion pioneers fiddling around the corpse for souvenirs, one man gleefully obtaining a ring from a finger (which came away with the ring). The thing was slightly bloated, held together only by the clothing. I can't remember seeing the face, only the uniform. The standard food carrier was a sandbag and to keep these safe from the depredations of rats, the sandbag would be suspended from the roof of the dugout. Nevertheless, I awoke one night with a rat on my chest, and I'll swear his whiskers tickled me into wakefulness. Food was rough and ready, with a minimum of that desirable commodity, bread, so emergency biscuits were issued. We experimented with these by soaking and cooking and placing in handkerchiefs to form a sort of pudding. I revolt at the memory. We rarely saw a live enemy, just a bit of something over a parapet. We held no opinion about them, except that we hated them; cursed them for our discomfort; fired at them with enthusiasm; and had no knowledge of them. It was a miserable existence. Trench feet, poor rations, continuous cold, no blankets when in the line. But, on coming out of the line, exhausted, the Regimental Band would turn out to meet us, and the weary men would respond to the stirring music in an unbelievable manner. For the last hundred yards, when the Regimental march past was played, arms would be sloped and the troops with head erect would carry themselves proudly for the final distance. This I remember very vividly.

"We had no steel helmets then, but I think we had the Mills bomb. The earlier bombs were home-made, just jam-tins with two rings of guncotton and any old nails or iron, with a detonator stuck in the top. We were armed with the short Lee Enfield and the long bayonet—a damned unwieldy thing that interfered with shooting. We were issued with the Lewis light machine gun here in place of the Vickers, but its bogey was jamming. The German artillery firing a very low trajectory shell was always a source of irritation. The firing of the gun and the explosion of the 3-inch shell in the parapet was almost one noise—'Whzzzzz-Bang!' Hence we called them Whizzbangs, or Pipsqueaks. The heavy German shells, 5·9 and 8-inch, were called Jack Johnsons and Coal-Boxes because the explosive caused a black smoke. Our own shell-smoke was yellowish, because the explosive was lyddite. The German mortars were broad and stubby and we called the bombs 'Pisstins' because they were like urinal tins. The principal activity on this part of the line, by both sides, was sapping; and we had several saps blown during our tour. The pick-work underground was audible to those in the line and had a bad effect on morale. You could hear them digging away in the chalk beneath you, and when they stopped, you knew it would not be long before they blew. Although we were continually on the alert, the blowing of a sap always seemed to come as a surprise. The result was always a large crater and the object of both sides was to get to the farther lip of the crater, first. So there was hand-to-hand fighting, and bombing, a grim little time. On one occasion, our front line were surprised, and in their eagerness to get to the far lip of the crater, some lost their gumboots in the sticky mud and scrambled on in stockinged feet."

One of the men who worked underground, tunnelling through the chalk, was Frank R. Crossland of the Yorkshire Hussars Yeomanry, attached to the Royal Engineers. "I helped to blow many mines at Vimy," he recalled. "Out of the line, we slept in cellars at Neuville St. Vaast, where there was only one well with clean water; all the others were full of dead bodies, mostly French. At evening, we walked up to the front line, then crawled on our bellies over the top to our barbed wire. Here we would dig a hole some four yards square and four yards deep. Into the hole we would put a winch with a wire rope. Then as we dug towards Jerry, we would put the earth and chalk into sandbags, to be drawn up by the winch and emptied over the top. The sap we dug would be about four feet high and there would be about twenty men in it, some dragging bags of earth to the rubber-wheeled bogey, others winding them up, some emptying them into a shell hole when it was dark. The air was awful at the sap face, and we had an old blacksmith's bellows by the winch to blow fresh air down the sap. We used candles for light and a special listening device, when we thought we were under Jerry's trenches. Jerry was also digging towards us, and if we heard him coming, we would try to blow his sap in. But the object was to finish a sap under his trenches, stemm it with explosives, then blow it up, making a hole like a quarry. When we blew one, our artillery would blaze at it for a while, then over we went to consolidate the crater with bombs and bayonets, kill or be killed. I get tired and weary now, but I can remember it all as yesterday, and it was a lot more dreadful than I can describe. The trees all black stumps as we crawled out each night, the ground all shellholes and with thousands of rats jumping among the dead bodies, the mines going up and Jerry coming down like confetti among the star shells. It was hard going— but I would do it again for England."

German casualties were heavy, the quiet Vimy front had become an irritation. They decided therefore on a limited attack, to capture the British front line and the entrances to the mine shafts. Above ground, however, only the night raiding had an appreciable effect on the enemy; feeble attempts to stir up the Germans with a bit of firepower, especially mortars, in which they had superiority, were as inadvisable as putting one's hand into a wasps' nest. J. B. Priestley, the novelist, who was then serving on the Souchez sector, described in his memoirs what happened: " It had been quiet recently around there until we British arrived, but of course we had to hot it up for the sake of our morale, to keep our fellas on their toes, in spite of the fact, not hard to discover on the map and all too obvious to any staff officer who went to see for himself, that if we did start anything the Germans, higher up, well dug in, and in places not more than twenty yards away, would have the best of it. So very soon, having asked for it, God knows why, we caught a packet. Outside any plan of campaign, without any battle being fought, any honours being won, we went through the mincer. It was not long before our own B Company, with a nominal fighting strength of 270, had been reduced to a grim and weary seventy. Two hundred men had gone somehow and somewhere, with nothing to show for it."[3]

On 21 May, 1916, the Germans launched their limited attack to cancel out the success of the British mining operations. Their barrage began early in the morning, wrecking the British positions and smothering them from view in a cloud of dust; at evening, their infantry swept forward and captured 1500 yards of the front-line and support trenches; and under cover of a further artillery bombardment, the Germans settled in and re-fortified the positions. They were ready for the British counter-attack when it came, on 23 May. At a cost of nearly 2,500 casualties, incurred in three days' fighting, the British achieved nothing whatever; some of the troops never reached the German trenches, those who did were driven out. The sting of this defeat irked Lieutenant-General Henry Wilson, the corps commander responsible for it, and he began to plan a repetition on a larger scale. Fortunately Haig, then intent on gathering resources for his coming offensive on the Somme, vetoed Wilson's attack. But the incident was decisive in that it brought the problem of Vimy Ridge and its potential threat to Arras into relief in the mind of the British Commander-in-Chief. He ordered preliminary plans for the capture of the Ridge to be made, to be carried out at some future date in conjunction with an offensive from Arras. It was to be nearly a year before these plans were to become reality, in April, 1917.

The forces to be allotted then to the capture of Vimy Ridge were to consist of the entire Canadian Corps, comprising the 1st, 2nd, 3rd, and 4th Canadian Divisions, with the 5th Imperial Division[4] in support. It was this latter division which in March, 1916, had taken over from the French the line between Arras and Roclincourt, from where they could clearly hear the daily

---

[3] *Margin Released*, by J. B. Priestley (Heinemann, 1962).
[4] In Canadian nomenclature ' Imperial ' meant ' British '

bombardments on the sinister hogsback, so much so that it spawned the daily witticism. " They're moving the furniture again at Vimy." None could guess that they were to be present at the final removal.

CHAPTER TWO

PORTRAIT OF AN ARMY

The Canadian Corps

Although commanded by a British General (Lieutenant-General Sir J. H. G. Byng, later Viscount Byng of Vimy), the four divisions which assaulted the Ridge in April, 1917, were in effect the new National Army of Canada. Vimy was their watershed. The appointment almost immediately after of a Canadian, Lieutenant-General Sir A. W. Currie, to command the Canadian Corps, was the mark that they had crossed it. Vimy was much more than a test of fighting ability. No one had ever doubted the prowess of Canadian soldiers, but a conflict between great industrial powers is not a Zulu War. When the Kaiser in 1914 had referred to the 'insignificant' (or 'contemptibly small') British Army, he had put his finger on the real weakness of the British Empire as a land power. Of necessity, no British General had any professional experience of commanding the masses of men and material normally committed in a European war; no British staff had experience of the problems of such violently swift expansion as was to be necessary.

In 1914, on the Western Front only, the Germans had eighty-seven infantry divisions, the French sixty-two divisions. The British contribution, six divisions, was equal to that of 'poor little Belgium'. In Canada, the Permanent Force was hardly the equivalent of a Brigade even. It consisted of 3,000 men, formed into one infantry battalion, one battery of artillery, two squadrons of cavalry, and some technical services. Its chief role was to organise the military training of the volunteer Non-Permanent Active Militia, a task rendered unduly difficult by the fact that the then Minister of Militia and Defence was a N.P.A.M. officer hostile to the regulars. In these circumstances Lord Kitchener was able to maintain, with some appearance of reasonableness, that no Canadian officer was fit to command anything larger than an infantry brigade. However, he later conceded that Canadians could command divisions after they had proved themselves in the field as brigade commanders, which they did during the Second Battle of Ypres.

Consequently, at the turn of 1916, the corps commander, Byng, was a British regular with service in South Africa. The commander of the 1st Division, Major-General A. W. Currie, was a Canadian-born insurance agent who had served in the N.P.A.M., roughly the equivalent of the British Territorial Army. The commander of the 2nd Division, Major-General R. E. W. Turner, V.C., was a Canadian-born wholesale grocer who had served in the N.P.A.M. and fought in South Africa, where he had won his Victoria Cross. (At Vimy, this division was to be commanded by Major-General H. E. Burstall, formerly corps artillery commander.) The commander of the 3rd Division, Major-General L. J. Lipsett, was a British regular who had been attached to the Canadian staff for some years before the war and had served with them in the field during the war. The commander of the 4th Division, Major General D. Watson, was a Canadian-born newspaper proprietor who had served with the N.P.A.M. The three Canadians were all Territorial, or part-time soldiers, none of the Canadian regulars of the Permanent Force having been given the command of anything larger than a brigade.

Of the infantry brigade commanders, three had served at one time with the North-West Mounted Police, two subsequently joining the Permanent Force; the third had graduated from N.C.O. in the British regular army to N.C.O. of the N.W.M.P. and thence to officer status in the South African Constabulary, before joining the Canadian Army. The remaining nine brigadiers came from the N.P.A.M. and were mostly Canadian-born.

At the time, the distinction between 'Canadian' and 'Canadian-born' was a very real one. Lieutenant-Colonel Harwood Steele, M.C., author of "The Canadians in France, 1915-1918," who has been generous with his advice to the present author regarding these points, states that: "British immigration to Canada during the years just before the war had been the highest in the country's history. It included many well-educated, adventurous types fond of hunting and other activities which make them half-soldiers already, and a large number of ex-regulars, Territorials, South African War veterans, etc. Many of them joined the N.P.A.M. in peacetime and nearly all ' joined up ' at once, the best getting commissions.[1] The Canadian-born officers were of the same type and of a very high physical and intellectual standard. Moreover, those in and out of the N.P.A.M. when the war began included many farmers, civil engineers, lumberjacks, miners, etc., who were also well fitted by experience for active service and for units such as the Engineers. The British Army regulars on loan included some who rose to very high positions in World War I and World War II, notably Dill, E. de B. Radcliffe, Harington and Brooke (eventually Lord Alanbrooke). They were with the Corps because of a shortage of highly trained Canadians to do their work (chiefly staff) and because the advantages of serving with it were so great that places in it were much desired. These officers played a very important—one might almost say decisive—part in the success of the Corps. Officers of non-British stock were comparatively few. They included those of the only French-Canadian battalion in the field. However, a sprinkling of French-Canadians was to be found throughout the Corps. Probably the majority of the junior officers had no pre-war military experience. The other ranks included few, if any, British Army regulars on loan; but otherwise they came from the same sources, were of the same racial stocks, and had the same military and/or civil pre-war experience as the officers. They too were of a very high physical and intellectual standard and at the time when they took Vimy Ridge had no conscripts among them.

" With the full approval of the British Government and of Sir Douglas Haig, Commander-in-Chief of the British Armies in France, the Canadian Government wisely decided that Canada should not over-extend herself but maintain the Corps always at full strength with thoroughly trained personnel and plenty of the best weapons, equipment, etc. (Note the exceptional strength in artillery and machine-guns held as ' Corps Troops '.) Even before Vimy, such encumbrances as the over-fragile Ross

[1] See also *Canadian Expeditionary Force 1914-1919*, by Col. G. W. L. Nicholson (Queen's Printer, Ottawa, 1962), which gives the background to this, and much more, in very great detail.

rifle had been discarded. Welfare services, with provision for entertainment, sport, regular mail deliveries, etc., were also very good. When the Corps took Vimy, its divisions had been fighting in France for periods of from over two years, in the case of the 1st Division, down to eight months in the case of the 4th Division. The Corps had not only seen much static warfare (holding the line) but had also taken a leading part in the Second and Third Battles of Ypres and the Battle of the Somme. In consequence, it had by this time been welded into a really fine fighting force around the nucleus provided by its British and Canadian active and ex-regulars, its veterans of previous campaigns, and its ex-members of the North-West Mounted Police and N.P.A.M., and fortunately its casualties, though heavy, had not as yet unduly drained it. Thanks to the natural self-confidence of the types serving in the Corps, reinforced by hard-won assurance that they could defeat the Germans on any fair field, and strict discipline combined with high spirits, the Canadian morale at Vimy and elsewhere was always exceptionally high. Slanders that they were a disorderly, unsoldierly lot are completely false. They went about their work with a silent and often very grim thoroughness, insisting that nothing but the best results would do for the Canadian Corps." This extreme self-confidence generally, and in particular the confidence that they would take Vimy where everyone else before them had failed, stands out both in the Canadian narratives and also in the comments of British eye-witnesses, and was probably a major factor in their success, for the plan was to depend upon initial speed and dash over ground, and in conditions, not exactly conducive to it.

*   *   *

The first Canadian unit to arrive in France did so in 1914, and it was not the sole regular battalion, the Royal Canadian Regiment, but a unit which had not existed before the outbreak of war and had, moreover, been recruited by a private individual at his own expense, in the Twentieth Century an almost mediæval proceeding. This was the Princess Patricia's Canadian Light Infantry, named after the daughter of the Duke of Connaught, then Governor General of Canada. It was raised by

Captain A. Hamilton Gaunt, who had served in the South African War and paid $100,000 towards the cost, and was composed of ex-soldiers most of whom had recent fighting experience. The battalion joined the British 27th Division in the line on the night of 6-7 January, 1915, two months ahead of the 1st Canadian Division. When they lost 400 men in two days during the Second Battle of Ypres, the gaps were filled by recruits from McGill University. The battalion still exists and is at present stationed in Germany.

The last Canadian formation to arrive was the 4th Division. The projected 5th and 6th Divisions were to be scrapped in favour of keeping a four-division Corps at full strength, and with four battalions per brigade, at a time when the British were to be compelled to reduce this figure to three because of their heavy losses in the war of attrition. The Canadian policy was certainly more economical in staff and administrative units, and it meant that the Canadian force was much stronger than an equivalent British or German formation; was in fact a miniature army.

The 4th Division was formed at Bramshott Camp, the new Canadian training area in England, in May, 1916. One of the voluntary civilian helpers at this camp was Mrs. Daisy M. Barnard, an English schoolteacher whose husband, serving in France with the Hampshire Regiment, was wounded during the British occupation of the Vimy sector. The atmosphere was quite different to that of the Second World War, because everyone knew that the soldiers would be going overseas in a matter of months and that the chances of survival were not good. Indeed, her most affecting memory is of the night they left for France and she was asked to sing one of their favourite melodies, " The Song That Reached My Heart," the emotion of the moment being so great that many of them were in tears.

Other memories were wry, or amusing. There was the soldier who made a date with one of the girls serving at the CYMCA hut. Assuming that she was a domestic servant, he went round to the servants' hall of her stately home and enquired for the dame with the honey-coloured hair and the blue eyes, or whatever the description was! On another occasion, Mrs. Barnard was able to help with a compassionate case, a soldier on draft for

France whose pregnant wife had become so worried that she had been put into an asylum. Under the stern regulations of the time, his OC could do nothing about it. Luckily the General who could was an incurable tea addict who used often to slip into the CYMCA hut after closing time for a quick cuppa. So Mrs. Barnard waylaid him, with a miserable expression on her face, causing the General to exclaim, " Hallo, you don't look happy? " That was her cue to mention the case and to ask how the man could be expected to go off to fight with this worry on his mind. The soldier got compassionate leave, the wife recovered completely—and the General got his tea!

A more trying experience with a Canadian General occurred after Mrs. Barnard had cashed a cheque for two soldiers, rather doubtfully, for she had seen a curious look pass between them as she handed over the money. Some weeks later, she was told that if this pair attempted to cash any more cheques, she was not to do so, but to hold them. One of the men duly came in, and wrote out a cheque in front of her. She refused to cash it, and informed the duty officer. In due course, she was chief witness for the prosecution—the only woman in court—and faced by a Presiding General who was deeply suspicious of the accuracy of a woman's testimony, especially as none of the other witnesses were at all sure of their identifications. He challenged every statement she made, asking how did she know this, that, or the other, and each time Mrs. Barnard had her answer. She stuck to her guns, maintaining that she could identify both the man and the cheque.

" I'm very observant," she explained. " It pays to be, with so much money passing through my hands every day."

The General thought he saw a weak point, and pounced. " On an average day, how much? "

" About 2,000 dollars, in money, cheques, and postal orders," she replied.

" How could you remember one particular cheque out of so many? " snapped the General, sarcastically.

" By its peculiar colour," retorted Mrs. Barnard. " It's very uncommon."

The General then pressed her to describe the colour, in a belittling sort of way, casually picked up the cheque, muttered,

"Hmmm! Something like my own," and ordered his batman to bring him his own cheque book for comparison. When he did, it was the General's face which turned a peculiar colour—for the cheque which the soldier had attempted to pass across the counter had come from the General's own cheque book! After that, the trial proceeded to a quick conclusion, with the other witnesses getting the rough edge of the General's tongue and Mrs. Barnard the commendations.

Among those who passed through Bramshott Camp in 1916, en route to Vimy Ridge, were Arthur and Eddie Farmer of the 71st Infantry Battalion. Brothers, and part of a family of five, they were orphaned when Arthur was five years old and Eddie was nine. At that age, they had found themselves inmates of an orphan asylum in London. After a few years, Eddie was faced with a man's decision—join the Navy, stay at the Home and learn an industrial trade, or emigrate to Canada. He chose the latter and the next word Arthur had from him, he was on a farm in Ontario. Two years later, Arthur made the same decision and found himself on a farm some eight or ten miles away from his brother. Eventually, Eddie managed to get himself a job as hired man on a farm next to where Arthur was living, and the brothers were re-united. When war came, they still managed to stay together. "Across the country, from Halifax to Vancouver, units of the Non-Permanent Militia volunteered en masse for active service in France," Arthur Farmer recollected. "These were joined by thousands of other young Canadians who clamoured to be admitted into the fighting forces. My brother Eddie was enlisted into the 71st Battalion in London, Ontario, under the command of Lieutenant-Colonel D. M. Sutherland, a doctor, in the early summer of 1915 and I joined the 71st in November, being enlisted into the Signal Section. Throughout the winter training was carried on, and in March, 1916, the Battalion embarked for England." In May, however, came the bad news. The 71st was to be broken up in order to reinforce other units. Eddie Farmer was transferred to the 102nd Infantry Battalion from Kootenay, British Columbia, while Arthur Farmer was posted to the 11th Brigade Machine Gun Company, a new unit forming under Major Blair Clark of Toronto. This was not as bad as it might have been, for the

102nd was part of the 11th Brigade which, with the rest of the new 4th Division, embarked for France that August. They went straight into the Battle of the Somme, but the brothers were not able to meet again until the morning of 9 April, 1917, on Vimy Ridge, and it was to be for the last time.

CHAPTER THREE

CANADA TAKES OVER

' The March 1st Gas Raid '

"On 14 December, 1916, the 11th Brigade M.G. Company was in position in front of Vimy Ridge, while the Canadians were at this time mainly in the Arras area training and preparing for what we did not know," recalled Arthur Farmer. "Our headquarters was at the entrance to a communication trench known as Tottenham Trench. During the winter much activity went on, excavating trench systems and tunnels until a complicated system of tunnels and caves, capable of billeting many hundreds of men, were in use. A narrow-gauge railway ran along the front of the Ridge, overlooked by the Germans but almost bombproof, as we were dug into the Ridge and nothing short of a direct hit from above could make us vacate our position. Here we stayed until preparations for the attack were complete."

"Whilst a trip to Vimy is illustrative, it cannot be the same as during the war. The ravages of war have mostly been covered, the roll of the artillery and the exploding shells, the drone of the enemy planes, and the constant sub-conscious fear of what might happen—is missing," wrote Mr. W. I. Fawcett, once a private soldier of the 7th Winnipeg Grenadiers. "The rats, too. One night I had to try and guard a dead soldier in a funkhole (that's a shelf in the side of a trench, covered with galvanised iron and sandbags above and rubber ground sheet over the entrance). Every time I heard a noise, I lifted the sheet and shooed away the rat. In spite of our best efforts, when morning came, one cheek was gone. Time and again, in the days of just holding the line, when the boys were sleeping in these funkholes, they were killed by direct hits; they did not know what hit them."

But the trip to Vimy *was* illustrative, in that recollections of the actual battle, which was brief, were subordinated in the veterans' memories to the over-riding business of *living* at Vimy.

Sitting in an Arras restaurant afterwards, discussing it in 1965, the rats and the lice were better remembered than the Germans. "Huge rats," said someone suddenly, "so big they would eat a wounded man if he couldn't defend himself." That stirred the memory of another man. "I remember, I once took cover beside a P.P.C.L.I. sergeant who had been dead about three weeks; there were two rats burrowing inside him. Put me off rats for life." Somebody butted in with an objection to puttees. They were no good, took too long to put on; whereas the Germans, if there was an alarm, could just jump into their half-boots. And everyone, without exception, mentioned the lice. The continual itch. Trying to get rid of them; going over the seams of their clothing with a match, and hearing the eggs pop.

Man was not made to live in the open, in a European winter, but that war millions did. "In late 1916 and early 1917 I was a so-called 'Staff Learner' attached to Corps H.Q.," recalled Lieutenant-Colonel Harwood Steele. "I was under Brigadier E. de B. Radcliffe and worked under Dill, who was G.S.O.2. One day Radcliffe handed me a huge mass of files containing previous plans for taking Vimy, and told me to co-ordinate them as a first step to the Corps producing its own plan from the resulting document. I accordingly prepared the tome required, then went back to my battalion, the 27th, to await a staff appointment. We held the Souchez sector, a frightfully bad one, as it lay in the valley of the Souchez River, right under the Pimple, and so was heavily waterlogged; with the Germans looking straight down on it and giving us hell with artillery and trench-mortar fire every day. The colds, etc., among the troops were so bad that no one was evacuated sick from these causes unless he had or was about to get pneumonia, the argument being that otherwise no one would be left to hold the line. Over two months of this proved too much for me, so I just missed the taking of the Ridge."

On the Ridge itself, in the 'crater line', so called because it was no more than a jumbled mass of mine-craters, with the Canadians holding one lip of a crater and the Germans the other, the armies were close. "You could hear the sentries talking in the German line," said Col. the Rev. Dr. Kilpatrick. "I remember one man telling me, 'The fellow opposite me,' he says, 'has got a terrible cold. I'm making it worse because I've shot holes in his dipper, so that he can't bail it, and he is standing in water to his knees '."

" The winter of 1916-17 was a nasty one with hard black frost that hardened the mud like stone, alternating with thaws that restored the normal depth of gooey mud to one's knees," recalled Gus Sivertz of 2 C.M.R. " But after the Somme and the battalion's experiences at Moquet Farm, Courcellette, Pozieres and Hessian trenches, almost anything was not so bad—by comparison. So in January the battalion took over from the British 6oth Division, a good but green outfit that was determined not to disturb the Hun too much. The front was in the general area of Ecurie and Roclincourt, slightly north-east of Arras, and gave a good view of the slopes of Vimy Ridge. On January 4 we relieved the 4th C.M.R.s and the mud was so impossible in the communication trench that the relief was made overland— without any casualties, thank God. At that time no one thought that within three months we would be storming up that formidable slope just in front of Neuville St. Vaast. That dour-looking ridge looked like it would be a permanent German possession—and he was welcome to it. The road from Arras to Mt. St. Eloi (with its twin spires first smashed in the war of 1870) and thence up into the coal villages of the Pas de Calais was in open view of Heinie and we always felt he was looking right down our necks as we marched along the slippery cobbles. On the enemy side of the road, engineers had stretched camouflage of wide burlap in the vain hope that the Hun couldn't guess what we were doing."

When young Harwood Steele (he was then nineteen) had set to work co-ordinating the previous plans for an assault on the Ridge, he had been told to regard the job as " more than *Most Secret*." But this was to be a ' set-piece ' battle behind a perfectly timed and intricate barrage and counter-battery programme, requiring thorough rehearsal of the troops and the massing of enormous quantities of guns, ammunition, and stores of all kinds. Although, in 1934, it was revealed by Colonel Wilfrid Bovey that there had been a spy in the Corps—a man who had joined the Canadian forces, claiming to be a Texan, and then crossed the lines with information five days before the attack—the only real secret was the date.

The experiences of 2 C.M.R. were typical. They came out of the line and marched to the little mining village of Rimbert. "It was a good little place with the kindliest people we ever met in France," commented Gus Sivertz. "Here, we started a schedule of the most intensive training, mainly over taped trenches in an area that simulated the slopes of Vimy on a small scale. Every few days we were visited by the Big Brass who watched as we practised attacking at a slow walking pace . . . no wild charging at a gallop . . . while officers rode ahead carrying little flags that moved at a speed that they hoped the barrage would move. When Sir Julian Byng, the Canadian Corps commander, came up, there wasn't the slightest doubt about what was in the · offing. Of course we knew pretty well that a big show was up-coming. Madam Chips, kindly Mrs. Turnelle, who provided us with endless dishes of eggs and chips, had told us:

' I tink big push soon come.'

And the padre's batman, who was first to know everything, let it out that we were to storm Vimy Ridge. And he was seldom wrong.

"But unlike going into the Somme the men were full of zip. There seemed to be a spirit of full confidence despite the dour look of the ridge and what we had heard about the Hun defences on it. A strange thing among footsloggers was our confidence in our divisional commander, Major-General J. L. Lipsett, who had commanded a battalion in the April, 1915, gas attack at Ypres."

Most were confident, but not all; some could remember only too well the fate of previous offensives. "The battle arrangements were purely criminal, time and again perpetually the same mistakes," pointed out Mr. W. G. Smith, who had started the war as a gunner private and ended up a battery sergeant-major. "Butchering the poor bloody infantry and knocking the light artillery to pieces. The generals could be excused for First Ypres, Loos or Givenchy, they had to learn their trade, the same as we did, but to continually repeat those mistakes stamps them as fools who should have been court-martialled, not honoured.

We who had long service became similar to dumb animals, obeyed orders, no longer caring what happened."

Another witness, E. B. Elgood, who was with the 7th Brigade Signals at Vimy, shrewdly suspected that it was precisely this established incompetence of the Allied High Commands which, by making the Germans over-confident, lost them Vimy. " A gradual slope from Mt. St. Eloi through Neuville St. Vaast," he wrote, " brought you to the front line of the 3rd Div, and beyond that 1,000 to 1,500 yards to the crest of the Ridge, from which the Germans dominated our positions from Hill 70 near Loos to just north of Arras, an area in which the British and French had lost tens of thousands of men, and from which they appeared confident we could not oust them. From early March, by observation of our mounting piles of ammunition and supplies of every description, the tremendous activity on the roads, and our mounting artillery action on his trenches and rear positions, his wire and strongpoints, he certainly knew we were preparing for an assault—but could only guess When? So, because of his confidence in the strength of his defence, and because of his thought that it was taking US a long, long time to realise that flesh and blood—as at Loos and dozens of other futile troop attacks—was just a form of slow suicide, he apparently did very little reinforcing of his position." German records show that this appreciation (in an unpublished MSS based on a contemporary diary) was basically correct. " By this time," went on Elgood, " I had put in eighteen continuous months around Ypres, the Somme, and the Souchez-Vimy areas, mostly in front of our guns, and had very few illusions or ambitions left—except that I might some day get back to the Salmon River Valley in British Columbia, and farm. A far off Dream."

" The private soldier and the non-com in the British Army was not a fool, he knew when he was abused and wasted," wrote W. G. Smith, angrily. " In the first three years of the war—1914 to 1916—I never thought we would win," said John Cornish of the 3rd Canadian M.G. Company. " You need dominating fire-power. Shock them, knock hell out of them, get their M.G.s. We didn't have such fire-power then." For the German soldier, as distinct from the German war machine and its overwhelming fire-power, there was not the exaggerated respect that tended to occur in the Second World War. "Mainly, I believe, to the terrific show put up by the 1st Canadian Division at Second Ypres, we had no fear of the German soldier," wrote Smith. "We knew that given anywhere near an equal chance we could hold them, or beat them, so there was little brutality engendered by fear. There was occasional killing of prisoners, but it would be of necessity, or caused by the behaviour of the prisoner himself. Actually it was hard to hate a man who suffered the same punishment you did. This may surprise you, but I believe the private British soldier hated his own commanders and staff people more than he did his opposite number in the German trenches. He soon knows whether his superiors are intelligent or not."

But Vimy was destined to be the first British attack which was even a half-success, and some inkling of this was apparent in the power and thoroughness of the preparations. Captain Ulric Nisbet was subsequently to write in *The Ypres Times*, April, 1936: "The 13th Brigade, consisting of my own battalion (1st Royal West Kents), 2nd King's Own Scottish Borderers, and 14th and 15th Royal Warwicks, together with our (5th) Divisional Artillery had been attached for the operation to the 2nd Canadian Division, and for a week or two we had been practising daily over specially marked out country behind the line. Although this bore little, if any, resemblance to the ground we were to fight over, the tapes and flags with which it was accurately bedecked not only familiarised us with the names and relative positions of trenches and woods on the Ridge, but also inculcated in all ranks an instinctive sense of direction that no amount of map reading would have done. In fact, there is no doubt that these elaborate preparations, coupled with the perfecting of the creeping barrage time-table, were responsible for our immense confidence and contributed significantly to the overwhelming success of the whole attack."

David Layton, M.M., then a sergeant in the 15th Royal Warwicks, also part of the British 13th Brigade, was to make the same point. "The outstanding reason for the success of this attack was, of course, the accuracy of the creeping barrage laid down by the artillery and particularly its synchronisation with the 'maximum rate of advance' of the infantry over that particular terrain. In spite of the blizzard, for the snow fell heavily on the Ridge itself that morning, the attack—*for the first time in the war*—went forward like clockwork. Coupled with the creeping barrage was, of course, the fantastic dash and elan of the Canadians. I should like you, in your book, to pay them this tribute from me; no troops could deserve higher praise."

Layton was also an experienced soldier by this time, alert to the smallest nuances which could be the difference between life and death. "After Vimy," he wrote, "I had a 5·9 shell drop about a yard from me—but before it dropped I went flat on the ground and fortunately for me the blast went away from me. Now this is a strange thing but *true*, for hundreds of thousands of Ex-Servicemen will tell you—and experts and generals, too—that you can't hear a 5·9 coming as it travels quicker than sound. Don't believe them! At the end of my first year in the trenches, I couldn't myself although by that time I had become really expert at dodging German mortar shells. But *after* the first year, I gradually became more and more like an animal—my hearing became abnormal and I developed an animal's sixth sense. This in part accounts, I think, for my optimism at the beginning of the Vimy do. When things were going to turn out badly, I sensed it and I was always right."

"The first signs of a build up for it were the large numbers of ammunition piles alongside the roads in the back areas," recollected Maurice Bracewell of the 102nd Battalion, the North British Columbians. "They stretched through Camblain le Abbey, Grand and Quay Servins, and Hersin Compigny right back to St. Pol. The shells were stacked by the thousands in earth pits, like farmers' turnip or potato pits, covered with straw and earth. Day in, day out, during the three months prior to the attack, the ammunition trucks were streaming along the main roads. A light railway system, similar to that used in mines, was put in to run supplies up to the base of the Ridge itself. Mule skinners also used to work all night making similar deliveries, and the noise of their shouting, cursing, and even singing, used to fill the air all night long as they reeled off the histories of the antecedants of the various mules at the top of their lung capacity. We heard the case histories of those mules broadcast so often that we knew their names off by heart. Those mule-

skinners seemed to think that they were fighting a great war as
long as they were shouting their guts out, but when Fritz used
to try to knock them out it was generally us who got knocked
out instead."

As the build-up proceeded, so did the tunnelling out of troop
quarters, dressing stations, and other accommodation in the
chalk of the Ridge itself; and, for once, British dugouts became
as good as German. "A person has to be fair in dealing with
people," wrote W. G. Smith, "and I believe the German soldier
was more industrious than we were, though he was not cramped
by consideration for French property. It paid off, for his dugouts
were safe and, to our standards, luxurious, and I do not believe
the daily German wastage of men in ordinary Western Front
conditions was even a fraction of ours." But now, as Maurice
Bracewell wrote, "The troop accommodations in the Ridge itself
were the best we found anywhere in France. Huge tunnels gave
off into large rooms that held about forty or so men, and the
chalk walls were covered with all manner of carvings, figureheads
and Regimental crests. There was electric lighting, but the water
had to be brought in in empty gasoline cans from wells or
springs and they all seemed to be in highly exposed positions,
and the noise of all the tin cans, loud conversations, etc., naturally drew both artillery and sniper fire. The tunnellers, who
were of course miners in civil life, were also continuously at
work running saps out under the barbed wire and listening for
the counter activities of the German troops. They used to claim
that they would lay up at the end of a sap and listen to Fritz
working on the other side and after he had quit work for a while
at that particular spot, they would break through and take out
the explosives that he had put in, and I suppose Fritz would
more than likely be doing the same. They had to prepare some
very big ground mines for the attack, to blow entrances out into
No-man's-land to get our own reinforcing troops out close to his
front line and to get the wounded and prisoners down under
cover."

"There was a great deal of tunnelling and blasting going on,"
said Lieutenant A. C. Pearson of the P.P.C.L.I. "This meant
that the man out on sentry-go didn't know whether the enemy
were right under his feet, blasting, or whether it was our own

blasting. It was a very, very trying time for the men on sentry-go. When the thing blew, they were just buried in it, and you could hear the shrieks of the men who had been manning the line."

" Then the battalion scouts started to go out on night patrol into No-man's-land, dressed in white coveralls," recollected Bracewell of the 102nd. " Local credit was given to the scout-officer, a Lieutenant Dimsdale, who was a very fussy little chap but demanded and got all his scouts could give. He was an engineer in civil life. To my mind, the most enervating job you could be detailed to do was that of being tail-end, or last man, on a patrol; you always had the feeling that the last man was most likely to be picked off by Fritz. The next hardest thing on your nerves was litter in No-man's-land. The tin cans, the sheets of corrugated iron, the hundreds of seemingly loose pieces of barbed wire which always turned out to be solidly anchored at the other end and so sent you sprawling among all that lethal and noisy junk. There was this noticeable atmosphere of prepara-tion for some three months, and there were also smaller though related actions that took place before the main attack."

The most elaborate of these took place on the night of 28 February/1 March, 1917, and in the memories of those who took part, and survived, is thought of as the ' March 1st Gas Raid '. It was carried out by 1700 men of the 4th Division and its object was a reconnaissance in force of Hill 145 (where the monument now stands) and, by achieving surprise, to damage the German defences of this commanding height. As bombardment or wire-cutting would alert the Germans, the raid was to be covered by clouds of poison gas. From 12 Brigade, the 73rd and 72nd Battalions were to be employed; and on their right, from 11 Brigade, the 75th and 54th Battalions. So Bracewell was lucky.

" We were more than lucky," he wrote, " for we and the 87th Montreal Battalion were at rest billets just behind the lines, the battalions chosen being the 54th Kootenay and the 75th Toronto. Cylinders of chlorine-gas were placed in groups of three along the firing-steps of the front line trench, and the gas was to be fed over the parapet into No-man's-land through short lengths of hose from each cylinder. A steady, gentle wind blowing directly into the enemy lines was necessary; too strong a wind would disintegrate the gas and blow it away. When the time planned for the raid arrived, wind conditions were unfavourable so it was postponed for three days. At the end of that time the weather was still unfavourable, so a further delay of two days was made. When the third time set arrived, the weather was still terrible, with a strong wind blowing *directly into our lines*! The Army Brass ruled, however, that the attack must go as planned irrespective of what happened. The colonels of our attacking battalions were reported as having protested the ruling most vehemently, but the Army Brass were adamant in their stand. Lieutenant-Colonel Kemball of the 54th Battalion, in defiance of orders to the contrary, went over the top with his men and shared their fate; his body was later found in the barbed wire. The German staff knew all about the impending attack and were sitting waiting for it. Colonel Kemball's conduct was the essence of valour but that is not the kind that wins official citations unfortunately. But one could almost imagine the unknown author of the following lines had been there:

' Come, my sons, aye come—the Battle dawn is nigh
And the screaming crump and thundering drum are calling
thee to die!
Fight as thy fathers fought—fall as thy fathers fell
Thy task is taught, thy shroud is wrought
So Forward! and Farewell '.

What happened was tragic indeed. Our own front lines got all the gas, the front trenches were saturated with it. Our men were wiped out. The whole front area was in such a state that a 36-hour cease-fire had to be arranged to get it cleaned up. Our own battalion received a hurry-up call and we moved right up and set to work to clean up the mess. We worked night and day on burial parties and even traded dead with the Germans. Such is War! After, it was claimed that the tragic results were not caused by faulty staff work but by the front trenches being too far apart."

Captain Harvey E. Crowell was one of the four senior officers from the unblooded 85 Battalion attached to units of the 4th Division for this raid. " I went to the 72nd, on February 28th, and can only write about my own tour. I was attached to a company i/c, Lieutenant Colquhoun, a splendid officer, nearly six feet tall, and wearing his leopard skin over his tunic. He took

me along and we made rounds to left of his extensive, thinly-
held front line, and out in front for three or four listening posts.
Everything was quiet but the German flares were up all the
time. Zero hour for the Gas Attack was to be midnight that night.
Everybody was anxious about the wind, there was hardly any.
Lieutenant Colquhoun told me to take charge of his HQ and
report that he had gone up the line about 2300 hours. I stepped
out a couple of times to judge the weather, and it seemed to me
that the wind was north instead of west, and a misty atmosphere.
Certainly not the night to release our gas which was supposed to
put the enemy out of action, not only his front line and second
trench, but right over the Ridge. (In all units there had been
nothing but growls and considerable rumour that the Huns had
captured one of the Engineer Sappers and likely knew all about
Canadian plans.)

    " Within a minute of the ' hour ' the Germans put on their
artillery and *lots* of it. They had every trench registered. Their
artillery and machine-gun fire were so immediate at midnight
that the 12th Brigade parties did not reach most of their objectives, except a very few prisoners from isolated listening posts
in No-man's-land. It was a terrific bombardment. International
Avenue in the evening was the best-built communication trench
I ever saw. It ran diagonally up hill for 200 yards, and in thirty
minutes it was all levelled out. Lieutenant Colquhoun was killed
by machine-gun fire and within the first hour. Normally the
troops were not to advance until the gas had blown towards
the enemy, but our own men got the worst of it. Some cylinders
were still leaking gas all morning, and it was making many
quite ill. At the time it was estimated that, with our own gas
casualties, each Battalion lost about 300." There was no
' Armistice ' on the dangerously weakened front of the 72nd,
according to Crowell, but one certainly did take place where the
54th was concerned.

    The Regimental History (*Cinquante-Quatre*, by Major J. B.
Bailey) is discreet, but states: " Colonel Kemball, foreseeing the
failure of the gas cloud, personally led the battalion over the
top in an endeavour to carry out the orders as laid down . . .
One of the most memorable and pleasant features of our fighting record occurred on this day, which showed that a few of the

Bosches at least had decent instincts. Realising the sacrifice made by Col. Kemball, and recognising in him a valuable and noble opponent, they proposed to stop all fighting on our and the adjoining fronts in order that we might obtain his body. This was agreed to and they immediately brought his body over to near our lines, treating it with all due respect and tenderness. It was a fitting recognition of Colonel Kemball's brave and gallant action." Such chivalrous actions did occasionally occur. Colonel Harwood Steele recalled of Canon Frederick George Scott, Senior Chaplain of the 1st Division, that " he was always going into the thickest of the fight with cigarettes, etc., and, just before Vimy, astounded everyone by going into No-man's-land at the height of the Somme fighting to search for his dead son's body. He failed to find it, but the Germans, realising that something queer was afoot, stopped firing at him."

Referring to the March 1st Gas Raid, the Canadian Official History by Colonel Nicholson admits that the enemy had indeed been alerted (by a preliminary discharge of tear gas); claims the capture of thirty seven German prisoners for the loss of 687 Canadians, including two battalion commanders; and states that part of these casualties were caused by German shellfire which smashed open some of the lethal chlorine-gas cylinders. The latter incident is not mentioned by Major Bailey, who states: " After the first lot of gas was liberated the wind shifted, and instead of drifting across to the Hun lines opposite us the gas went down No-man's-land and entered the Hun lines opposite the 3rd Division on our right. Consequently, when we came to make our raid the Bosche was ready for us and managed to prevent us from getting across to his lines."

The next time there was a slight miscalculation at staff level, Maurice Bracewell was right in the middle of it. " A new front line trench was planned," he recalled. " It ran up close to the German front line, and an Engineer officer was sent up to supervise. He was a huge man, about six and a half feet tall and correspondingly broad of build. The position of the new trench was marked out on the ground at night with *brand-new* white tape about two inches wide, which was pinned to the ground with wire staples, and the rough outline of the fire-bays were shown. That white tape stretched as far as we could see and at night it seemed to glisten as it moved in and out of the German barbed-wire. There was no immediate move made to dig the trench. That white tape was left there for *forty eight* hours for Fritz to sit and look at it and draw his own conclusions—to say nothing of preparing to deal with whatever was the sequel to its being there. He made the most of his time, as we soon found out. When the seeming lethargy of our 'Staff' had run its course, men were given picks and shovels and lined up on top of the Ridge and told to dig!

" All Hell broke loose! The Germans promptly put a Box-Barrage of high explosives all round us to keep *us* in and reinforcements out! while they went to work to clean up on those of us who were inside the curtain of fire. Luckily for me, I was detailed to work with the scouts. We lay out ahead of the diggers in shell-holes or the remnants of trenches of other days. We had bags of hand-grenades and were supposed to protect the diggers from direct attack. But Fritz had no need to attack, all he had to do was to mow the boys down with his machine-gun fire, which he surely did as fast as they stood up, and when others stepped up to replace their comrades—he did it again.

" The huge Engineer officer was running up and down the front, shouting, cursing, gesticulating, and urging on the digging operations. One minute he would be at his full height, hands open, arms outstretched, *pleading* with the boys to 'Dig! Dig!' The next he would be crouched, fists closed, arms bent, shouting and cursing at them to 'Dig-Dig-Dig!' He looked as big as a house and I have no doubt he felt even bigger! How anyone could continuously run up and down the front, yelling, cursing, waving his arms around, and *live*, while scores were being mown down all round him, is one of the mysteries of war! At dawn they had the trench down a scant waist deep in places. No men had ever tried to work harder but everywhere was so littered with dead and wounded; it had been a terrible night. They gradually managed to get some of the wounded out along the shallow depressions left by old trenches. As they got the new trench down a bit, the casualties eased off a bit, but Fritz did not ease off at all in what he was pouring into us.

" He brought up more trench mortars to try and knock us out. Some of the heavy mortar shells we nicknamed ' Rum-Jars '. They came in varying lengths from two feet to three feet six inches, and were about as big around as a nail-keg. They had a time fuse at one end and a very heavy explosive charge for moral effect. They were filled with all manner of scrap-iron, just about everything. You could hear them coming through the air —swish, swish, swish!—and you could see the sparks from the time-fuse sputtering as it went end over with the mortar shell in flight. Any that seemed close overhead, you naturally figured were going to land on *you*! We of the scouts would cry out a warning to the diggers when we thought any of the mortar shells were going to land near them.

" One night, my partner yelled out such a warning—' *This is IT, Boys!*'—and he and I attempted to drop back and flop around a zag in the new trench, but that Rum-Jar exploded in our faces. It seemed as if the earth must have exploded, the concussion was terrific and felt as if it was tearing us apart. All I could see was fire, nothing but fire, and we in the middle of it. When we came to again, the boys had dug us out and were holding us against the side of the trench. We had taken the full force of that explosion and concussion, but the boys each side of us got all the shrapnel, for it killed five and wounded seven more. Then we went back to our shellhole to carry on.

" Later that night, just as the first streaks of dawn were beginning to creep across the sky, the ground under and around us started to rock. You could see the tremors running in waves, just like water when a stone has been thrown into it. We had time for quite a look around, between the initial tremors and the actual explosion, though I know it must sound incredible. It seemed as if there must be scores of giant moles at work beneath the surface. I remember yelling to my partner—' *He's Blowing the Ridge!*'—when the ground opened under us and we went hurtling through the air. When we picked ourselves up again, where our shelhole had been was now a huge crater, forty to forty five feet across, and in what seemed like no time at all there were machine-guns on opposite lips of it, German and Canadian. They were so busy with what they were doing, fortunately, that they did not appear to notice us as we crawled back to safety. We were both badly shaken up, having taken two lots in one night. I lost the use of my left arm for a while from heavy bruises to the shoulder and upper arm.

" We were sent back to the reserve line to rest up a bit ready for the big attack. Those of us who had put in the new front line did not go over in the attacking waves at Vimy, they figured we had done our show, but we were right up front just the same. We had to wade through water up to our hips to get past the support line, which was Music-Hall Trench. The attacking troops going in on that line had to wade through the water and then stand all through the cold night in the jumping-off trenches, soaking wet, loaded like mules with full battle-kit, extra ammunition, hand grenades, etc., packed like sardines, watching and waiting for dawn and zero hour, then over the top and God Knows What! "

The trenches of this war were different, and more vulnerable, than those of the Second World War, which very often were simply two-man slits in the ground. " You must remember," wrote W. G. Smith, " that you had to carry stretchers, trench stores, duck boards, revetments, anything you used, through them. Their width was governed by that need. Always the German trenches were best, for they retired, or originally settled, on high ground, we beneath them mostly in every section. Their construction was largely governed by the drainage and condition of the ground. Sandbags easily rotted in the wet, and the trenches were continually in need of repair." And, pointed out Maurice Bracewell, " The communication trenches that snaked their way up to the front line were usually not kept up as good as the front trenches. They usually had duck-mats in the bottom, they kept your feet up out of at least part of the mud and water, but they were a tangle of phone and signal wires, etc., and as these trenches were not of full body depth you had to develop a technique of trudging rather than walking, in a stooped position. That is why so many troops would rather climb out on top and run like blazes to wherever they needed to go." On one occasion, they were led up the communication trench by the platoon sergeant, a burly, rough-tongued Irishman, followed by a brand-new young officer who kept tripping over the tangle in the bottom of the trench and then, nervously, drew his revolver. That made the sergeant nervous, for the young officer's gun hand was making wild gyrations behind his back as the lad stumbled and tripped behind him. Finally, he turned and blazed out, "Look, son! I wish to God you'd turn the spout of that damn thing the other way!"

At dawn on 17 March, 2 C.M.R. marched out of their friendly billets at Rimbert. "Every soldier had a girl on his arm and in some cases a whole family marched along with some chap whom they liked, until we had left the confines of the little town," recollected Gus Sivertz. "We marched to Villers-en-Bois from where we got a good view of that long, sinister hog-back that General Byng wanted us to get for him. It was easy to understand how the poor French had lost thousands of men in their attempt to take it. There wasn't any time to worry about that, as it appeared we were expected to become pack mules and lug picks, shovels, bath mats, wire, water cans, cases of S.A.A. and Mills bombs, up the line. It was a brute. My little pal, Jimmy Duffield, was slushing through knee-deep mud just ahead of me when he slithered off the duck board and went armpit deep into a sump hole. It wasn't funny. It took three of us pulling on his rifle to haul him out of the goo. And when we got him out, he had no puttees . . . just muck. That night it froze, and the poor kid looked like a solid pillar of mud." For a former cavalry unit—C.M.R. stood for Canadian Mounted Regiment—this was unromantic work, but, despite the visions of South Africa lingering in the minds of the staff, Vimy was to show once again that there was no place for the horse in modern war, except as a beast of burden.

"Next morning, 22 March, had bits of sun and, in a quiet moment, I rolled over a trench lip—a communication trench, of course—and stretched out in the warmth," recalled Sivertz. "But not for long. I heard our O.C., Lieutenant-Colonel G. C. 'Whizz-bang' Johnson, and Major W. W. Foster talking a few feet away; they were watching our shelling (on Thelus, I suppose), when a sharp spurt of Lewis-gun fire burst out from No-man's-land. We all stood up on the top and saw a group of Germans disappear into the big Chassery crater while our Lewis gunners spattered them—without doing any damage, unfortunately.

" This is what had happened. Each of us held opposing lips of the crater by outposts connected to the front lines by saps. Well, these smart Huns had angled over their crater lip under a good sniper fire, captured two of our men and shot the rest of the post. The Colonel was so mad he was all for rushing into the crater himself. The men captured were a fat chap called Burgess and his pal, A. F. Hastings. I think Hastings reached a German prison camp but we never again heard of poor old Burgess, although in the attack eighteen days later we found a copy of his interrogation in which he had lied like a true trooper . . . told the Hun that our morale was terrible, food was short, and things in the Canadian Corps at a low ebb . . . I think he was ' done in '. A note stated that he was a ' low intelligence type.' We retaliated a few nights later with a fast raid on the Hun front line behind the crater, and killed the whole garrison in the area. Lance/Corporal Johnny Morton got on a high spot and, with his Lewis-gun crew, wiped out an attempted counter-attack.

" By 5 April, we were in battle positions and still playing the role of pack mules by day while at night digging new jumping-off trenches that Heinie and the pelting rain wiped out every night. We didn't know the date of the attack but our dumbest blank file knew it wasn't far away. Funny about that, I think very few men are much concerned with fear of death. Fear of mutilation—a shell splinter in the belly, for example— seemed more real. In fact, I took my entrenching tool from the back of my web belt and hooked it up in front. Of course, men with wives and children had reason to worry. The night before we were to go over—that was 8 April—I looked up some pals in a nearby dugout just to hear what they would find to talk about. They were mainly Scots, of my brother's platoon, and all from Victoria, British Columbia. I could hear their voices through the gas blanket. There was Al McKinnon and Jimmy Nairn and Jimmy McKeown arguing like billy-bedammed about . . . soccer! They were good men to have with you in a tough spot."

George Hancock of the P.P.C.L.I. recalled that the Germans were confident, too. "A German officer was captured on a raid, and he said, ' We know you're going to attack Vimy Ridge. We know all about your plans.' He says, ' You might get to the top of Vimy Ridge, but I'll tell you this, you'll be able to take all Canadians back to Canada in a row boat that get there.' Fortunately for us, he was wrong."

CHAPTER FOUR

BIG-GUN BUILD-UP

'Red Knight' Moves

The little biplane came speeding down the valley below tree-top height, the snarl of its engine re-echoing off the slope of the Vimy Heights. Amazed soldiers, expecting to see only the accustomed red-white-and-blue roundels of the R.F.C., saw instead the black Maltese Cross of the Imperial German Air Force. And thought, ' Richthofen's here! '

" That was about two days before the kick-off, and we were laying extra telephone lines at the time," recalled Donald Patrick, M.M., of HQ 8 Brigade, 3rd Division. " He flew right up the centre of the valley so low that nobody dared to shoot. He was so close to me that I felt the wind from his propeller. I could have hit him with a stone if I had had one. He must have got an eyeful."

The Richthofen Circus had indeed arrived on the Vimy front. Patrick's identification was based, however, not on aircraft recognition, but on the daring shown by the pilot. " There were certain common beliefs about Richthofen," he pointed out. " As Germany's top Ace he had a prestige that Allied flyers didn't have. His flyers were supposed to be all hand-picked by himself for extra daring. They sought, and were given, the toughest missions. This low-flying reconnaissance would be right in their mitt. Also they were kept right up to date on the latest and fastest planes, and as a challenge they were always painted mahogany red, hence the name ' Red Devil '. I don't think there can be any doubt that the flyer on that occasion was one of Richthofen's men or, perhaps, even himself as was suggested by some at the time."

" The German aeroplanes became much more aggressive than in 1916," wrote James A. Iveson, now a Major, O.B.E., M.C., but then a Lieutenant of 145 East Cheshire Heavy Battery, in a contemporary account. " In 1916 the British aeroplanes un-

doubtedly held command of the air and two or three German
'planes would scatter and run for it on the appearance of one
British 'plane. Either their morale or their machines, or perhaps
both, had by the early months of 1917 undergone a considerable
improvement for, for some time, the position appeared almost
to be reversed. I think that probably the squadron of red 'planes,
commanded by Baron von Richthofen, was responsible for this
state of affairs. These 'planes were known as 'the red circus'.
They were reckless in the extreme and before our batteries were
supplied with Lewis guns for anti-aircraft protection, I remember
running out of the mess dug-out to see what I expected was a
British 'plane flying very low over the battery position, only to
find, to my amazement, that it was a German 'plane which had
just skimmed over the battery and was far away by the time the
gunners had brought their rifles to their shoulders. There was,
however, a very sad side to aerial warfare. I do not know whether
our fighting 'planes did the same, but the German fighting
'planes would often attack and bring down one of our solo
artillery 'planes which had no chance whatever against them and
could only at a speed of perhaps 80 m.p.h. endeavour to make
its way to our lines with the much faster German 'plane hovering
over it like a hawk over a pigeon."

For many weeks, there had been a new and ominous note
in the reports, official and unofficial, of Royal Flying Corps
pilots. " 22 *March*. Lidsey and a sergeant pilot brought down by
the 'red hun' today; the sergeant may live, but it is rather
doubtful . . ." " 24 *March*. I saw two absolutely red huns today
and kept my eye on them; they are very fast. We are badly de-
ficient in the way of protection owing to the changing of
machines in our fighting squadrons. This should be remedied in
three or four days. Three F.Es. do seven hours each a day to look
after us. We work in batches. Owing to the huns, we are not
able to go over the lines with the same ease that we used to . . ."
" 25 *March*. Halligan was sent up during the afternoon to make
another effort and while over Vimy was chased by a hun. He
went down in spirals, stalls, etc., thinking he had got to his own
side of the lines. Instead of being our side, he was over Lens at
500 feet. He saw the huns as plain as day. They were pulling
their guns out of the emplacements and popping off at him

machine-guns and every conceivable thing was firing at him. He crossed the trenches under 1,000 feet, twisting and turning the whole way with the result that they only punctured the machine in three places. It was a great effort. Halligan is an old soldier, he was a sergeant-major in the Dublin Fusiliers and he said it was the tightest corner he had ever been in, so it must have been pretty warm . . ." " 28 March. Knight and Lloyd were attacked by two huns; they succeeded in putting a nasty one through Lloyd's thigh, fracturing the bone. But the vets say he will be all right. Knight had the skin knocked off his finger so that makes the third time he has been wounded. They were very unfortunate, as while they were spiralling round things went all right, but on coming out of it, about three bullets went through the machine, one of which got Lloyd. Bishop was attacked, but Mackenzie succeeded in putting two drums into them, whereupon they sheared off. Four of the devils attacked the three F.E.s and succeeded in puncturing the tank of one—he was obliged to return, the other two were less fortunate. One F.E. was brought down our side of the lines, but the other followed a hun over the other side and was shot down by the remaining three. So we have had a bad day. Brooke-Taylor was wounded in the arm with a piece of shrapnel but has not gone sick . . ." All these reports are from No. 16 Squadron, R.F.C., which had been attached to the Canadian Corps for the special purpose of artillery spotting, with the idea of knocking out the German batteries. And the air battle was to increase in concentrated violence over the Vimy-Arras battlefield so that the following month was to go down in the history of the Royal Flying Corps as ' Bloody April '.

There was a logical order in these events, but the arrival of Richthofen was their culmination, not their starting point. The process began, naturally enough, with the order for the offensive. This could not succeed unless the enemy's wire, the enemy's machine-guns, and the enemy's batteries were blown apart. That would require the concentration of a mass of artillery of all calibres. This artillery, and especially the heavy guns engaged in counter-battery work and the knocking out of selected strongpoints, would require to have their fire accurately directed. That would be done by observers of all kinds—in Forward Observation Posts on high ground, in stationery balloons, and in aeroplanes. And the counter to the concentration of observation balloons and spotting aircraft was, for the Germans, the concentration of fighter aircraft to raid the former and intercept the latter, under the direction of a system of ground control posts equipped with mounted telescopes and direct telephone lines to the fighter aerodromes. Only in this way could they hope to counter the Allied counter-move of concentrating superior numbers of fighters. That spring of 1917, the Allies had an overall numerical superiority in aircraft of three to one; but by a freak of invention and production, they had fallen behind the Germans in technical excellence by a matter of a few months only. The new crop of German aircraft were already in service in numbers, whereas their Allied counterparts were entering action only in driblets and with many 'teething troubles' still uncured. And many of their pilots were untrained, under-trained, or inexperienced.

But the first move was the move of the artillery. In all, nearly 1,000 guns to support the assault on Vimy: one heavy gun to every twenty yards of front; one field gun for every ten yards. Virtually wheel to wheel.

When on 5 February, 1917, Captain E. J. D. Routh, an experienced Army Co-operation pilot, was posted from No. 34 Squadron on the Somme to No. 16 Squadron at Vimy as a flight commander, almost the first thing he heard was the local astounding story—"There's an Admiral commanding a 60-pounder battery down here! His name is Eyres, and he's really a Major." Not only was it true, but on 14 February he was doing his first 'shoot' with this unit, 145 (East Cheshire) Heavy Battery.

James Iveson, who joined the battery in 1916, well recalled his first meeting with his new CO. " Admiral Cresswell John Eyres, D.S.O., was at this time well into his fifties and his uniform was covered with field glasses, compasses, haversacks, gas masks and all kinds of appliances, as he strode into the courtyard where we met. His stern, clean-cut, naval face, looked very much like business, and he made a very definite and forceful impression on everyone with whom he came into contact. His history had been already somewhat remarkable.

" When war broke out the Admiral had already retired after about forty years' Naval service. But the war-horse smelt blood and it was not long before he was firing at the Germans with a 4·7″ gun from barges in the Flanders canals. Following this he proceeded to the Dardanelles and became Beach-master at Helles on the Gallipoli peninsula where, I was told (and can well believe it), he used to walk the beach entirely regardless of the Turkish shells with which it was regularly swept. For his services the Admiral was awarded the Croix de Commandeur of the Legion of Honour; and the red rosette and ribbon of this decoration frequently brought the Admiral some recognition from the French peasantry who would take off their hats to an officer wearing a decoration so important in their eyes. After his return from Gallipoli I understand the Admiral asked for more war service, but was told that he was too old for further active service but could either be appointed Senior Naval Officer on the Tyne or, alternatively, he could proceed to Russia and endeavour to re-organise the railways. The Admiral, who felt that he had waited forty years for such an enjoyable war as now presented itself, was much grieved and hurt at the prospect of being deprived of active participation in the present very promising campaign, and after rejecting the Admiralty's offers proceeded immediately to the War Office where, in view of his long naval experience as a gunnery officer, he was soon made a Lieutenant-Colonel in the Royal Artillery. The Army despatched him to Salisbury Plain for training, but he very soon demanded that he should be immediately sent to France to fight and, on their protesting that he could hardly expect to command a Brigade in the field on so brief a military experience, the Admiral asked if he could not be reduced to the rank of Major and sent out to the Western Front in command of a Battery. This the War Office agreed to do.

" Major Davidson (First Lieutenant with 145 in those days) assures me that his somewhat extraordinary story of the sailing of the Battery is perfectly true. The Battery had embarked at Southampton, following much difficulty in getting on board the 240 or so horses. The Admiral, somewhat weary after his efforts, had retired to his cabin when it was announced to Davidson and Elliot, the two subalterns on board, that His Majesty the King was already on the ship in the course of an inspection of the Port and the transport arrangements. Neither of the two subalterns fancied the job of waking the Admiral and they tossed up. Davidson, having lost the toss, apprehensively knocked. When advised that the King was on board, the Admiral did not seem at all perturbed and casually proceeded on deck, failing however to don his Sam Browne belt. Despite this omission and the fact that his uniform was somewhat soiled after his labours, he saluted with the remark, ' Good day, Your Majesty ', to which the King replied, ' Good day, Admiral Eyres ', immediately following which the Admiral held out his hand to the King and they shook hands, exchanging at the same time the friendly greeting, ' How are you, Cresswell? ', ' How are you, George? ' It seemed that they were old friends in the days when the King had served as a Naval Officer, but such a revelation of this long standing relationship staggered those who were not prepared for it."

The Battery moved into positions at Bray and Anzin, near Arras, and the first night there was a night to remember, for Iveson. " The Admiral left me in charge of the guns for a short time whilst he retired to his dug-out, ordering me, whether he was back or not, to open fire at a fixed time. When that time arrived the Admiral had not turned up, so I opened fire. A few moments later a dishevelled figure blundered forward from the darkness. It was the Admiral who, having lost his way, found himself in front of the guns when fire was opened. This was a most unpleasant and alarming experience at any time. Nevertheless, the Admiral applauded me for having obeyed orders to the letter, and it proved a happy, rather than an unfortunate, incident from my point of view. We soon learnt that the Admiral enjoyed an utter contempt for danger and liked nothing better than that the guns should be fired under his command at the same time as the Battery position was being shelled. On the burst of a shell, he would say, ' Don't duck, don't duck, what are you ducking for? ' Once, he was rudely brushed aside by one of the men who became excited and exclaimed, ' There goes my b------- dug-out!' The Admiral did not address the man, as this would not have accorded with his ideas of discipline, but reproved the subaltern in charge, coldly directing him to restrain his men.

" The Admiral was once asked by the Brigadier General commanding the Corps Heavy Artillery, to become a Colonel on his staff, thinking no doubt that the Admiral would regard this as welcome promotion but the offer was firmly and, indeed, contemptuously declined by the Admiral with the words, ' I have been on the staff of Admirals, I have been an Admiral myself, I have been an A.D.C. to the King and, at my time of life, you ask me to be on the staff of a Brigadier General. *No, sir,* thank you.'

" He ensured that his officers were thoroughly trained by making them give orders for an imaginary shoot, using a stop watch to ensure that they were given both accurately and speedily. He would ask you problems, such as ' Aeroplane sends B—what reply do you give? ', with a view to ensuring that you were thoroughly acquainted with the ground signals, given by white strips laid near the Battery position, with which we communicated with the aeroplane in reply to its wireless messages. The position was peculiar, in that whilst attached to our Battery were two or three Royal Flying Corps personnel, who received the wireless signals from the aeroplane, there was no means, except by putting out ground strips, by which we could reply to the aeroplane's signals."

The use of aircraft as mobile observation posts was then highly experimental, but vitally important to the conduct of a battle, especially a ' set-piece ' affair such as Vimy was going to be. There were four distinct tasks which could be set: Contact patrol, photographic cover, artillery shoots, and ground strafing. Ground strafing was not at this time a serious occupation, as there were no proper forward-firing machine-guns on the B.E.2cs. and B.E.2es. mainly used for the work and they could carry 20 lb. bombs only. The photographs were taken with large plate-cameras lashed on outboard of the pilot's cockpit, which was behind the observer's. Unless very careful note was made at the time, it could be difficult to pin the pictures together in the right order afterwards, because a typical battlefield after the artillery had been put on to it looked like a featureless morass—which it was—with few if any recognisable features. At the conclusion of the Somme battle Captain Routh was told that a Guards battalion had lost sixteen men, by exhaustion and drowning, while coming back out of the 'trenches'; one of the men had been trapped up to his neck in liquid mud for forty six hours before being rescued, only to die fifteen minutes afterwards from the effects of his ordeal. Naturally, an offensive conducted by such methods could never 'break through', but must always break down; the artillery, which helped the infantry forward initially, provided the built-in brake to prevent them ever getting out of bottom gear, so to speak. And, eventually, the exertion of merely existing left neither time nor inclination for fighting. A contemporary note, for the Somme, dated 12 November, 1916, reads: "The Bosche are on very friendly terms. Rifle shooting never occurs, provided you do not commit an act of hostility, such as watching them or their immediate reserves with glasses. If you show signs of doing this, the Bosche will slowly put up his rifle and tell you to leave off."

Generals could no longer stand on a hill and personally watch the progress of a battle, nor could they keep even in rudimentary touch with it by telephone, because almost invariably the enemy's counter-fire cut the lines. In the past, men on horseback could quickly convey messages to and from the General, but this, too, was no longer possible in the battle area. Messages could only go by men on foot, struggling for hours through the morass, and perhaps dying in it. The staff were no longer in contact with the battles they were supposed to conduct. Hence the 'Contact Patrol' by low-flying aeroplanes, designed to re-forge the link, but, on the Somme in 1916, operating a system insufficiently rehearsed and in many quarters definitely mistrusted. Much rehearsal was required, because the means of air-to-ground communication, and vice versa, were extremely primitive. For instance, there had been a proposal that aeroplanes should drop smoke bombs as a signal from the General to the infantry, that the battle could begin; this was because of the difficulty of synchronising watches. But once the battle had started, the task of the aeroplanes was to find out where the infantry had got to, what was happening, and what they wanted. The aeroplane signalled for a report from the infantry by making noises on a Klaxon horn. The sequence of events, as noted from the air, would all too often be:

(a) red flares from the old position (which, being interpreted, meant, " We have got nowhere ");

(b) a strip message on the ground reading " XX " (" held up by m.g. fire ");

(c) a strip message on the ground reading " OO " (" barrage wanted ").

The aeroplane observer would then write down a detailed message, put it in a message-bag with long red-yellow-blue streamers attached, and drop this at Corps HQ. The message might contain other information, such as the progress of the tanks. For instance, Captain Routh was flying over the first tank attack ever made, that at Flers on the Somme, 15 September, 1916, and from above the whole picture was plain. The tracks of the tanks over the morass could be followed until the eye reached the tanks themselves—one stranded in the mud by Posieres, two at Martinpuich—one of these flying a red flag to denote that it was out of action, the other proceeding to the rear, apparently damaged; another tank stuck in a German trench at High Wood, and burning; two more lying on their sides in the British front-line trench, having fallen over in the morass. And so on . . . In fact, an excellent and most graphic lesson in how *not* to handle armour—in penny packets and over unsuitable ground. Nevertheless, eight tanks were to be allotted to 2nd Canadian Division for the Vimy assault.

In order to carry out their task, the aircraft had to fly very low; preferably at between 2,000 and 2,500 feet, but often a low cloud ceiling would force them down to 500 or even 350 feet. Even at 2,000, the sound of the British guns firing and of the German shells exploding underneath could be plainly heard above the noise of the clattering and unreliable engine. They were fired at from the ground by rifles and machine-guns, and could actually see the men who were firing at them, but this was not half so alarming as flying, as they had to, within their own barrage, hearing and occasionally seeing British shells go past them as thick as rifle bullets, the machine rocking and bumping in the wildly disturbed air, and with the conscious fear of a hit. Once, over the Somme, Captain Routh was actually watching two of his friends flying a Morane Parasol a short distance away, when it was struck. " A shell appeared to strike the wing, which immediately folded up, the machine going into a spinning nose dive and continuing in this manner until the ground was reached. They must have been killed instantaneously. It was a horrid sight," he wrote shortly afterwards.

The B.E.2e was not unlike a Tiger Moth, which was in fact descended from it. Apart from being almost defenceless, it was extremely slow, and in a high wind hardly moved over the ground. As the prevailing wind on the Western Front in summer was south-west—that is, blowing *into* the German lines, the return journey could be awkward. " It takes such an infernal time to get home," noted Captain Routh. " You do about twenty m.p.h. land speed instead of sixty. And take thirty five minutes to do a ten minute trip." Sixty m.p.h. was the cruising speed; if everything was perfectly adjusted, they could just about touch eighty m.p.h. with throttle wide open. Even so, the greatest barrier to the acceptance of the value of aeroplane observation was a belief strongly held in many important quarters that an observer moving swiftly about the sky must necessarily be unable to note anything on the ground below. For instance, a contemporary impression of the Somme battle, 28 July, 1916: " Some of our heavy guns have not been given a target for ten days, simply because some divisions do not believe that the R.F.C. can see anything from above. It shows an awful lack of knowledge on the part of the senior gunner officers, i.e., those on Corps and Divisional staffs. The gunners were very annoyed because the Corps had plenty of targets which the R.F.C. had sent down, but they had not taken the trouble to send them on to the Batteries." And later, on 7 August: " The whole trouble with infantry is that they do not realise how much we can see and consequently do not trust us." Of course, these people were thinking in ground terms, perhaps of the motor car, but more likely of the horse; and it was true that, from a horse going across country at sixty m.p.h., one would not see very much. Without actually ascending in an aeroplane, it was impossible to grasp the fact that the contraption appeared to be standing still, the only indication of motion being the way the leading edge of the lower wing crept slowly forward over the ground.

To do them justice, some of the staff were made to realise this, and, at the last moment, actually during the battle, ordered senior officers, from divisional generals downwards, to attend Contact Patrol exercises and go up for flights.

But it was still a very novel experience for the generals concerned. For instance, Routh (attached to R.F.C. from the K.R.R.C., the 60th Rifles, as a lieutenant) was laying down the law at a demonstration to the commander of 5th Division, General Stephens (also ex-Rifle Brigade), the commander of 13th Brigade, and many lesser lights, when the demonstrating aeroplane suddenly landed. At this, the whole ' class ' deserted and, like big schoolboys, ran " hell for leather to look at the intrepid aviator," who turned out to be a young gentleman who appeared to be about sixteen and had just been violently air-sick. Next day, Routh gave flights to signallers from 15th Brigade of the same Division, and these he thought intelligent men, for they had already grasped the fact that German shellfire dropped markedly when R.F.C. aircraft were about, because the Germans did not want to risk their gun positions being located and subjected to observed counter-battery fire. On the other hand, a ' scheme ' with a different division was an utter failure because, although the aeroplane went through the motions, the ground troops did not reply to the signals. " After half an hour I landed and went to see if I could find some responsible person," wrote Routh later. " I found the Brigade Major, who knew absolutely damn all about flares, sheets, signals. I then went up and saw the Brigadier, who knew a little less than the Brigade-Major."

With six months experience in the trenches with 3rd Battalion of the 60th Rifles, followed by seven months of contact patrols, photography, artillery observation, and bombing, with the R.F.C., Routh was promoted and posted as Flight Commander to No. 16 Squadron for the battle of Vimy Ridge. Appropriately, there were a number of Canadians in the squadron. On 18 February he attended a Wing Conference, where the artillery programme for the coming battle was outlined, including the large allotment of heavy and super-heavy guns, with plenty of ammunition. The work of the spotting planes was obviously going to be vital to the success of the assault, and this pleased Routh as it meant that his hard-gained' experience was to be

put to use. He soon learned also that the almost defenceless B.Es.
were to be protected by F.Es. The F.E.2b and 2d was a 'pusher'
aircraft with the engine at the rear and the observer/gunner in
the nose able to fire ahead, unobstructed by the propeller,
whereas the observer in the B.E. was caged in by wings, wires
and whirling blades, having such limited fields of fire that it
was hardly worthwhile giving him a gun. The slow speed of the
F.E. would in this case be an advantage, as it would enable the
escort to keep close attendance on the spotting machines. However, the advantages of speed and height (which meant surprise)
and of twin machine-guns synchronised to fire through the propeller, would lie with the new high-performance German inter-
ceptors, the Halberstadt and what was then known as the
Albatross 'destroyer'. They would have the initiative. For the
airmen, and for the artillery, the Battle of Vimy Ridge did not
start on 9 April, but many weeks before.

" Things began to move very rapidly now and hosts of Batteries took up their position in front of the Vimy Ridge so that,
in parts, they were almost wheel to wheel," wrote Iveson. " For
a month or so a concentrated strafe on the Bosche line continued.
Thousands upon thousands of rounds were fired and the poor
wretched village of Thelus must have been a good place to
avoid, for on occasions there would be a concentrated strafe on
the village for five minutes during which every gun on the front
that could bear, fired as hard as it could go into the dilapidated
ruins. The 30th March is given in my diary as one of the days
when Thelus was heavily strafed by heavy guns." This was no
exaggeration. Michael Volkheimer was there with Bavarian Reserve Infantry Regiment No. 3, and he recalled, " After several
days of uninterrupted barrage from artillery of all calibres, the
enemy finally levelled our defensive positions, the 1st Line, 2nd
Line, 3rd Line, and all the connecting trenches as well. We
sought shelter in the dug-outs which were deep below the ground,
but soon the entrances were blown in and many German soldiers
buried alive." The last week before the assault, the Germans
were to call 'the week of suffering'. Both reinforcements and
rations failed to get through. The shocked, exhausted men were
without food, let alone hot food, in the bitter cold and with the

barrage raging above; when it ended there would come, not relief, but the assault.

To smash the deep dugouts and the concrete strongpoints on the Ridge, the British moved up their heaviest guns; not for barrage fire but for the knocking out of selected targets with a few carefully ranged and observed rounds. The heaviest of all were the 15" howitzers of the Royal Marine Artillery Brigade, which had been designed originally at the Coventry Ordnance Works for use in monitors against the German-held Belgian ports. It is this gun which is the subject of the Royal Artillery War Memorial at Hyde Park Corner in London. The real thing weighed some twenty tons. To shift it, with its stores and ammunition, took nine tractors each pulling one, and sometimes two, trailers. Their speed on the level was about eight m.p.h., but in icy conditions they would often refuse to negotiate hills and had to be winched to the top. These guns were never close together, but were emplaced separately a mile or so behind the front line. No. 9 Gun was sited at the Bois-de-la-Haie, near the headquarters of 4th Canadian Division. " The first job was for the gunners to dig a gun-pit, two feet deep and twenty feet square," recalled Mr. G. P. Roberts who served with this gun. " Then sixteen iron bedplates, about four feet square and two inches thick, would be laid on this and fixed together. On top, two rows of girders would be placed crossways and bolted. Onto this would be bolted the gun carriage in two parts; then the gun muzzle, also in two parts, one of them an inner casing; and lastly, a derrick would be rigged for hoisting the shells. This would take a whole day in favourable conditions and I have known it take four days. The parts would be brought up one at a time, so as to avoid giving a clue to any enemy planes, and after the gun was erected, it was camouflaged." Such care was not always taken. The ' Admiral ', for instance, insisted on having his guns brightly polished, and Captain Routh noted that aggrieved complaints from III Canadian Siege Battery, that they were being shelled, was explained by the fact that every gun was plainly visible from 2,000 feet, whereas the guns of 58th Siege, which had not been troubled, were much better concealed. As an object lesson, No. 16 Squadron flew some of the gunners over their own gunsites; and what they saw astonished them.

While the 15″ howitzer was being erected, there would be only two breaks from work, of fifteen minutes each, for dinner and tea. " Dinner was mostly bully beef soup, with potatoes if you were lucky. Tea was always the same: two slices of bread and marg., sometimes jam, with a big enamel cup of tea." After dark, they would look around for somewhere to sleep, digging a hole in the ground, if no old dugout was available. " We found no trouble sleeping on the ground after the first two or three times, one got quite used to it," commented Mr. Roberts. " The general atmosphere of the war used to help. There was a great spirit of comradeship and rank, though respected, was not made apparent. No spit and polish, not surprisingly, as our shirts always housed little crawly insect families. On the whole, strangely enough, there was much I enjoyed about those times, sometimes frightened, sometimes wet and miserable, but generally, we were cheerful and jocular. At Vimy we had a pet jackdaw which had a damaged wing. No one knew how it had joined us, it just came. It could not fly, but would not leave us, I suppose because we fed it and made a fuss of it. We had a lot of fun giving it a ring or some other object—it had to be shiny—and watch the jackdaw go and bury it. The bird went as mysteriously as it came, but was missed the same day as one of the officers went on leave. Very suspicious.

"It took twelve men to man the gun: (1) gunlayer, (2) breach loader, (3) fuse worker, (4) barrel cleaner, (5 & 6) elevation of muzzle, (7 & 8) deflection of gun, (9 & 10) shell loaders, (11) cordite worker, (12) spare man working anywhere. Every man knew his job exactly and specialised in it. 5 ft. 10 in. was the minimum height, and most were over 6 ft. They were a fine body of men, fitted for the heavy work entailed. Working full speed, it took them five minutes to load and lay the gun. The shells were rolled up along a miniature railway and the day after preparing this we would begin ranging on our targets. We could not of course afford to waste many rounds of this calibre. The ranging would be done either by aeroplane, observation balloon (blimps, as we called them), or by our own trained observers in a strongpoint or pillbox with good observation over the enemy lines, who took morse code signalling apparatus with them. On receipt of a message from them, the gunnery officer would make a quick calculation as to weight of charge, deflection and elevation of the gun, and give it over a megaphone to the gun's crew. Generally about four or five rounds would get us on target, but as all this spotting depended on visibility, sometimes it would be four or five days before we could register. The targets were scattered—crossroads and strongpoints, one of which was a slag heap near Lens which had been converted into a machine-gun nest. We also succeeded in doing considerable damage to a group of German pillboxes in their support lines. Most of this work was done in the four days prior to the assault, with a few left over for luck on the actual day. We took no part in shelling their front lines, as owing to the area of explosion this would have been dangerous to our own troops. It seemed to me that there were certain drawbacks in our preliminary fire on defined targets, as it must have given the enemy some indication of an impending big assault, but it was necessary to destroy these strongpoints beforehand, as spotting would have been impossible and too late on the actual day. I got mumps after going to a Canadian barber and was sent to hospital the day before the assault, but was told it went off all right as far as we were concerned."[1]

Some Batteries preferred to observe by balloon, as they considered it the most accurate possible. At any rate, they were not likely to run out of petrol, or suffer engine failure at the critical moment. But they were very vulnerable, and balloon observers —unlike the occupants of aeroplanes—had parachutes. These were tied to the basket of the balloon in casings which soon rotted and were sometimes reinforced with string. This had led to the death, on the Somme, of a notable character on the Western Front, Basil Hallam, the musical comedy star famous for the 'hit' song *Gilbert the Filbert*. Lieutenant W. G. Dreschfield, who during the Arras-Vimy offensive commanded No. 36 Balloon Section, had been in Hallam's unit at the time. " This charming man killed himself most unfortunately, having forgotten to cut the string we used to hold our parachutes in their rotten casings," he recollected. " Hanging thus below his basket, he raised his arms over his head to cut it free, and the loose harness he wore

[1] No. 9 Gun fired 26 rounds on 3rd April, 50 on the 5th, 10 on the 6th, 30 on the 7th, 15 on the 8th, 16 on the 9th, 9 on the 10th, and 2 on the 12th. Lighter guns were firing up to 100 rounds per day to cut the German wire close to the Canadian trenches.

slipped over his head and down he came without a parachute. Before the Vimy battle, we registered the guns on or about their future targets, with a minimum of shots on easily-visible points such as cross-roads, church steeples and railway stations, so as not to give away either the positions or the numbers of our guns. Being connected by telephone to the Batteries, we directed their fire by direct visual observation, informing them simply if their shots were short or over, or so many degrees left or right, the degrees being marked on our field glasses. The Vimy battle followed the usual practice which our brilliant Allied staffs had inaugurated on the Somme and which I continued to witness later at Ypres, etc. Thousands of lives were regularly sacrificed to a war of attrition on the grounds that as we outnumbered the enemy we would eventually win. In fact, if the Americans had not arrived we would never have succeeded because with the idea of never giving up an inch of trench we kept our front lines heavily manned, whereas the Boche kept very few men forward, counting on counter-attacking to retake the positions, but only if they were of importance, thereby regularly losing fewer men."

Iveson's Battery also made use of the ' balloonatics ', as they were called, especially a character known as ' F '. " It was always a sign that he was becoming a trifle merry when he commenced to sing, ' Raspberry, strawberry, I am fond of pudding, I am, give me a little bit of roly poly roly poly jam '. He was a rummy character and full of pluck. One of F's passions was an undying hatred for the staff to which he would give vent with great eloquence and much force. He used to say that the best sight he saw on the Somme in '16 was two Brigadier Generals lying dead in the same shellhole."

Although, daily, Vimy Ridge was erupting with British shellfire, there was a puzzling lack of reply by the Germans. Mr. Roberts recalled it as a " quiet time "; No. 9 Gun had only two casualties, both slightly wounded. " Curiously enough the old Bosche, like Brer Fox, lay low and did little by way of retaliation," wrote Iveson. " I think he was saving his ammunition for a wonderful counter-strafe during what, he imagined, would be the last week of the bombardment. I believe he was much misled by a prisoner, who gave him April 16th as the date of the attack whereas, of course, it was made on Easter Monday, exactly a week before. The British High Command seemed to have no real idea of surprise attacks. That dour Scotsman, Sir Douglas Haig, preferred to deal the enemy hammer blows and the attacking policy of the British Forces consisted first of a few weeks of colossal artillery bombardment of the enemy lines and positions, followed by a mass attack at dawn, for the purpose of attaining certain defined objectives. Once the defined objectives were attained, there the attacking army must come to a full stop, whatever the position might be, and I think the Vimy Ridge attack, whilst on the whole successful, was a very good example of the weakness of this policy."

On 4 April, it was planned that the R.F.C. would start an offensive to obtain air supremacy over the battlefield, with the object of ensuring full artillery observation and contact with the assault forces on the day of the attack. The night before, an R.F.C. pilot wrote: " Tomorrow if fine should see Fritz with his tail firmly between his legs, as endless aeroplanes will go over to fight him on his own ground; scraps should be numerous, his aerodromes will be bombed, and he will have a lively time." ' Boom ' Trenchard, the R.F.C. general, had 369 spotting machines and 385 fighters—754 in all. The Germans, by denuding their other fronts, could put up 150 spotting machines and 114 fighters—264 in all. The German interceptor force of 114 fighters was outnumbered by more than three to one in its own kind and, overall, was facing odds of seven to one. Only the most economical use of their superior and speedy machines could be considered. Therefore, the tactics were to fight over their own territory as much as possible and to dive through the R.F.C. formations, picking off victims as they went, but not staying to engage in a protracted dogfight. As a result, in the four days before the attack—4th to 8th April—the R.F.C. lost 131 machines destroyed, of which seventy five were shot down (with the loss of 105 aircrew) and fifty six completely written off in major accidents. At the time, only the loss of twenty eight machines in the first forty eight hours was admitted, but even this caused a storm at home. ' Bloody April ', in which von Richthofen alone was to claim thirty personal victories, had begun. Trenchard knew that most of his machines, and many of his men, were out-classed, but they would have to carry on and take their losses. They did. Of one of his British victims at this time, Richthofen wrote, " This was once more a case of splendid daring. He defended himself to the last."

CHAPTER FIVE

PLAN AND COUNTER-PLAN

" All Troops Fully Fit To Fight "

Thus far, the build-up for the battle as it evolved—as it actually appeared to the participants at the time. But, simultaneously, another struggle was being waged at the Governmental and High Command level, just as involved and long-drawn-out, with many intricate twists and turns; although its end product was the ruin of the French Army and the near-ruin of the British Army, it touched the Vimy assault at a few points only and therefore need not be considered in detail. Briefly, a planning conference was held at French GHQ in November, 1916, at which it was de-cided to make 1917 a decisive year for the Allies. There were to be great offensives all around the besieged perimeter held by the Central Powers: The French, the British, the Italians, the Russians, all were to strike in one long blaze of battle. And decisive the events of the year were most certainly to be. The Italians were too weak to attack, the French Army did attack—and mutinied, the Germans (with some help from New York) arranged for a revolution in Russia, and America for the first time entered a European struggle for power. The results are with us yet.

On the Western Front, the British were to attack out of Arras while the Canadians secured their flank by capturing Vimy Ridge; this two-handed operation was designed to draw German reserves away from the areas, further south, where the French were to attack. And then Haig would transfer his forces north for the main British blow of the year, out of Ypres, in an attempt to capture the Belgian coast (this battle was to be known in his-tory as Passchendaele). But between the thought and the execu-tion, fell the shadow. Firstly, between the conference and the battle, the French changed their commander-in-chief. The old man, Joffre, had intended a French version of the Somme—another attrition-slaughter. The new man, Nivelle, promised a breakthrough, a decisive mobile battle, and a pursuit. Technically, this was to be based on new artillery tactics which had been brilliantly successful, on a small scale, at Verdun (and which were to be copied for Vimy); strategically, there was to be surprise. From the Somme to the Aisne, the German line bulged out into a great salient fifty miles deep into France. German reserves were to be drawn to the head of the salient by direct attack, then a second but unexpected offensive was to surprise them by striking quickly, violently, and brutally from the flank of the salient at its base, thus rolling up their flanks and throwing them into confusion for the final kill. There was nothing wrong with the principle of causing disruption by speed, violence and brutality, as the Germans were to demonstrate in 1940, but Nivelle expected to achieve it with unarmoured, boot-shod infantry carrying rifles at one or two m.p.h. Then fell the shadow. The Germans, anxious to conserve manpower, withdrew up to fifty miles from that great salient into defences prepared previously at leisure—the Siegfried Stellung, or 'Hindenburg Line'. They had taken the point out of the attack by removing the weakness, they had shortened their line so that it could be held in greater strength, and in the areas they vacated they left a desolate, booby-trapped wilderness through which the Allies advanced slowly and painfully to regain contact. Nevertheless, Nivelle persisted in his plan with that suicidal stubbornness which marks First World War generalship; however, his ruin, and the final ruin of the French Army, is not our story.

The points of contact are three: that the artillery technique used to take Vimy owed much to him; that Vimy had still to be taken because it was not included in the German withdrawal but, instead, virtually marked the northern hinge of a retirement which, for once, really was 'according to plan'; and that the Arras-Vimy offensive was still intended to draw away the German reserves from the areas to be attacked by Nivelle.

The offensive which began on 9 April, 1917, is usually referred to by the British as the Battle of Arras, confusing for Canadians who associate this title with a more memorable affair in 1918. To the Germans, it is known as *Die Osterschlacht bei Arras*. Sometimes it is called the Battle of the Scarpe, from a small river which runs through Arras. By whatever name it be called, the assault on Vimy Ridge was a limited and separate part of the main attack. The task of the Canadian Corps was to capture the Ridge, and then hold it; they were to advance no further. The rest of the First Army, of which they were a part, was to advance past the Ridge, which would then be guarding their flank, across the plain towards Douai, while the Third Army broke through to the East of Arras and advanced towards Cambrai. Therefore, it was only the Canadian part in the offensive which was limited. The overall idea was a breakthrough of some proportions, which would be exploited by massed cavalry held ready and waiting behind Arras. In the event, nothing so stirring occurred, the offensive failing in its main aims, so that the Canadian capture of Vimy Ridge stands as an achievement in its own right.

*   *   *

Viewed from the west, the Canadian side, Vimy Ridge was not a spectacular feature; long, gentle slopes led up to the three high points which, reading from north to south, were the 'Pimple', Hill 145, and Hill 135 near Thelus (the two latter being 145 and 135 metres high respectively, hence the designations). But, on the eastern side, the side farthest away from the Canadians, the drop into the Douai plain was steep and wooded. These woods were the German gun area. One other peculiarity of the terrain needs to be noted. The crest of the Ridge did not run parallel to the Canadian front lines. Starting very close to them in the north, where the 'Pimple' dominated the Souchez valley from the south, the crest angled away at nearly forty five degrees until, near Farbus, it sloped gently down to the Scarpe near Arras. Because Hills 145 and 135 were the dominating heights, and, furthermore, gave each other mutual fire protection, it was decided to divide the attack into two phases. The main attack would consist of the Southern Assault, to take and hold Hills 145 and 135, together with the ground they commanded. If this Southern Assault was successful, then a separate Northern Operation would be launched against the 'Pimple', which would complete the capture of Vimy Ridge and place the Allied line along the heights at all points, the Lorette spur on the north side of the Souchez river having been captured by the

French under Petain in 1915. Even so, the Southern Assault would, in effect, advance across a triangle: at the apex, the infantry would have a mere 700 yards to cover; but at the base, they would have to move forward 4,000 yards. The front of the advance (that is, the near side of the triangle) stretched for some four miles, but the troops on the right would have much further to go than those on the left.

The Canadian Divisions were lined up in order from right to left— the 1st, 2nd, 3rd, and 4th. The 2nd was judged to be not quite strong enough for its task, and was therefore alloted an extra brigade—the 13th Brigade of 5th Imperial Division—for the assault. The two remaining brigades of the British Division were to be held back on the first day, acting as the reserves to the Canadian Corps, but the divisional artillery was added to the Canadian effort.

Facing them, initially, were five German regiments, roughly equivalent to British brigades (of which there were three to a division). They were; reading from right to left also: Bavarian Reserve Regiment No. 3 (of 1st Bavarian Reserve Division), Reserve Regiments Nos. 263, 262, and 261 (of the Prussian 79th Reserve Division), and Bavarian Regiment No. 11 (of 16th Bavarian Division). Bavarian Reserve Regiment No. 3 had been at Vimy, as we have seen, since 1914, but the units of 79th Reserve Division had previously served on the Russian front, while the 16th Bavarian Division was a new formation. All three divisions were part of the 1 Bavarian Reserve Corps. In general discussion in 1965 one veteran remarked that the Canadians disliked both the Prussians and the Bavarians, but liked the Saxons —probably because they could push them around!

The Canadian plan was intended to ensure that they pushed the Prussians and Bavarians around also. In the first wave of the attack, 15,000 men were to assault positions held by 5,000 men; then 12,000 Canadian reserves were to be put through to meet 3,000 German reserves.

On 8 April, there was to be a night approach march by the assault troops into the trenches and craters of No-man's-land; they were to get as near to the enemy as possible, and wait there.

On 9 April, two large mines were to be exploded in the German lines and their guns deluged with counter-battery fire, plus a brief three minute barrage on the German front line. After those three minutes were up, this barrage would ' creep ' forward at the rate of 100 yards every three minutes, with the infantry following as close behind it as possible. This barrage was to be thickened up by a hail of bullets laid down by 150 machine-guns sweeping a zone 400 yards ahead of the infantry. Simul-taneously, to quell the German guns, and disorganise their reserves, the German batteries and dumps, already ' registered ', were to be swamped with high-explosive and gas shells. And, in places, a smokescreen was to be laid down by the heavy mortars.

The entire scheme was based on the fact that the German defensive arrangements on Vimy Ridge were out of date, almost necessarily so. Out of date, that is, in German eyes; for the Germans had learnt the lessons of the Somme and of Verdun. The Allies insisted in attacking in line; if one unit was held up, every other unit halted, too, fearful of flank attacks; a parade advance behind an artillery barrage after an immense bombard-ment. Clearly, it was vulnerable to dislocation by means of scattered strongpoints; and if these were sited well back and the front regarded as a lightly held buffer zone instead of as a rigid trench line to be defended to the last man, then two advantages would follow. The heavy losses among the infantry from the Allied bombardment would be largely avoided; and the losses of the field artillery, too, for this also would be held back, out of range of the enemy field guns. The enemy advance would tend to come to a halt, all along the line, merely because here and there a unit was held up by a strongpoint and by that time, too, the enemy would have come on beyond the protective range of his own field artillery, and therefore be ripe for counter-attack.

But Vimy Ridge offered little room for deploying such an elastic defence—it was the last of the heights, and had to be held in fair strength fairly far forward. Behind it, there was only the plain, and five miles or so in rear the as yet incomplete ' stop ' position of the Wotan II Line (known to the Allies as the Drocourt-Quéant Line), which butted up to the Siegfried (or Hindenburg) Line. Vimy had been turned into a Gibraltar, with underground tunnels and dugouts, and belts of wire forty yards wide; and as a Gibraltar, it must stand or fall. What made it especially vulnerable was the fact that all the deep dugouts and tunnel entrances were inside the first 700 yards of German front line to be attacked. The British and Canadian planners had seized on this weakness, and their assault, long anticipated by the Germans, contained one staggering element of surprise. The preliminary bombardment was to be unexpectedly, unprecedentedly short; all these positions were to be rushed, while the Germans were still deep down below, firmly convinced that, at the least, many hours, and possibly several days, must elapse before the attacking waves came over. Whereas, it was to be a matter of minutes only. Unaware of this, and made arrogant by their long and successful defence of the Ridge hitherto, contemptuous of the obvious blunderings of their opponents in the past, the defenders of Vimy—at staff level—had become grossly over-confident.

*　　*　　*

Over the entire front to be attacked by the British and Canadians, some dozen miles in all, the defences of General von Falkenhausen's 6th Army were not in accord with the new principle of defence in depth: they were completely out of date. The dugouts and deep shelter tunnels were in the front line instead of well back and the trenches in a poor state of repair; and the artillery also was well forward, their dispersal to the rear having only just begun. Worse, the reserve divisions intended for counter-attack were held very far back. In effect, there was a hard crust with very little immediately behind it, and a breakthrough was possible, provided the Allies mastered the technique of forward flow, so that fresh divisions were fed smoothly into the break and supplies came up as if by conveyor belt, instead of—as was normal—getting helplessly snarled up in their own traffic arrangements. Nevertheless, an atmosphere of confidence reigned. It started at the top, with the Army Group Commander, Crown Prince Rupprecht, who announced: " The great spring offensives are imminent, and, especially on the front of the 6th Army, we must expect the attack any day. I am firmly convinced that this year also all enemy offensives will fail, provided every one of us does his best. The reserve divisions will remain where they are and will not move without a personal order from me." Major Mende, who had been ordered by the

High Command to report on the situation in the area of the 6th Army, was equally optimistic: "Group Souchez: defence measures well advanced. Group Vimy: preparations well advanced, defence well organised. Group Arras: preparations still behind." And of the two groups which were not to be attacked: "still retarded, but the possibilities for an effective defence are at hand." Von Falkenhausen's own appreciation was: "Divisions up to strength and holding a small area, spread out in depth and with a defendable trench system, familiar with the tactics of a defensive battle, and with quite presentable artillery support and services, will perhaps lose part of their front line, but cannot be over-run in their entirety. It will have to be accepted that the reserve divisions will not arrive until the second day of the battle."

5 April was the day the Germans became worried. The Allied artillery fire had doubled in intensity, compared to March, and continued to over-power the German artillery. On 4 April, the Germans fired 23,000 rounds against an estimated 79,000. On 5 April, 30,000 against an estimated 90,000. On 6 April, 24,000 against an estimated 80,000. And most of the German fire was directed against actual or potential raids, very little of it was counter-battery. Remorselessly, the German trenches were flattened out, and great gaps torn in their wire. British and Canadian infantry raids were constantly being carried out in great strength, to check on the effects of the bombardments. By 5 April, the Germans knew that the attack was coming, not in the next few weeks, as they had previously thought, but within the next few days. And realised that they had been caught with their preparations far from complete. That afternoon, General Ludendorff asked for the state of artillery reinforcements for the threatened front, and when told that most of the batteries allocated were not yet in position, he issued urgent orders for a speed-up. Next day, 6 April, he ordered a concentration on counter-battery work by the artillery already in position. The groups promptly asked for more ammunition, and Ludendorff gave permission to expend stocks. That day also, there were the first reports of cavalry massed behind the British lines— almost sure indication that Haig intended a breakthrough. The ruthless disregard for losses by the R.F.C. in an obvious attempt

to gain air supremacy over the battlefield, and the destruction they were able to cause by bombing in the back areas, was another indication.[1] Von Falkenhausen authorised the use of gas shells, previously held back for counter-battery work at the last minute, because existing stocks were small. Pioneers, Labour Corps units, tunnellers, and defence-construction units were ordered to concentrate in the 6th Army area to help build new defences. 6th Army were told that 233 horse-drawn and twenty eight motorised units were on their way, and would be available —as from 10 April.

By 7 April, the deployment of the fighting troops had been practically concluded, except for the artillery. Many of the batteries allocated to the 6th Army, and particularly the heavy guns which were being reconditioned, were not ready, and would not be ready—until 10 April. Or later. And the field artillery of the divisions lying well back in reserve was still back with those divisions, instead of forward where it could help the defence. Those fresh batteries which had been moved in were not yet fully operational, because the system of observation posts and telephone lines upon which they depended were not yet ready, or bad weather had prevented them from registering upon their intended targets, or insufficient ammunition had been brought up. The infantry units were under-strength, but reinforcements of ten machine-gun sharpshooter units had arrived to support them.

Nevertheless, the German High Command did not consider the situation really dangerous. This was because the power of their own artillery seemed unshaken, and must increase from day to day. Up to 5 April, the German artillery losses for the whole front were: one man killed, eighteen wounded; five guns destroyed, ten damaged. That left Group Vimy with 297 guns (seventy batteries) still available. On 6 April, this figure was reduced by British fire to sixty nine batteries, and Group Arras lost thirteen of its 352 guns. Unimportant losses, which would be more than made good as fresh batteries moved into position. On 7 April, the 6th Army appreciation was: " The three divisions

[1] According to German computation, the R.F.C. lost fifty aircraft between 1st and 9th April—a very modest estimate, less than two-thirds of the actual figure for combat losses alone. Normally, reports by all sides claimed three machines shot down for every one actually shot down.

in the line are fully battle-worthy, although the men seem to be mentally and physically less alert after the strain of the last few days bombardment, but should be capable of withstanding a major offensive." After a conference with the Chief of Staff of the Groups at Douai, General von Nagel reported in similar terms, but with one important proviso: " I believe it possible to bring their first wave of attack to a halt, but we must expect that in places the enemy will break through the front line trenches. A counter-attack may suffice to halt them. However, the demands on the troops in this first stage of the offensive will be so great, that they will have to be relieved immediately it is over. They will be unable to withstand any further attacks."

Expecting, from previous experience, to be able to halt any British advance at an early stage, the German High Command thought that the British might intend a limited operation against Vimy as a preliminary. The bombardment was taking place along a twenty kilometre front, as against forty kilometres on the Somme the previous year, when it had broken down with the most appalling casualties in the history of the British Army, then or since. Von Falkenhausen still did not move the reserve divisions forward to positions from which they could intervene quickly; this was because he did not want their training interrupted and because the forward areas were congested. One of these divisions, the 17th Infantry Division, was in fact being used as a labour force to hastily complete the Wotan Line. On 5 April, however, he did order preparations to be made to transport forward in case of emergency two divisions only—the 1st Guards Reserve Division and the 18th Infantry Division. Next day, Ludendorff was urging the Crown Prince's Army Group to get von Falkenhausen to move forward all his reserve divisions, except the one labouring on the Wotan Line. And on 7 April Major von Xylander, G.S.O.1 of 6th Army, was reporting by telephone: " The 18th Division and the entire Guards Reserve Corps will be brought forward today and tomorrow behind Group Arras, as there's no room anywhere else. At the moment, it looks as if the enemy intends to take Vimy Ridge as a springboard for further attacks. It can't be the ' Big Push ' yet, the area's far too small."

At 1400 hours on 7 April, 6th Army (having obtained permission from the Crown Prince) ordered a half-hearted move forward of the reserve divisions: The 18th Infantry Division was to move up as far as Douai in support of Group Vimy, and the two divisions of the Guards Reserve Corps were to march their infantry as far as the Lille-Douai road, during 8th and 9th April, but leaving their divisional 'tails' behind them. These three divisions would still be some twenty kilometres (about twelve miles) behind the front on 9 April. The reason for this was the German basic appreciation that the Allied offensive was likely to take the form of an attack on a narrow front to capture the Vimy Heights, which would meet the fate of all such assaults in the past; and that in any event this would be followed later by a much more powerful offensive, not merely from south of Vimy in the Arras area, but perhaps also north of Vimy towards Lens. In that case the reserve divisions were well stationed and would have plenty of warning anyway. On 7 April, it was reported to 6th Army that intercepted enemy telephone messages showed British cavalry massed behind Arras, normally indication of a 'Big Push', but this information had to be weighed against the narrow, twelve mile front of the bombardment. The possibility that this was a feint and that the main offensive might take the form of a surprise assault in the north at Wytschaete, could not be disregarded, as there had been much patrol activity in that region. But that some offensive action in the Vimy-Arras area was imminent was clear, from the interrogations of prisoners, who stated that the bombardment was the preparation for an attack. The German estimate of the number of British and Canadian troops facing them was that the force consisted of twelve to fourteen divisions. As against that, the retirement to the Hindenburg Line had freed some twenty German divisions to the general reserve.

The British and Canadians might achieve some initial successes, but they would never break through. On the evening of 7 April, 6th Army reported to the High Command: "All troops fully fit to fight." But there was one ominous little footnote, concerning the three divisions of the Group Vimy, which read: "Although the effect of the last few days can be clearly seen, the troops are still battleworthy in the event of a major offensive."

CHAPTER SIX

EASTER SUNDAY

" I Hates the Sights of You Canadians!"

Early on Sunday morning, 8 April, there was a raid on the 1st Division front, put in by the 10th Battalion of 2 Brigade. Major-General D. M. Ormond, who was at the time commanding the 10th Battalion, later recalled: "We did a raid to examine the wire in front of us. The ground observation had said the wire was cut. The air reconnaissance reported the wire was heavy, but they couldn't come down close enough to see because it was on the apex of the ridge, so General Currie personally came up, and he suggested we should find out. So we put over the raid, and we reported it wasn't cut. Then the trench was cleared for a thousand yards on each side of our front and back for four hundred. Then General Currie turned the whole artillery onto it and cleaned it up, and when we went over on the morning of the 9th the wire was no obstacle." It turned out that the ground observers had been unable to see the uncut wire in front of them because of the masses of earth thrown up by the craters. A new fuse (the 106) had been devised specially for wire-cutting, and was effective, but nevertheless it was no part of the programme to destroy all the wire or the entire German trench system by 'saturation' fire, because the enemy defences were far too extensive. Instead, there had been selective concentration on individual German strongpoints and on registering for counter-battery work. The Germans were saving their ammunition, and especially their gas shells, which were in very short supply, for what they called, literally, the 'big hit'; designed to strike the attackers at the most vulnerable moment—in the open, at the start of the assault. The essence of counter-battery, which was a French conception, was to have such effective knowledge of the enemy's artillery dispositions that his batteries could be swamped, harassed and hampered by a deluge of accurately aimed H.E. and gas shells just before the critical moment of the assault and while it continued. In short, hit him in the stomach just before he hit you, then keep at it. But this was easier said than done, and only the morning of the 9th would show whether the long, technical, and intricate preparations would prove adequate.

The 8th was spent by different people in very different ways. Sergeant Charles W. Evans, of the 3rd Division's Ammunition Column, for instance, had anticipated spending the day in bed —a real iron bed with a mattress of real straw, in a real civilian room. Along miles of light railway track, the Mule Trains of his unit—six mules to a train—had completed the previous day the immense task of bringing forward the ammunition necessary for the assault and had pulled back well behind the line. " Well! here I was, eight miles or so behind Vimy," Evans recollected. " Easter Sunday tomorrow. All nice and quiet. I turned in about eight p.m. and, on the first iron bedstead I have seen for a year, fell into a sound and peaceful sleep. Suddenly, I was awakened by a voice calling, ' Messieur! Messieur!' I looked at my wrist watch, which showed it was five fifteen a.m. on the 8th. And there at the bedroom door stood the batman of a British officer who was attached to our unit and at that time on duty at an observation post known as the ' Steel Tree ' (because it was a dummy tree made of steel)." And that was the end of a peaceful Sunday for Evans.

He reported to the Sergeant-Major, who was in bed. A Sergeant-Major's bed, with white sheets and pillows, too. The batman brought in a bottle of Scotch, and the Sergeant-Major spoke.

" Now, Sergeant, these are your instructions. Get your horse saddled up. When you've had breakfast, take two nosebags with you and that bottle of Scotch. Proceed to Signals HQ at Villers-aux-Bois, where they will give you four D3 telephones and four coils of telephone wire. You will then proceed to the Horse Lines of No. 4 Section at Marveuil, where you will leave your horse. Then, with the phones, wire, and bottle of Scotch, you will proceed on foot to the Steel Tree O Pip somewhere over the Black-heath Tunnel in the Quarry Line and you will there report to Captain X. Got it? "

Sergeant Evans spoke. " Yes, Sergeant-Major."

All went easily as long as the horse was carrying the load.

Then Evans transferred it to himself for the last stage. First, four heavy coils of telephone wire, two to each shoulder. Then two nosebags, one to each shoulder; one holding two heavy field telephones and the other two heavy field telephones and a bottle of Scotch. Finally, Evans' own haversack and gas mask. From there on, Evans did not so much walk as ' mush ' through the mud, until he turned onto a track leading to La Targette. This appeared ominously quiet and empty. Two M.F.Ps. stepped suddenly out from behind a tree.

" This road is closed. Where are you making for? "

" The Quarry Line," replied Evans.

" Well, you'll have to go in the trench."

Evans obediently got into the communication trench, found himself up to his knees in mud and water, and waded on for another three hours until he had reached La Targette. Here, he had to call for help to get himself out of the mud, in which he was stuck fast. After a brief breather and a mug of char, he waded on to the Quarry Line, arriving spent, soaked, mud-splattered, and littered with equipment at Blackheath Tunnel, where an old friend spotted him and called out, " Hello, Charlie! going on your holiday? " Blackheath Tunnel was a subway, dug out of the chalk and leading forward underneath the three trench lines, giving covered access to them. But it also served as troop accommodation and was now occupied by most of the 7th Infantry Brigade—the Royal Canadian Regiment, the ' Princess Pats ', and the 42nd Battalion. Evans found his way impeded by thousands of men, some trying to sleep, others writing last letters, in terribly congested conditions. As he forced himself forward with his load, the gas alarm sounded, and they all put on gas masks. Evans, impeded by the loads round his neck, was about the last to do so. Then he trudged on, breathing heavily through the mask and with the eye-pieces misting up from his exertions. At last, as Evans passed one of the outlets leading up to a trench above, he saw soldiers coming down it who were not wearing gas masks. So he took his off. He then discovered that he had trudged past the Third Line trench exit, and so he had to trudge back. And when he eventually arrived, " Hello, Sergeant! " said Captain X. " Did you get lost? And did you bring the Scotch? "

Canadian infantry advancing across Vimy Ridge, 9 April, 1917.

Before the bombardment, this was a German gun position in a wood on the top of Vimy Ridge near the Arras-Lille Road. Its state on 9 April shows what counter-battery fire directed by aircraft and balloons could achieve.

BELOW: Canadian shells bursting on Vimy Ridge during the preliminary bombardment, April, 1917. MIDDLE: Inside a knocked-out concrete gun emplacement on Vimy Ridge, 9 April, 1917. EXTREME RIGHT: Men of the 19th Battalion consolidating in what, before the bombardment, had been a German trench.

ABOVE: The Arras Offensive, 13 April, 1917. A tank hopelessly bogged in a muddy gunpit and, in the background, the cavalry waiting for the breakthrough which never came.

LEFT: Bogged down—as usual. Even after off-loading, these ammunition lorries are firmly stuck in the morass of the battlefield, graphic evidence of the drawbacks to an 'artillery battle'. The picture was taken on a road leading to Vimy Ridge, April, 1917.

Light trolleys on a narrow gauge track, and pushed by prisoners, was one answer to the problem of getting the wounded back across the torn-up ground. Vimy Ridge, April, 1917.

" Yes, sir."

" Good man. Put it here, and then get down to the Signal Pit and have a rest."

Evans spent the night there, being too exhausted to go back immediately. It had been a mild day, comparatively, that is, but became colder and cloudier towards nightfall. Another soldier who also made his way up there was E. B. Elgood, who was to be attached to the 11th Brigade Signals Section for the attack. He had come up with a party the previous day, in the middle of an artillery duel, to what was known as M.G. Fort in Ross Street Trench, and " being missed by our flying driving bands and prematures, and Heinies probing for our ammo dumps and supply columns, and seeing our guns almost wheel to wheel and (about the only time) a galloping gun team coming into position," as he put it.

" Any complaints? "

" Yes, sir, I would like to go home! "

The Brigade Signal Office turned out to be " a dug-out room about 20 × 30 feet, which was also a thoroughfare for the Brigade staff, runners, linemen and battalion men, pigeon men, etc., looking for anywhere to sit down and rest. Each step to the trench was being used, while to add to the luxury a stream of muddy slush trickled down from Ross Street above to keep the stair-occupants' bottoms cool. This was also a bed, sitting, and dining room for the Princess Pats, and their band, who, rumour said, were going to play the boys over the top (and their pipers did pipe them up and over, though I doubt they could hear them, as the din was too deafening). Grant and I got the Fuller-phone working to forward Division HQ. No talking phone, just Morse code signals, as Heinie can pick up anything in water-soaked ground (took our V.I.P.s a year or more to learn this, and act on the knowledge). But Heinie gave his secret away (we learned from Captain Lodge, a nephew of Sir Oliver Lodge) by sticking up a large sign in his front line: " WE HOPE CAP-TAIN SMITH GOT HIS WHISKY." How did they know Captain Smith had actually ordered whisky for the Officers Mess? Two and Two were put together, and for a wonder, they came to three: " They must be hearing us!! Ye Gods!!! "

" To say we were cramped is putting it mildly. One chicken wire bunk for four men, and at night men trying to sleep anywhere, leaning against walls, lying on the damp ground, while every hour someone is running the Primus stove, heating tea water, or frying when anything to fry—rations are on the short side except bully beef and cheese, Quartermasters saving it up to feed prisoners ... We enjoyed all that for two days and nights with only one warm meal, and a good rum ration, which is a wonderful gut warmer. We had dropped our equipment and stores on the muddy floor when our Brigadier-General Macdonnell came through, tired and grouchy. ' Ha! ' he said. ' I thought you were Canadian soldiers, looks more like a pig pen. Serge, get organised, eh? ' " This was one of the two famous Brigadier Macdonnells, one of whom was reputed, early in his Canadian Army career, to have boasted: " I'm the first goddamm private who walked into the *Sav*-oy Hotel and said, ' Damn you, give me a room! ' "

" It had been rumoured the attack would begin on the 7th," recalled Elgood, " but this was postponed on account of the atrocious weather. Again, the 8th was supposed to be it, but weather worse and sleety snow, and more artillery smashing of wire and strong-points could be used. Rumour changed to almost certainty on the 8th, as officers' batmen had orders for calls to those who could sleep for two a.m. to four a.m. on the 9th, and finally learned Zero was for five thirty a.m. Strangely, the night was unusually quiet until five thirty, but by the 10th we had a nice assortment of corpses piled up near our entrance."

Captain Ulric Nisbet, of the 1st Royal West Kents, had been appointed liaison officer with the Canadian 29th Battalion, and reported to them on the evening of the 8th, " dead beat " and after " several sousings in liquid mud." The Canadian C.O. let his battalion have a 15-minute start, then announced that he intended to get ahead of it. As he was carrying absolutely nothing whatever beyond two gas helmets, it seemed likely he would succeed, but for Nisbet and his batman, Flynn, both heavily laden, it was a nightmare! " After a while we left the road," he wrote, " and struck across fields near Neuville St. Vaast, guided by a line of tape. Parallel to it the tracks of tanks could be dimly seen." There were eight of them, in fact, from No. 12 Company, D Battalion, Heavy Branch Machine Gun Corps, and all were to assist the 2nd Division. " We passed some batteries that were being gas shelled. Box respirators were adjusted, and we crept along at a snail's pace until the air cleared again. At last the trench system began, and, after losing our way once or twice, we reached the dugout that was to house us 'till dawn. There had been twenty days' intense bombardment of the enemy's front and rear positions, but this had quietened down on the night of the 8th-9th to allow the troops to get into position with as few casualties as possible from retaliatory fire. So far as the battalion I was with was concerned, there were only two or three wounded. In spite of the hard going everyone was in high spirits, and although the French were commonly reported to have lost 60,000 killed in their assaults on the Ridge, failure was unthought of."

Next to them, on the 1st Division front, things were different, at least after dark, by which time the units had moved up. " We were quite unmolested until it got dark," recalled George R. Alliston of the 7th (British Columbia) Battalion in the 2nd Brigade. " Then the enemy must have smelled a rat because he began sending up Verey lights so fast after each other and opened up his artillery, all calibres, plus mortars, right on our front lines. So our officers took most of the attacking troops back down the communication trench. In the meantime, one of our machine-gun posts out in front, just behind the wire, had got a 5.9 shell which left only one man out of five of them alive, Sergeant Gunn, and him yelling for help.

" So four of us got out of the trench and headed for him. We got to him O.K., but had to get him to the dressing station, two trenches back and down a deep dugout. At last, we put the stretcher down in front of the doctor (who was working overtime by this time). He told us to take him out, he was through.

" Then I got back in the front line trench, when, lo and behold, another call for our small gang. This time the doctor wanted water. A sergeant directed us where to find it, piled up in two gallon cans in the communication trench. ' Each man two cans, and you know where the doctor is working '.

" Sure I know where he was working, but those Germans were changing the contours of the land thereabouts, and my two cans and I travelled on to the jumping off trench before I knew it. Too close to Jerry for comfort. So I sat down in the mud (scared, did you say?—could be, brother, could be). After a long time, it seemed, I heard a slosh-slosh noise coming my way, then a heavy whisper, ' Who's that? '

" (Water Boy, just Water Boy). It was Sergeant Scout this time, and what language for a sergeant. Furthermore, he accused me of being unobservant. ' Darn you, can't you see anything? Right above your head, a box of primed Mills grenades ready to be picked up at dawn! '

" Well, I delivered my water to the doctor's dugout, and one of my bugler pals just got carried in. (I was a Corporal Bugler, by the way, in more pleasant times). Billy Cross had just got the result of an exploding shell, but no metal, concussion only.

" Then I am back in the front line again, and next thing is some fellow, whimpering, come up to me, so I said, ' What's the matter, Jack? '

' I'm wounded,' says he.

"And so help me and he had one through the wrist. I said to him, ' How did you get that one? '

' Cleaning my rifle.'

" Now of all the lame reasons to give! I'll eat my shirt. Pitch black night, cleaning his rifle. So I took him to the dressing station and he got a pretty little S.I. ticket (' Self-Inflicted '), but he had to wait until daylight before he could get away."

Water was one thing wrong with Vimy, it was always short because the chalk formation would not hold it, and therefore vast amounts had to be brought up every day. George Stebbing, of 4 Field Company, Canadian Engineers, was one of those who spent the night of 8th April bringing up a supply in horse-drawn limbers, to the reserve trenches of the 2nd Division. The Germans were doing their best to interfere. " The shelling was heavy and continuous," he recalled, " and while my load was being transferred to the dugout cookhouse, a shell landed amongst an ammunition column. All hell was let loose. The stampeding horses crashed into us, throwing my assistant and myself into the roadway. While we were spreadeagled in the roadway, the stampeding horses and limbers went right over us, how we escaped I do not know." As their own horses and limbers went racing away into the night, Stebbing and his comrade picked themselves up, and ran after them, the light of the gun flashes their only illumination. The terrified animals were still moving, when they did sight them; and there ensued a midnight chase which ended when the two soldiers drew level with the limbers and were able to put on the brakes. That didn't stop the horses, but it slowed them, and they were able to jump onto the watercart and climb forward to the driving seat. " But our troubles were not over. As we turned back to get out of it, we picked up a soldier with a broken leg, hoisted him onto the cart and took him to the dressing station. Apart from being a mass of bruises, for a wheel had gone over my chest, I was all right after a day's rest."

Behind the front of the 4th Division, John Cornish of the 3rd Canadian M.G. Company spent most of the day in the woods near Mont St. Eloi, where the horse lines, transport, and main dumps were. He had the job of loading sixteen Vickers machine-guns, with 20,000 rounds of ammunition per gun, onto a mule train; and, after dark, taking it up to Cavalry (or Cabaret) Rouge, where the forward dump of the 72 Battalion (the Seaforth from Vancouver), to which his unit was attached, was situated. The name, ' Cavalry Rouge,' was rumoured to be associated with the fact that whenever anyone dug there, they always came across the rotting cloth of red trousers—the bodies of French troops dressed in the original uniform of 1914 and 1915.

The Vickers machine-gun was used at Vimy as an artillery piece and in three important roles. Firstly, before the battle, to fire on fixed lines at night, at targets like road junctions, so as to make hazardous the bringing up of food supplies and reinforcements, the relief of units in the line, and so on. This was massed fire by many guns, with each gun firing hundreds of thousands of rounds. Secondly, this massed fire was to be used again, thickening up the barrage at the moment of attack. And thirdly, some of the guns were to move forward with the infantry, to give flank-covering fire, and finally dig in on the last captured position so as to guard against counter-attack. More than 150 machine-guns were to be used, and they were directed by Brigadier General R. Brutinel, a French-Canadian who had served in the French Army, and was responsible for this innovation, which meant that the guns would be handled like artillery to give concentrated, centrally-directed fire.

" Machine-guns, especially the fixed-platform Vickers, required specially trained men, not because the mechanism was especially complicated, but because they were used in effect as artillery pieces," explained John Cornish. " Thirty two M.Gs. might be firing on points ordered by telephone. This required knowledge of map reading, target and range-finding, prismatic compass, etc., and allowance for safety angles, especially when giving indirect fire in support of a moving infantry attack. It was a heavy gun, in two main parts—barrel and tripod—and particularly useful for holding off counter-attacks. British machine-guns used to be very noisy and had a large, giveaway flash, until we copied the German methods of flash-concealment and semi-silencing. They were water-cooled, better than the Colt M.G. with which the Canadians were at first equipped; and not too much affected by mud and grit (unlike the Lewis), the main cause of a jam being faulty ammunition. The high rate of fire meant that movement forward of ammunition supplies was essential and could be critical, especially when the ground was a morass of muddy craters."[1]

This was, of course, the case at Vimy and the reason why these guns and their ammunition were being brought as far forward as possible on the night before the attack. The woods by Mont St. Eloi were full of mule-trains with their heavy loads. John Cornish had been there for some hours, smoking cigarettes, his mule-train loaded, just waiting for dark and his turn to move off in the queue that led forward to Cavalry Rouge. He was a new Canadian, having gone to school at Eversley in Hampshire, emigrating to Canada only in 1912. As the leading trains began to move, Cornish heard another team behind him obviously having mule trouble, and a man swearing in the broadest Hampshire, his own dialect, so that he laughed aloud. The cursing soldier looked up—and they recognised each other. It was Ernie Taylor, who had been in the same school, in the same class in

[1] The Vickers was still in use during part of the Second World War as a means of stopping counter-attack, from fixed positions. It could actually fire about 500 rounds a minute, because of the belt-feed system. Light machine-guns, such as the Bren, with 30-round magazines, could get away only about 150 rounds per minute, although their rate of fire was about 450; nor did the normal bipod mounting allow of the deadly ' scything ' effect obtainable with a tripod. They were, however, capable of being carried and operated by one man, an essential for mobile warfare.

fact, as Cornish, but had joined the British Army instead of the Canadian. " I remember you. I remember you going to Canada," burst out Taylor. " I hates the sights of you Canadians."

" Why, Ern? "

" Because we go wherever you go, and wherever you go there's always hell to pay! What trouble are you going to stir up now? "

" We're going to take the Ridge."

" You're going to have some guns behind ye," commented Taylor, and they continued talking all the way from Mont St. Eloi to Cavalry Rouge, where the unit dumps were, each one marked with the distinctive ' flash,' or sign, of that unit. There they had to say goodbye, and Taylor put out his hand.

" Anything I can do for yer? We'll bring up the ammo and rations tomorrer—and take the stiffs back. Hope I don't take you."

" Yes, there's something. If you can run over there to our ' flash ' tomorrow night and ask if I'm alive, and let 'em know."

He meant let them know at home, which was easy, for Cornish's mother still lived at Eversley in Hampshire, a few hundred yards away from Ern Taylor's mother.

The next night, the night of the 9th, Taylor did turn up at the unit sign of the 72nd Battalion, the Seaforth of Vancouver, and asked after John Cornish of 3rd Canadian M.G. Company. On the night of the 8th, there had been twenty men in that company. Now there were four. John Cornish was one of the four.

Ern Taylor sat down to write a brief note to Mrs. Cornish:

" Pleasure met Jack. All right. 9 April, 1917."

CHAPTER SEVEN

EASTER MONDAY—BARRAGE BEFORE DAWN

Captain Routh was not called until four a.m. on 9 April, as it was impossible to take off before then. When he did, he logged " Rain, sleet and snow drove us down to 300 feet." There was to have been a bombing programme by other squadrons, but this was cancelled. The temperature dropped still further shortly before dawn, and the only comfort in that was that the bitter wind was blowing from the north-west. The defenders of Vimy would have the snow and sleet in their faces. But it also prolonged the darkness beyond Zero hour, which had been set for first light, five thirty a.m. By that time, some of the men had been standing in the jumping-off trenches for thirteen hours, with full battle kit on and up to their knees in water. The 102nd Battalion endured this experience and were grateful for the little tot of warming rum they got before going over. They were still known as the ' Pea-soupers ', because the rum ration for the whole of the 11th Brigade had been stopped temporarily and a ration of hot pea-soup served instead while in the line, partly because of misconduct in the serving out of the rum ration by some officers and sergeants, partly because the officers were able to fill their water-bottles with rum, which the men were not able to do. A friend of Bracewell's had a man standing next to him with a mickey of rye whisky (smuggled up in a loaf of bread), and this man, whom he knew only as ' Bill ', offered him a share during the long and bitter wait. ' Bill ' only made forty yards of the forthcoming trudge up the Vimy slope. Most men got only the small, official tot, and some refused even that, saying they wanted a clear head for what was going to happen, but for the average man the ration was enough only to produce a momentary warmth in the stomach, gratefully received.

A. E. Barker, of 4th C.M.R., had made sure he would have a good, hot feed the night before, by buying half-a-dozen eggs and frying them before his battalion moved off to spend the night in Goodman Tunnel. Although packed tight in the tunnel, they escaped the bitter sleet and snow until five a.m., when the tunnel entrance was blown to give an exit direct to No-man's-land, and they went through and spread out, lying down in the icy mud. Gus Sivertz, of 2nd C.M.R., in the same Brigade, was already in the line. " I found something to eat," he recollected, " and got a tot of rum; had a word with Sergeant Jock MacGregor (who was to win the DCM a few hours later) just for the comfort of his great presence; and, then, soon after three a.m., we started to worm out into our assembly area, a field of mud which we solemnly cursed as we lay, side by side, elbows touching. In addition to rifle, bayonet, and extra bandoliers of ammunition, I had a huge pick stuck down my back. The prongs were wider than my shoulders and the damned thing was always catching in wire or in my pals' equipment. Everyone had something extra to carry and it was just my bad luck to win a pick. The night was pitch dark and fairly quiet. Our side popped over a few shells now and then but nothing out of the ordinary. Then, for no darned reason at all, Heinie sent a salvo of shells right among us. Fountains of muck blasted upward and then fell back on us, and in that moment we blessed the mud that had so effectively cushioned the bursts, for Sergeant Oram counted noses and not one man had been hit. Heinie didn't repeat, so the salvo was probably a sheer accident."

A mile ahead of him, near the ruins of Les Tilleuls, the staff of Reserve Infantry Regiment No. 263 were also grateful for the comparatively quiet night. It facilitated the relief of the staff at the *Felsenkeller*, the deep dugout HQ of Sector Arnulf-South. They thought of it as sort of dungeon, damp, mouldy, stinking of old cooking, spirits, hot candlewax, and dried blood from the casualties who had been dragged in there for first aid during the three weeks' bombardment they had suffered. Hauptmann Schmidt-Eberstein, with his Adjutant and Signals Officer, had formally taken over. The men who had been reprieved, temporarily, Hauptmann Güinzius, Lieutenant Thiel and Lieutenant Richter, turned and began to walk towards the steps which led up onto the shattered streets of Les Tilleuls. Then the earth shook with the roar of continuous explosions, and one of the sentries posted above came clattering down the steps, shouting " Gas attack! " For them there was to be no way back.

That was the moment that Gus Sivertz, having synchronised watches with Lieutenant J. H. Christie, his platoon officer, started to say something—forgot it, and dug his nose in the dirt instead. That was the moment when a German officer, on watch in the Third Line trench of Sector Arnulf-North, and waiting for dawn, literally looked into the mouths of a thousand guns. " Slowly, the veil of darkness lifted. Snow danced lightly across the torn and cratered landscape. It was unusually quiet. Suddenly, all along the horizon from Arras to Lens, the sky was ablaze with an immense, flickering light. Verey lights? Explosions? Then, as if on the word of command, the sound. So abrupt, so continuous, that the discharge of the shells, and the explosion of them, were indistinguishable."

The barrage had, indeed, started on the word of command. " We and the infantry had synchronised all watches," recalled Sergeant W. G. Smith, then serving with a 2 Division 18-pounder battery. " But we were sure to remember this item. The attack time was to be taken from a signal gun back of Mont St. Eloi. I can hear it yet, for it was not a bark, or a roar, but like a big cough or whoosh. It must have been a big howitzer, and also every gunner on our side must have had his hand on the lanyard or the firing lever. Everything started on the split second."

" The front had been silent for a short time beforehand— the lull before the storm," recalled Sergeant Layton of 15th Warwicks. " At five thirty a.m. precisely the whole atmosphere was rent by screaming shells passing overhead, every gun seemingly having been fired as if by clockwork. The German front line was erupting along its entire length and seemed to be enveloped in sheet lightning. The fact that it was still only half dawn added to the effect." " The sky at our back was lit up by the gunfire," said Percy Boxall of the 49th Battalion, " and just in front of us a curtain of shells was bursting, like water off a tin roof in a heavy thunderstorm." " The whole of the top of the Ridge, as far as we could see," wrote Captain Crowell of the 85th Battalion, " suddenly out of the blackness became one bank of smoke of every colour imaginable, with the heavy explosions of mines puncturing the continuous roar of the artillery barrage."

In front of the 72nd Battalion, Love Crater was blown. " A big sheet of flame," recollected John Cornish, " and a roar and a rumble, but not a big bang—we had expected to be knocked down by it." " When our bombardment opened up, Fritz immediately filled the air with golden rain—amber coloured flares which broke into clusters of sparks or stars," recalled Donald Patrick of HQ 3rd Brigade. " This was his S.O.S. call for artillery support. His whizz bangs responded at once with a barrage on our front line, but our infantry were already lying out in shell holes which had been deliberately made in No-man's-land for that purpose." Gus Sivertz, lying out in front next to Lieutenant Christie recalled: " I looked ahead and saw the German front line crashing into pieces; bits of men, timbers, lumps of chalk were flung through the air and, blending with the shattering wall of fire, were the Hun SOS signals of all colours. We didn't dare lift our heads, knowing that the barrage was to come flat over us and then lift in three minutes. That queer empty stomach feeling had gone . . . I don't think anyone was scared . . . instead one's whole body seemed to be in a mad macabre dance . . . I felt that if I lifted a finger I should touch a solid ceiling of sound (it now had the attribute of solidity). I guess it was perhaps the most perfect barrage of the war, as it was so perfectly synchronised. Then, suddenly, it jumped a hundred yards and we were away."

That was the assault battalions only. The reserve battalions, which were to advance through them when, inevitably, they became tired, decimated, disorganised, watched the spectacle for a moment and then sat down to breakfast. " From our position we could see lines of dark figures and tanks advancing behind the barrage, and, beyond them, the coloured rockets of the enemy, calling for help," wrote Captain Nisbet of the West Kents. " The din was so continuous that one soon forgot it, and after a scratch breakfast of sardines and tinned ham, we set off up the trench to the front line. The first prisoners now appeared with some of our wounded, whom they were helping along. One of them was wearing the ribbon of the Iron Cross. They were obviously very thankful to have got through alive."

From above, it all seemed very leisurely. Major William Bishop, a Canadian fighter pilot who had won the M.C. a few days before and was to gain the V.C., wrote: " The waves of attacking infantry as they came out of their trenches and trudged forward behind the curtain of shells laid down by the artillery were an amazing sight. The men seemed to wander across No-man's-land, and into the enemy trenches, as if the battle was a great bore to them. From the air it looked as though they did not realise that they were at war and were taking it all entirely too quietly. That is the way with clock-work warfare. These troops had been drilled to move forward at a given pace. They had been timed over and over again in marching a certain distance, and from this timing the ' Creeping ' or rolling barrage which moved in front of them had been mathematically worked out."[1]

The real reasons for the leisurely pace of advance were the twin facts that the men were heavily laden and that the ground that they had to traverse was peculiarly difficult—a vast sea of sticky mud interspersed with enormous and impassable craters and the upheavals from them. To avoid any risk of their ' losing the barrage ', the timed rate of advance was dead slow—three minutes for each 100 yards.

" We felt so safe with that rolling barrage in front," said H. Campbell of 14th Battalion. " You could see the thing beating. It was just like a lawn mower, you know, when you're cutting grass." In addition, 150 of the Canadian Corps 358 heavy machine-guns, were firing a thicker barrage of bullets close overhead; and they moved forward, with the attack, leap-frogging, and especially covering the flanks. " The machine-gun fire was so thick and heavy and persistent that I saw balls of barbed wire rolled up there and beaten as hard as iron," said Colonel E. S. Russenholdt, then with the 44th Battalion.

The real reason why the barrage went rolling forward remorselessly like a machine, and the infantry flooded through behind it like a slowly rising tide, was that the enemy's powerful artillery had been over-powered, both numerically and tech-nically. A German gunner officer who had come up to the Ridge to look for an O.P., was taken prisoner during the attack. A map he had on him showed that two only of the German batteries in the area had escaped notice. All the others had been plotted

[1] *Winged Warfare,* by Major W. A. Bishop, 1918.

accurately, by sound ranging or by aerial photography, and heavy fire was being brought down on them now. " Most of their barrage batteries were neutralised throughout the engagement," wrote Captain Routh. " I managed to send down fourteen ' N.F.' calls, which was great fun. (' N.F.' is code for ' guns firing in position at . . .') After ten minutes shells could be seen falling all round the located batteries. I should think that our casualties from German artillery were small, as every time a battery opened fire it was immediately zone called and shelled to hell. Nor did our own batteries seem to suffer very much from hostile shelling." One of 16 Squadron's machines was brought down while flying low through the barrage; Elgood saw it crash. From an O.P. covering the flanking advance of the 51st Highland Division, Major H. Smithson saw no less than three R.F.C. machines brought down by British shells. But the work was vital: it ensured that the German infantry was isolated. The only help the German artillery could give, was to put down some fire on the original Canadian front line. This cut up some of the reinforcements, but hardly affected the initial assault.

The German official history recorded: " The batteries could not follow the continuously changing course of the battle, especially since their communications with the front lines had been cut. Mostly they put down barrage or harassing fire on the enemy's former front lines. Nor was there enough ammunition, because it had been impossible for some time to bring up the usual daily quota. This had become more critical later on, when the roads and the batteries themselves were brought under a continual heavy fire. Therefore, from the very beginning of the battle there was a shortage of ammunition, which meant that the German infantry had to fight alone without effective support from the artillery."[2]

On the front of the 1st, 2nd, and 3rd Canadian Divisions the dictum that " the artillery conquers and the infantry occupies " for once came true; the advance proceeded as nearly " according to plan " as is ever likely to be the case. But on the right, where the 51st Highland Division was to have kept pace with the Canadian Corps, and on the left, where the 4th Canadian

[2] *Der Weltkrieg: 1914 bis 1918*, Vol. 12 (1939).

Division had only a short distance to advance, things went wrong and the final objectives were not gained that day.

The 1st and 2nd Canadian Divisions had the furthest distance to advance—some 4,000 yards. Therefore they were to go forward with two brigades up and one in support; this third brigade would advance through the two leading brigades at about the halfway mark and continue the attack, their axes of advance tending to converge on the final objectives near the crest of the Ridge. As this was to be a tightly-integrated 'set-piece' battle, the ground in front of these two divisions was divided into strips by marking the maps with four different-coloured lines—a convenient method for indicating just which stretch of heavily cratered and featureless mud had been reached at any one time. The nearest was the 'Black Line', which more or less corresponded with the German Third Line trench; all four divisions were to take this line. The next was the 'Red Line', which included the remainder of the German 'layback' or II Position (part of which, together with all the forward trenches, would have fallen once the initial 'Black Line' had been gained). All four divisions were to reach this line also. But, for the 1st and and 2nd Divisions only, there were two further lines of advance, the 'Blue Line' and the 'Brown Line', which were to be taken by the support brigades of those divisions. This was necessary because, on this part of the front, Vimy Ridge angled away from the original Canadian front line, but still maintaining a high and commanding elevation around Thelus.

The assault actually divided into a series of carefully spaced attacks. Starting at 0530, all four divisions were allowed thirty five minutes to gain the Black Line, where there would be a forty minute pause to allow the by now disorganised infantry to reform. All four divisions would then advance again, being allowed twenty minutes in which to reach the Red Line. The time now would be 0705 and the tasks of the 3rd and 4th Divisions completed. But the 1st and 2nd Divisions would be barely halfway, so they would be allowed a two and a half hours pause on the Red Line to bring up their reserve brigades for the final phases of the assault. They would then advance to the Blue Line, halt for ninety six minutes there, and finally carry on to the Brown Line, just beyond the Ridge, which they would reach by

1318 hours. From there they would push out patrols 500 yards in front to cover the consolidation of the captured ground. And the main part of the battle—the Southern Assault—would be over. Next day, 10 April, the Northern Attack would be launched by the reserve brigade of the 4th Division to take the ' Pimple ' height overlooking the Souchez valley. With the Vimy Heights securely held all along their length, the British would continue their flanking advance to a. breakthrough from Arras, and un-leash Haig's mass of unused cavalry for mobile war on the plain. Up to that point, the plan was both thorough and rigid. Every-one knew in very precise detail what had to be done on the first day; beyond that, little had been thoroughly thought out, let alone thoroughly prepared, nor was there any allowance for unexpected success. Considering the previous British record, this was perhaps understandable. But success there was, and it came early. At Vimy, on the fronts of the 1st and 2nd Canadian Divisions, it was there already by 0715. Less than two hours after the assault had begun.

*　　　*　　　*

There have been a number of short studies of the Battle of Vimy Ridge, including the British Official History by Captain Cyril Falls (1940), the Canadian Official History by Colonel G. W. L. Nicholson (1962), two Reicharchivs histories, *Der Welt-krieg* (1939) and *Schlachten des Weltkriegs* (1929), and unofficial but valuable works such as *The Canadians in France* by Colonel Harwood Steele (1920) and *The Shadow of Vimy Ridge* by Major Kenneth Macksey (1965). Some of them describe the battle from left to right, which is logical, because the entire Arras offensive hinged on the left with the attack of the 4th Canadian Division. Others describe the battle from right to left, which is also logical, because the formations and units were aligned from right to left, the flank duty lying on the left. Most attempt to describe the battle by stages, reading quickly either right or left, which is logical but proves confusing even in a brief account, and also awkward, because the divisions with the furthest distance to go reached their final objectives much earlier than did the 4th Divi-sion on the extreme left. To meet this difficulty, almost all the authors preferred to describe later and separately what happened to the 4th Division. In the first full-scale work, which this is, all these complications are magnified. There is in fact no way of describing adequately and yet simultaneously an advance along a front which stretched for four miles, and which met different opponents and varying fortunes, at the same or very closely related times. The 'Square Four' technique of football reporting will not do; because there was not one football, but hundreds, in play simultaneously. Also, if we use the line or time method laterally along the front, we lose by this the sense of continuity of experience by the many witnesses, as they trudged forward through the defences. The least confusing method appears to be to divide the battlefield into divisional paths of advance, but grouping closely together the two divisions which had the furthest to go—the 1st and 2nd—and considering separately and at length the fortunes of the 4th, which affected the 3rd. Because the battle ended much earlier on the right than it did on the left, the battle will be described from right to left, which coincides with the numbering and alignment of the actual formations and units, twenty one battalions advancing in line to storm one of the strongest fortresses on the Western Front.

CHAPTER EIGHT

EASTER MONDAY MORNING

Advance of the 1st and 2nd Divisions

The 1st Canadian Division, commanded by Major-General A. W. Currie, attacked on a frontage of more than a mile with two brigades up and one in reserve; and, in the brigades, three battalions up and one in support for mopping up. On the extreme right, beside the 51st Highland Division of the British Army, was the 2nd Brigade (Brigadier F. O. W. Loomis) with three battalions in line—the 5th (Lieutenant-Colonel H. M. Dyer), 7th (Lieutenant-Colonel W. F. Gibson), and 10th (Lieutenant-Colonel D. M. Ormond), with the 8th Battalion (Lieutenant-Colonel J. M. Prower) in the support role. Next in line was the 3rd Brigade (Brigadier G. S. Tuxford) also with three battalions in line—the 15th (Lieutenant-Colonel C. E. Bent), the 14th (Lieutenant-Colonel G. McCombe), and the 16th (Lieutenant-Colonel C. W. Peck), with the 13th Battalion (Lieutenant-Colonel G. E. McCuaig) in support. That was the initial attack force, reading from right to left. The reserve, which would continue the attack from the halfway mark, the Red Line, was the 1st Brigade (Brigadier W. A. Griesbach) which would also assault with three battalions in line—the 1st (Lieutenant-Colonel J. H. Hume), the 3rd (Lieutenant-Colonel J. B. Rogers), and 4th (Lieutenant-Colonel W. Rae), with the 2nd Battalion (Lieutenant-Colonel T. L. McLaughlin) in reserve.

Their opponents were the original victors of Vimy Ridge—Bavarian Reserve Infantry Regiment No. 3, of 1st Bavarian Reserve Division (General von Reitzenstein), the major part of which was committed to the south against the simultaneous British assault out of Arras. Their triple line of forward trenches had been flattened by the bombardment, and the survivors were crouched in dugouts with multiple entrances; nevertheless, in some cases, the men had been completely buried. The attack,

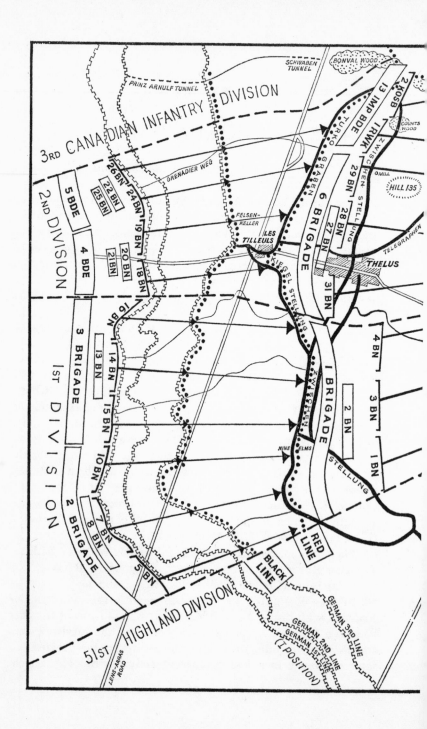

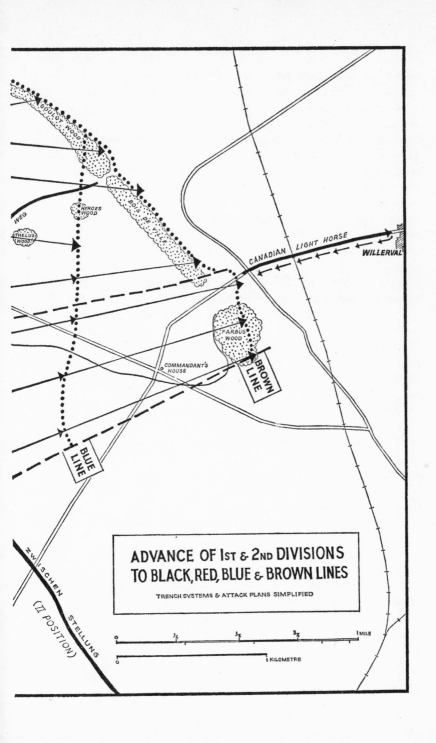

GOULOT WOOD

BOIS DE VILLE

HEROES WOOD

THELUS WOOD

WEG

CANADIAN LIGHT HORSE

WILLERVAL

FARBUS WOOD

COMMANDANT'S HOUSE

BROWN LINE

BLUE LINE

ZWISCHEN STELLUNG

(II POSITION)

ADVANCE OF 1ST & 2ND DIVISIONS TO BLACK, RED, BLUE & BROWN LINES

TRENCH SYSTEMS & ATTACK PLANS SIMPLIFIED

0   1/4   1/2   3/4   1 MILE

0   1 KILOMETRE

coming so swiftly on the heels of so brief a barrage, was utterly unexpected. And, in many places, the lines were very close.

George R. Alliston was with 7th Battalion in the first line of the assault by the 2nd Brigade. " Half our outfit were men from the Cariboo Trail, otherwise known as the Klondike Trail— prospectors, cattlemen, bank clerks, store clerks, construction men. Fine men, the flower of the land, you might say; those are the people who are the backbone of the country in peace or war, so that way Vimy was just a big loss to us. Well, all of a sudden those 18-pounders started up their drum-fire, it was like ten thousand thunders. Such a wonderful boost to those going on an uncharted trip. After a few moments, there were two excessive explosions. Our miners had mined the enemy front line, and this was the result. Before the stuff had stopped falling, we had to man the lip of the crater that was caused. While on the way to man this thing, my next-door pal Georgie Brown (another bugler), from Glasgow, Scotland, keeled over and fell into the crater. I knew he was hit, so I went down, turned him over— but the poor lad had paid the price. Above was an officer, point- ing his revolver first at me, then skyward, meaning ' Get the heck out of there! '—*which I did*. Going through the wire was not bad, our artillery had busted it up fine. Our objective had been a stump of trees called Nine Elms, and we were favoured, because the Scottish Division on our right, they had it tougher than we did, and we got to our objective first. Our artillery was going full blast yet; now and then we would have a dud shell explode behind us, but in the main our presence was discovered by the Germans a little bit late."

Nine Elms was where the Augsburger Weg communication trench slanted in towards the Zwischen Stellung, the German II Position and more or less the Red Line, the halfway mark. The three forward lines had been over-run, the dugouts surprised and summarily dealt with. " All that ground was full of German dugouts, and when we'd come to a dugout, we'd just throw three or four Mills bombs down into it, and carry on," said Jack Pin- son, also of the 7th Battalion. " I remember one fellow standing at the top throwing bombs down; he'd say, ' Come out, you sons of bitches ', and every time a man would come out he'd demand his watch," recollected F. C. Bagshaw of 5th Battalion. " He had about twenty watches." The 7th Battalion took 150 prisoners in the Augsburger Weg, and the worst was over. "We lost about fifty per cent. of our men on Vimy Ridge," said Pinson, "but we lost the most of them in the first half mile."

The trouble came almost entirely from securely-emplaced machine-guns further back. J. Gordon MacArthur, later to win the M.M. at Amiens in 1918, was going into his first battle with the 13th Battalion from Montreal, the support unit of the 3rd Brigade. "The Germans were hit with complete surprise," he recalled. "We were about 115 yards from them in trenches that had steps dug into the sides, and from there went over the top with bayonets fixed. Our artillery did a great job but it took them some time to silence the machine-guns in the pill-boxes, which seemed to be the only German guns firing. All our casualties were caused by the machine-guns. A sergeant right in front of me got hit by a machine-gun bullet and, as he fell, he nearly knocked me down. He was killed instantly. By his side were two dead Germans, one lying crosswise over the other. My first view of dead Germans, and it was pretty gruesome because one of the bodies was headless. I particularly remember one German popping up out of his trench with his hands up, pleading for mercy as I approached, giving him quite a scare with my bayonet. But he had no gun, so I motioned for him to go to the back lines where they were herding the prisoners, and I pushed on."

The concrete emplacements for the machine-guns were nearly flush with the ground, and very well sited; the only way to get them was by bombing. Crawl forward and hurl a grenade through the firing-slit, which was easier said than done. Private W. J. Milne, of the 16th Battalion, put a complete crew out of action, and was awarded a posthumous V.C. The 1st Division was ten minutes late on the Black Line, arriving at 0615 instead of 0605; but after that the advance speeded up and they reached the left half of the Red Line—the halfway halt—just after seven o'clock, almost dead on time. They did not close up to the right half of the Red Line until eight o'clock, however. It is obvious, in retrospect, that this was the critical moment of the battle, as it actually developed; but this was also the point where the inflexible artillery plan laid down a compulsory two and a half hours halt.

In fact, the Red Line fell with a rush. Masked by fresh flurries of driven snow, and by drifting smoke from burning Thelus to the north, the leading brigades of the 1st Division were upon Bavarian Reserve Infantry Regiment No. 3 almost without warning. At 0730, 1st Division reported to corps that what seemed to be a complete battalion of Bavarians was in hot retreat back to Farbus Wood! Michael Volkheimer was one of them. He saw the Canadians break through on his right, and realised that if they did not retreat now they would be cut off. He therefore headed down a communication trench slanting back towards the heights of Thelus, and warned the units on the way. He recalled: "In this communication trench, in front of a dugout, was a battalion command post, and on the steps leading down sat a sentry, sheltering from the barrage. I called out to him, 'Get out! The English are coming!' I then hurried on to the Regimental HQ on top of the Ridge, where I reported to the Regimental Commander, Maier, that, unless strong reinforcements were available to be thrown in from our side, the entire regiment would be taken prisoner. But no such reinforcements were available. So the entire Ridge from Vimy to Thelus fell into the hands of the enemy, and of our regiment only some 200 men managed to get away—and that *included* the men from the rear echelons, such as cooks, clerks, storemen, and carrying parties. Had the enemy used faster troops, such as cavalry—or even motorised troops—our front would have been torn open wider still."

But the time-table compelled the Canadians to halt until 0930. Even so, when the reserve brigades came through to renew the advance, there were only brief flurries of opposition here and there; mostly, it was unbroken marching, behind a barrage thinner now because it had outranged most of the field guns. The 1st Division advanced through the ruins of Thelus and up onto the high ground beyond, to join hands with the 2nd Division. As they did so, for a brief moment the sun came out, and the Germans saw the southern summit of Vimy alive with 'teller helmets', and knew that they had lost the Ridge. Then the 1st Division swarmed down the slope and into the German gun area of Farbus Wood. MacArthur of the 13th Battalion was one of those who reached the guns. " When we reached the big guns it looked as if the Germans went to them in a great hurry, as we found them sprawled in the mud, with their sleeves rolled up. The big guns were not manned, because our artillery knew just where they were and knocked them out first thing. All our casualties were caused by machine-guns." Even so, MacArthur did not realise the full significance of those silent guns with their dead crews lying around them. For Allied batteries to fall into German hands was nothing exceptional, but for Allied troops to capture German guns was almost unheard of. This was the first time, since siege warfare set in on the Western Front, that British forces had advanced deep enough and swiftly enough, to take the German gun area.

Not all the batteries were captured; some got away. But not the battery of 5·9s which was attacked from the air as it was withdrawing from Farbus Wood. The elderly B.E. crewed by Crowe and Durham of No. 16 Squadron was puttering about over the battle at 300 feet on contact patrol, when they saw the battery pulling out, one gun already limbered up and moving off behind a team of horses. Wings rocking in the bitter wind, the little biplane came stuttering down on the battery position, and opened fire. Some of the horses fell in a tangle of harness, three being killed and others wounded; and that was enough. In indescribable confusion, the remaining horses stampeded through and out of the battery position, and the motive power to remove the artillery was gone; only the gun which was already limbered up and moving, managed to get away. " Some Canadians were within shot at the time," wrote Routh, " and the guns, dead men and horses were found there shortly. It took some days before Maltby, our Major, could find men who had taken part in the advance over that particular ground, but then they bore out exactly what Crowe and Durham had said they had done. These two both received the Croix de Guerre for this affair, and General Haig presented one of the guns to No. 16 Squadron, as recognition of the first battery captured by the R.F.C."

On the captured ground, the troops dug in hastily against counter-attack, as laid down in the plan; some of the wounded were collected, but there was no time for the dead. Some of the badly wounded must have lain out, helpless and in agony, all day; perhaps for more than one day. Alliston of the 7th Battalion, because his name began with ' A', was among twenty men detailed to go out and search for wounded, and then get them back down to the original communication trench. Here, he came across traces of the man who had shot himself through the wrist just before the attack and had been given a ' Self-Inflicted Wound' ticket. " I came across our Self-Inflicted man's ticket on a poor wounded fellow who had tried to walk out, and just dropped there. I took the ticket back to the doctor and told him how the skunk had traded tickets with a real soldier, and the doctor passed this on. Mr. Skunk got five years."

The 2nd Canadian Division, commanded by Major-General H. E. Burstall, attacked on a front of 1,400 yards with two brigades up and two in reserve; and, in the two assault brigades, two battalions up and two in support and reserve. On the right was the 4th Brigade (Brigadier R. Rennie) with two battalions in line—the 18th (Lieutenant-Colonel G. F. Morrison) and the 19th (Lieutenant-Colonel L. H. Miller); one battalion in direct support—the 20th (Lieutenant-Colonel H. Rorke); and one battalion in reserve—the 21st (Lieutenant-Colonel T. F. Elmitt). On the left was the 5th Brigade (Brigadier A. H. Macdonell) with two battalions in line—the 24th (Lieutenant-Colonel C. F. Ritchie) and the 26th (Lieutenant-Colonel A. E. G. Mackenzie); one battalion in direct support—the 22nd (Lieutenant-Colonel T. L. Tremblay); and one battalion in reserve—the 25th (Lieutenant-Colonel D. S. Bauld). Because the front of the attack would widen when the crest of the Ridge was reached, owing to the configuration of the ground, there were two reserve brigades, instead of one, detailed to pass through the two leading brigades on the Red Line and continue the assault. There was, firstly, the 6th Brigade (Brigadier H. B. D. Ketchen), which would assault with three battalions up—the 31st (Lieutenant-Colonel A. H. Bell), the 28th (Lieutenant-Colonel A. Ross), and the 29th (Lieutenant-Colonel J. M. Ross); and one battalion in reserve—the 27th (Lieutenant-Colonel P. J. Daly). This was the normal, fixed strength of the Canadian Division. The extra brigade required was supplied from the 5th Imperial Division, and its British troops wore Canadian flashes for the attack. This was the 13th Brigade, which would attack with the 1st Royal West Kents on the right and the 2nd King's Own Scottish Borderers on the left; the other two battalions—15th and 14th Royal Warwickshire Regiment—being in support and reserve respectively. The latter would be relieved when necessary by yet another brigade—the 15th brigade—from 5th Imperial Division. The gun power of this division would also support the attack.

The Canadian divisional boundaries very nearly coincided with the boundaries of the German regiments they were to attack. The frontage of the 2nd Canadian Division meant that most of their opponents would be from Reserve Infantry Regiment No. 263 (Oberstleutnant von Behr), of the 79th Reserve Infantry Division commanded by General von Bacmeister, with a small part of Bavarian Reserve Infantry Regiment No. 3 on the Canadian right. In accordance with the new orders for defence in depth, the three regiments of the 79th Division were positioned in echelon, with one company of the resting battalion held forward. In this case, the reserve company was in Vimy village, behind the Ridge, plus one reserve machine-gun company. But, as the German official history dryly remarks, " as the companies averaged no more than sixty rifles each, their defence sectors were inadequately manned. The main task of defence lay with the machine-gun nests, sited at the most important points of the heavily-cratered ground, also in echelon, and protected by small groups of infantry." In the static German defensive arrangements, Regiment 263 was holding what was known as Sector Arnulf, with a northern command post in the Schwaben Tunnel near Bonval Wood (just inside the 3rd Division's assault boundary) and a southern command post at the Felsenkeller in Les Tilleuls (in the centre of the 2nd Division's advance). Still further to the south, Bavarian Regiment 3 was holding what was known as Sector Löen, with its HQ on the heights near Thelus, just inside the 2nd Division's boundary with the 1st Division. Although Vimy Ridge runs from north-west to south-east, the front-line trench systems were aligned roughly north-south, so that, from the Canadian point of view, the north was on their left, the south on their right.

Although small numbers of tanks were to be used to help the British infantry get forward in the Arras assault further south, eight only had been allotted to the Canadian Corps and all were to be employed to support the advance of the 2nd Division. The tanks were 'females' of 12 Company, 'D' Battalion, Heavy Branch Machine Gun Corps, carrying m.gs. only. It hardly mattered what their armament was. The ground was impassable for any vehicle of any kind, wheeled or tracked, nevertheless their orders were to support the infantry advance to roughly the crest of the Ridge and destroy the two thick belts of uncut wire which ran south-east from Count's Wood to Farbus directly in front of the German gun area on the reverse slope. All eight were bogged down at various parts of the morass, and three of them were shattered by shellfire. Either GHQ did not know what a tank looked like, or they did not know what Vimy Ridge looked like. Conceivably, they were ignorant of both.

Wilfrid Derbyshire was serving as a private soldier with the 19th Battalion, the left-hand battalion of the 4th Brigade in the initial assault. At the time of Vimy, he was just twenty years of age, and had been in France with the battalion since the autumn of 1915. Some Canadian soldiers were even younger, having disguised their true age in order to join up.[1] " Immediately opposite us was a battalion of the 79th Division," he recollected. " Their fellows offered no resistance and appeared to be dazed. We made good use of these prisoners as stretcher bearers. From what I saw of them, they appeared cheerful and willing to work; not so sullen as some of their previously captured comrades. The wounded were well cared for. We had a good supply of blankets for warmth, and an ample supply of stretcher bearers to carry the wounded to a narrow-gauge railway. Those badly wounded, or shocked, were treated in the dugouts."

Waiting in a tunnel under No-man's-land was Lieutenant Herbert Bradshaw of 145 East Cheshire Heavy Battery. He had under him a party of men detailed to lay telephone lines, equipped also for flag and lamp signalling. There were four

[1] One Vimy veteran, who died before he could be contacted by the present author, was William J. Nixon, of Dundalk, whose obituary notice showed that he was born on 21 October, 1901. He was therefore 16½ when he fought at Vimy, and younger still when he originally joined up, which seems to have been in 1915.

such parties to the Brigade of 2 Division which they were supporting, and their task was to go forward with the second wave of attack, in order to establish Forward Observation Posts on the captured crest for the heavy guns which, unlike the field guns, had sufficient range. He wrote down his impressions very shortly afterwards. "While waiting to go forward with the second attack, the men had a very trying time, as the wounded were brought back from the first wave. One of the signallers, a big coal-miner named Wells, actually fainted at the sights he saw. On the steps, leading from the tunnel, was a Canadian Engineer who had been shot in three places in the body. He had crawled in, but could not be moved as he was obviously dying fast. A runner came in and the man feebly asked for news. ' Things are going fine, we've got the Zwischen Stellung, our first objective ', he was told."

Cecil R. Macleod was with the 25th (Nova Scotia) Battalion of the 5th Brigade, which was assaulting on the left of the 4th Brigade. "We took one line of German trenches, then the other battalions leap-frogged over us, we in turn leap-frogged over them, and finally we took the fifth and last line of trenches on the crest of the Ridge, from which we looked down on the great plain with the smoke of the city of Lens far distant. There was no excitement of any kind at Zero hour, for we spent the whole night crawling over sunken roads and up communication trenches and it was about three o'clock in the morning before we reached the take-off trench. I have had people ask me if it was true that before we went into the battle we got well soaked with rum. Well, we got one stiff tot after struggling to reach the firing step of the take-off trench. If a man don't drink, the old Army rule is, he can still take it and if you are next to him, he can give it to you; that is the only way a soldier can get two drinks, and it has little effect on any man after the night march. Vimy was a big operation in fire-power, but to my mind the Somme was worse and we were harder hit; it was months before we were able to go into battle again. As to how it feels going over the top, there does not seem to be any emotion involved except to reach the objective alive. We follow the barrage (and at Vimy it was a beaut.), and the only scared men we met were Fritzies. To me, the German trying to become a prisoner was always a scared man. I have often thought that was because the German's way of treating P.O.Ws. was not quite so considerate as ours. As long as he dropped his rifle and stripped off his battle harness, he was safe from us. I don't say that he did not get the odd boot in the rump to put him in line to march to the rear; after all, we could not talk his language and some of the boys used rough signs. Fritz in mass formation was one thing, but on even terms he dearly loved to become a prisoner of war and eat white bread. I remember an incident at Vimy, when a German soldier (a mere boy) was doing his best to keep his hands in the air while at the same time falling on the shell-pocked ground. I took him to a large shell hole, and pushed him in, and there saw an odd sight: there were at least a dozen Germans ringed about that hole, and the boy joined them and began to do as they were doing—for every man jack of them were on their knees and praying.

" Another incident that stands out in my memory is of the kilted Imperial regiment that jumped over the 25th Battalion at the top of Vimy Ridge. They lined up in front of us, and then I heard a command that I could not understand: ' Right dress ranks '. And these kilted men dressed ranks under sniper fire. Dressing the line may look magnificent, and that German sniper must have loved it as he got his bullets home.

" I do not know if there is anything of value in this rambling account—I don't believe a combat soldier can give an overall picture of a battle; it is the chaps back in the elevation with powerful field glasses that get the real look at it."

From the overall view, it is clear where the ' Right dress ranks ' incident occurred. It was on the Red Line, where the two reserve brigades took over the assault. Confusingly, these lines did not coincide with the German trench system. The German II Position, or Intermediate system between the triple-line forward trenches and the HQ and gun areas, was like an ' X ', with the intersection point at Les Tilleuls. The stroke from top left to bottom right was the Zwischen Stellung (which south of the village was the Canadian Red Line and north of it the Canadian Black Line). The bottom left stroke was the Zwolfer Stellung (1st Division's Black Line) and the top right stroke the Turko Graben (2nd Division's Red Line). The task of the 25th Bat-

talion had been to carry the attack forward across the widening
gap between the upper strokes of the 'X', while the 21st Battalion took on the ruins of Les Tilleuls at the intersection point.
In the Turko Graben, the Nova Scotians of the 25th Battalion
took 400 prisoners, two 77 mm guns, and eight heavy m.gs.; and
lost 250 men. The 21st Battalion suffered almost equal loss, 215
men, and took 106 prisoners from the Felsenkeller, the command
post of Sector Arnulf-South, where the German relief staff had
been trapped by the start of the barrage. Soon after 0600, they
had received frantic calls from the third line of the forward
triple-trenches for reinforcements. Black with smoke and daubed
with mud, the reserve company, heavily laden, had struggled
forward, falling to the barrage fire and the low-flying aeroplanes.
All in vain, it was soon clear. The German official history
records: "Lieutenants Reinecke and Richter, still holding the
Felsenkeller, had to report to Hauptmann Schmidt-Eberstein,
the commander, that the enemy had advanced in the north well
behind the Third Line trench and in the south had crossed
the Lens-Arras road. Almost immediately, the first 'teller-
helmets' could be plainly seen there. The last two machine-guns
were brought into action by Lance-Sergeant Erdmann, and from
the twin entrances of the dugout they fired burst after burst into
the lines of advancing enemy. But hardly had they opened up,
when they were located and deluged with hand-grenades. Soon
one m.g. was silent, then the other."

This was where the Canadian dash showed itself; not in the
steady advance, which was timed, but in the rapid and intelligent rushes to subdue such strongpoints, when lesser soldiers
might simply have gone to ground for good, so that the assault
stalled and got out of gear. Typical of this, in the 2nd Division,
was Lance-Sergeant E. W. Sifton's initiative in spotting and
clearing a hidden machine-gun which was holding up the 18th
Battalion just before Les Tilleuls. He reached the gun entirely
alone, bayonetted the crew, and fought off their comrades until
supported. Like Private Milne of the 16th Battalion, his V.C.
was also a posthumous one; he was killed by one of the men he
had wounded. Not all Germans surrendered.

With Les Tilleuls taken and the Turko-Graben in Canadian
hands, it was time for the Canadian 6th Brigade, on the right,

and the 13th Imperial Brigade, on the left, to take the advance forward from the Red Line; not so much up the crest now, as across it, through the barbed wire uncut by the stranded tanks, to the Blue Line and finally the Brown Line by Farbus village. The time was now 0800, two-and-a-half hours after the start. The reserve brigades came up, and the assault recommenced at 0930.

Dead in the centre of the attack was Captain Ulric Nisbet, from the 1st Royal West Kents, right-hand battalion of 13th Brigade, who had been attached as liaison officer to the Canadian 29th Battalion, left-hand battalion of the 6th Brigade. Fortunately, he kept his maps and notes, which give an excellent idea of the problems of the battle at a level midway between private soldier and high command. The maps are, of course, large scale; if the whole of Vimy Ridge was to be depicted at that scale, then it would paper one complete wall of a large-sized room. This is one excellent reason why most military histories have comparatively inadequate maps. The configuration of the Ridge meant that these two brigades would be attacking into a triangle from the blunt end. Along the blunt end, parallel to the Turko-Graben and aligned nearly north-south, was Thelus Trench with its barrier of wire; deeper in, still parallel, was the Blue Barrage Line. The tip of the triangle was Farbus Wood and the upper edge of the triangle, from Farbus Wood to north of Goulot Wood, was the Brown Barrage Line. And parallel to that, almost at right-angles to both Thelus Trench and the Blue Line, were two dense barriers of wire which, it had been planned, the tanks would destroy. The Brown Line, the upper edge of the triangle, represented three factors of importance—the point where Vimy Ridge dropped steeply onto the far plain; a line of almost continuous woods; and the main German gun area. The triangle also contained, just north of Thelus, and under Hill 135, an elaborate deep tunnel system which housed, among other units, the HQ of Bavarian Reserve Infantry Regiment No. 3, to which Michael Volkeimer had made his way when it was obvious that the critical moment had arrived.

Nisbet, who was then a Lieutenant, wrote: " As we neared the front line we came under German shell fire, which was being concentrated on our advanced trenches. An officer a few yards ahead of me was killed, but I and my batman safely reached our reserve line, from which a deep tunnel had been dug up to the front. This was crowded with troops moving up, also with R.A.M.C. men, wounded, and stretcher-bearers. When at last we emerged at the far end the trench had suffered such damage from the heavy rains and shelling, that for a moment we could neither haul ourselves out of it, nor tell which way to proceed. However, we got through a gap and more by chance than skill found ourselves in No-man's-land. From here onwards the ground was a boggy wilderness of shell craters. The early morning drizzle had turned to snow. It needed all one's strength to drag one leg after the other. About half-way across this first stretch I just had time to hear that terrible sound of a ' dead-on ' shell when its wind bowled me over like a ninepin. This, and the violence of the explosion, convinced me that I was finished. It was therefore curious and somewhat disheartening to come back to the realisation that I was still alive without even a ' blighty '. There was nothing for it but to go on. During the next hour we covered a thousand yards, passing two derelict tanks which had been defeated by the mud, and reached our first (official) halting place—the Lens-Arras Road, where the troops detailed to attack the second and later objectives were forming up. The road, which was quite unrecognisable as such, was being heavily shelled, but both the West Kents and the Canadians were exceedingly fortunate, casualties being few. Great work was done here by the former's C.O. in getting companies sorted out, and all ranks behaved as though on parade. The result was that the leading waves were ready to advance precisely according to schedule."

Nisbet had a complete pad of notes, eleven pages of them, giving in detail the attack plans of the Royal West Kents, for the information of the O.C. 29th Battalion, who would be advancing alongside them. They were not in the least Napoleonic, merely the prosaic details of movements to be carried out at specified times, along specified axes of advance, to specified sections of certain objectives by certain specified companies, under fire, and meanwhile keeping in step both with the barrage and the units to left and right; easy enough on a parade ground, near impossible on ground so cratered and torn that most of the landmarks had disappeared. The overall objectives of the two brigades were: " Thelus and Hill in A·6 " (between Red and Blue Lines); " Bois du Goulot and Bois de la Ville " (the Brown Line along the wooded reverse slope of the Ridge). The parts of those objectives allotted to the Royal West Kents were noted in detail, together with the signals which would denote to Battalion HQ that they had been taken:

" Three white Very Lights will be fired by order of O.C. companies as follows:

C & D Companies when they have taken THELUS TRENCH.

B Company when it has taken edge of GOULOT WOOD.

D Company, advanced platoon, when it has taken CROSS ROADS.

A Company when it has taken edge of WOOD.

O.C. C Company will fire from his HQ three Gold and Silver

Rain Rockets when HILL 140 (MILL) has been taken."

The greater part of the military art consists of making such tight organisational arrangements in theory, and then carrying them out in practice under the most appalling conditions and with unexpected developments likely to occur. When there is a failure, it is most likely to be an organisational failure; some factor has not been allowed for, or insufficiently allowed for; or the practical difficulties prove overwhelming. The factor most likely to cause trouble, especially in a set-piece battle, can be summed up as: ' Where the hell has A got to? ' or ' Who holds X? ' It is quite unlike a game of chess, because the position of many of the pieces on the board is frequently unknown, their precise value often in doubt, and there is in any case no way of bringing down a God Almighty finger from on high to move them forwards, sideways, or backwards, as required. Once the battle has begun, the general more or less abdicates, leaving his reputation in the hands of some of the most insignificant of the pieces, lost somewhere in the smoke on the muddy, blood-stained chaotic board.

The acid test of the general, therefore, is whether his organisational arrangements are satisfactory; for if they are not, it matters little whether he has chosen the right time, place and direction of attack, or done his elementary sums correctly. Hence the multiplication of signalling methods, to ensure that if two

TRAINING: German storm troops practising new methods of attack, supported by flame throwers, on a training ground near Sedan in May, 1917.

THE REAL THING: Canadian soldiers sheltering in a hastily consolidated trench on Vimy Ridge during the battles which followed its capture in May, 1917.

ABOVE, LEFT: German soldiers in Vimy village. ABOVE, RIGHT: Ruins of Vimy village when in German hands. Both these photographs were picked up by Sergeant Roland Irwin after the battle. RIGHT: The French lost more than 100,000 men in trying to take Vimy Ridge. This is a German photograph. BELOW, LEFT: Vimy, after capture. BELOW, RIGHT: Napoo Corner, Lievin, one of the hottest spots after Vimy Ridge had fallen.

Gefallne-Franzosen

D. H. ('Steve') Keay

David Layton

Battle Flag of the 54
(Kootenay) Battalion wi
'Koots', the Regiment
Mascot.

Maurice Bracewell

George R. Alliston

fail, there is still one which might work. Therefore, in addition to the normal system of 'success' rockets for each objective taken, and also the simpler reverse sign of the same coin—" Heavy M.G. or Rifle Fire breaking out will be taken as an S.O.S."— there was the new method of contact patrol by aircraft, offering the possibility of restoring to the modern general some of the overall vision, albeit somewhat delayed, which Hannibal undoubtedly had most of the time; and which Marlborough and Napoleon had part of the time, smokeless powder being unavailable to them. (Given just one ground-radar set, Bonaparte must have become master of the world.) Therefore, orders to the Royal West Kents included the following additional paragraph: " There will be a contact aeroplane marked by two black bands under Righthand bottom plane and by two streamers. Flares will be shown at the time to be laid down in orders and when called for by aeroplane." The pilot dived and made noises with a Klaxon horn, when he wanted a unit to identify itself by flares or report by signal panel if it was held up, and if so, by what. There was also a simple code of tank to infantry signals, ranging widely from optimism to pessimism: R.W.G.—" Enemy retiring "; R.G.R.—" Infantry held up "; W.R.—" Thelus Trench captured "; R.R.R.—" Broken down ".

What was expected of the tanks is laid down in Note 21 of Captain Nisbet's memo pad: " Two Tanks will move forward with C & D Companies in attack on 1st objective. They will then move up wire shown between THELUS trench and TELEGRAPH WEG and pass over the latter trench after which they will not take any further part in the operations by this battalion (1 RWK) unless called upon." The Telegraph Weg was the important communication trench leading across the attack triangle and linking the German reserve units area of Farbus with the immense tunnel and dugout command post system at Contour 135, otherwise known as Telegraph Hill, between Thelus village and Thelus Mill to the north (sometimes called Hill 140). The German nomenclature is easy to read: all their communication trenches were designated ' Weg ', which simply means ' way ' or ' roadway '. The strong II Position or Intermediate lines were designated ' Stellung ', which simply means ' Fortress '. The deep dugouts were ' Keller ', or ' cellar '. The forward triple lines of trenches were designated 1, 2, 3, as was the British and Canadian practice.

"At the pre-arranged moment our great barrage lifted and moved forward at the rate of 100 yards every three minutes," wrote Captain Nisbet. "During practice we had thought that this might necessitate our waiting, very much exposed, in front of the objectives, but on the actual day the pace was quite fast enough for anyone. The accuracy of the barrage called forth loud praise from the Canadians. Co-operating with it were two hundred machine guns, firing over us at long range targets. Their combined effect was devastating. No sooner had the curtain of shells cleared an enemy trench than the leading wave dashed in, and the succeeding one passed through to continue the attack. Meanwhile, the weather remained atrocious; occasionally the snow became so thick that the Ridge was entirely hidden. At other times the sun shone brilliantly for a few minutes, but it was mainly dull and bitterly cold. Through all this our aeroplanes carried out their observation work, flying low over objectives. There were very few enemy 'planes about. By ten a.m. the Canadians were in possession of the village of Thelus. Nearby we descended a deep shaft and to our surprise found that it led to a vast underground system of dugouts and tunnels. So unexpected and rapid had been the advance that the inhabitants were blissfully cooking or awaiting their breakfasts. They offered no resistance. Among them was an artillery colonel, who owned a nicely papered bedroom and a feather bed with sheets. Above ground in the village itself, the troops captured several guns and then continued the attack towards the crest of the Ridge —a distance of about 4,000 yards."

Albert C. Woodward was a private soldier in the 27th (City of Winnipeg) Battalion, the reserve battalion of the Canadian 6th Brigade advancing to the right of the 13th Imperial Brigade. "Starting out from a trench near Neuville St. Vaast, our orders were: Follow the man ahead. The ground was a mass of shell holes, in most cases full of water; the barb wire entanglements had been destroyed, but the going was really tough. After some distance, ground conditions improved, and we passed through lines of troops that had attacked earlier. The sun came out. We could see trees to the right which marked the village of Thelus, and saw the 31st Battalion (recruited in Calgary, Alberta) take their objective. In front of their position was a wide band of barb wire. We waited for Zero hour, then advanced. Soldiers who had been detailed to cut the barb wire entanglements went forward and cut the wire with long-handled clippers. We followed through and advanced behind the artillery barrage. A section of my platoon had been detailed to search for dugouts and take care of any prisoners. Almost immediately they found a dugout with two entrances. The Germans refused to come up, so a smoke bomb was thrown down one entrance. Twenty eight Germans emerged from the other entrance, were stripped of weapons, and sent back. We could see for miles ahead, and to our right could see the whole line of our troops advancing, spread out in open formation, as far as Arras. We had advanced about two or three hundred yards, when a German machine-gun opened fire straight ahead of us. The troops hit the ground. A small section had been trained to insert a Mills bomb, with a small stem attached, into the end of a ·303 rifle. A round was then fired, which discharged the bomb about 200 yards ahead. The soldier firing the bomb could not aim it, but had to judge the right direction and elevation. To land within ten or fifteen yards of a target was considered good. It took only the one bomb. The three German machine-gunners threw up their hands and advanced towards and through our lines, searched by the section previously mentioned. The main body continued to advance and took our objective."

145 East Cheshire Heavy Battery had been keeping up a rapid and continuous fire until nine a.m., when their fire slackened. They had been engaging three enemy batteries. " Somewhere between ten and eleven a.m. the Admiral ordered us to register our guns on Thelus Mill so as to check the accuracy of our fire," wrote Lieutenant Iveson. " I had never seen it as a Mill, as it had been a white heap for as long as I had been on the front, but its position was so accurately located on the map and it stood up so well on the skyline, that it was a good mark on which to check the fire of our guns. We therefore went onto the hillside behind the battery, from which we could see the Ridge and the Mill, and were just about to open fire on the Mill itself when, fortunately, we were stopped by a

message from Bisgood at the Battery Command Post that British troops were in Thelus village on the Ridge itself. This, of course, was wonderful news, for the Ridge had been a bogey to us for so long, that it did not seem possible that we were in command of it. ' Cheers ', my diary records."

For the Germans, it was the beginning of the end, in spite of the long pause built-in to the attack time-table, as their official history records. " By eleven a.m. the 79th Reserve Infantry Division still held some parts of the front line, but the centre was already back beyond the crest of the Ridge, the left wing had been pushed back west of Vimy as far as the II Position and, further south, even as far as the railway embankment. There it was reinforced by the reserve battalions which had now arrived. The resistance of the small outposts up in front petered out one by one. With this, the most important part of the Vimy Heights, and especially the important south-eastern contour— Telegraph Hill—was lost."

" The enemy were now thoroughly demoralised, and by early afternoon we had gained the final objectives," wrote Nisbet. " For the first time since the early days of the War, our infantry looked down across the wide panorama of the Douai Plain. It was a sight for the Gods! We could see the German gunners working their guns, then limbering up and moving back. Transport wagons were in full retreat with hundreds of fugitives from the Ridge. There appeared to be nothing at all to prevent our breaking through—nothing, that is, except the weather. So appalling was the state of the battlefield that neither tanks nor cavalry could cross it. The day before, we had seen the cavalry massed behind our lines and were bitterly disappointed that they never came through to exploit what seemed to be a deep gap in the German front. I believe that the High Command never expected such an overwhelming success and had no plans for a breakthrough. My own battalion captured nine guns and a most realistic dummy, made up of two old wheels and a log of wood."

The British brigade saw the plain before the Canadians did. Being on the left of the triangle, they had the shortest distance to go to reach the crest, and once there, turned south-east to sweep through the woods. Sergeant David Layton's presentiment had proved reliable again; the battle had gone well and he had survived. His unit, the 15th Warwicks, had gone in as support battalion to the 13th Brigade, but because Vimy occurred in the middle of his fighting career—which ended in North Russia in 1919—he recalled only " trivial things, for in fact one's world is always the few square yards around one." The " exuberance " of 2nd Canadian Division. Passing on the way up a Canadian battery being gas-shelled. Coming under desultory shellfire and some sniping. British aircraft flying very low overhead throughout the battle. The 5.9 shell that, contrary to what the experts said, he heard in sufficient time to drop flat. " The scores of dead bodies lying around, one ignored, because there was nothing unusual in that; but I have a clear recollection of one of the K.O.S.Bs. walking back, having had a bullet through the top of his little finger, which was just hanging by a bit of skin, and I wondered: Was it a Blighty? Would he be lucky and get home with such a trivial wound? " And, some weeks later, after being forty eight hours without food, being given a whole 7 lb. tin of bully beef by a generous Canadian unit. After nearly fifty years, that memory still remained! And the after-impression that " neither the planners of the battle—nor the officers and men who took part—have received the acclaim they deserved." That was a studied judgment, based on considerable comparative experience.

As the British drove south-east, the Canadians wheeled left to meet them on the Brown Line and then, once established on it and overlooking the Douai plain, dug in against counter-attack. Not because any serious counter-stroke was imminent, but because it was laid down in the plan; and it was so laid down because, firstly, a rapid counter-attack (as opposed to a prepared counter-offensive) catches a newly-established attacking force off-balance and disorganised, and, secondly, because German doctrine always stressed this fact. However, at this moment, everything was wide open; the German reserve battalions which had come up in the meantime could not even plug the hole, let alone strike back.

Albert C. Woodward, of the 27th Battalion's ' B ' Company, was ordered down the steep reverse slope of Vimy Ridge to join a Lewis gun crew under Lance/Corporal Byrns which was posted some fifteen yards in front of a German communication trench which here marked the Brown Line. The back of the communication trench had been excavated at this point to make a gun position—obviously a heavy gun, because a hand-operated endless-chain elevator for lifting shells was still in place, although the gun was gone. On their left, where ' C ' Company was still moving on the crest, there was a sudden burst of machine-gun fire, and it was obvious that they were being held up. Sergeant Tetherington, of ' B ' Company, sized up the situation and thought he could get to the gun via the communication trench, so he called out, " Pass the word along for some bombers." Grenade-throwing was then a specialised art and during static line-holding periods there was a special section of each battalion devoted to it; in an attack, however, they all rejoined their companies. Woodward heard the shout, and called back, " I've got some bombs, I'll come with you." Then, just the pair of them, they moved along the trench towards the sound of the German machine-gun. " Throw a bomb as far as you can," said Tetherington. Woodward took out the pin, paused, then hurled the grenade like a cricket ball. The moment it exploded, they hurried on. The machine-gun had stopped firing, and they saw the reason—the crew were running like hell down the hill towards the ruins of Petit Vimy, leaving their gun behind them. Sergeant Tetherington then waved to ' C ' Company to come on and occupy the position (he was later awarded the D.C.M. for the affair), and Woodward returned to the Lewis gun where he started to dig a shelter in the rear (now the front) wall of the communication trench. It was to be needed.

" From our position on the Ridge we could see German troops retreating, and civilians' washing hanging on the lines to dry," he recalled. " A bomb or shell had made a direct hit on a freight train on a bridge on the Lens-Arras road, and a freight car was hanging precariously over the road. Later in the afternoon, German gun teams of horses were seen galloping up and pulling out guns." Up to now, the soldiers had hardly seen a German, but now they saw the whole panoply of war spread out before them on the Douai plain, some of it in terms of galloping gun teams which had seemed to belong to an earlier, and more romantic, era of warfare. " There were German guns out in the brickyards on the Mericourt plain there, and our fellows were doing the darndest to keep them from getting these," said another member of the 27th Battalion, L. R. Fennel. "And by Golly, the Germans came up there with four horses. Galloped up there and hitched them onto these guns and hiked them out. By Golly, I tell you, the shells were flopping around them, because we was trying to get them with the heavies, you see. Our field guns weren't up, so they couldn't fire."

G. Scott of the 29th (British Columbia) Battalion was told to find out if Heroes Wood, between the Blue and Red Lines, was occupied by the battalion, or whether there was a gap between the left flank of the 29th and the right flank of the Royal West Kents, which would mean that the Canadian brigade was out of touch with the British brigade. "I got to where I thought it should be on the map, and and I couldn't see anything," he said. "It turned out afterwards, there wasn't anything. With our bombardment, even the stumps had gone. The nearest woods I could see was Farbus Woods. At this stage it was very, very quiet, as frequently happened after an attack. I walked over the top into Farbus Woods, then I realised as soon as I got there that I had the wrong wood. I also realised that Farbus Wood hadn't yet been taken. There was nobody there. There was a field gun emplacement with nobody in it and very, very deep dugouts, so I went down in these dugouts, picked up the odd souvenir, and went along a certain distance and found a tunnel that ran out into the base of the Ridge on the German side. So I went to the mouth of this tunnel and, perhaps two hundred yards away, there was a German howitzer in full operation. So from back in the tunnel where I was perfectly safe, I fired some random shots in their general direction; and immediately they all left the gun, because they were just waiting for someone to give them a hint it was time to go away, and away they went."

Lieutenant Herbert Bradshaw, of 145 East Cheshire Heavy Battery, went forward with the Canadian Brigade from the Red Line, followed by his team of signallers, to establish an observation post on the crest and so keep his battery firing on observed targets. The field guns on this section of the front had mostly ceased fire, the advance having gone forward beyond their range. "About a hundred yards to the right flank of our O.P., an in-

teresting discovery was made. A four-gun battery position had
been dug and camouflaged. Inside it were four dummy guns
made of sheet metal. From these, wires ran to a battery in the
edge of the wood behind. There is no doubt that when the real
battery was in action, flashes were fired from the dummy in front
to deceive us. In fact, the 145th had fired hundreds of rounds
at the dummy position."

As the Germans began to pull out their field guns, in full
view of the Canadians, their heavier guns further back began to
shell their lost positions at Vimy Ridge, the ranges of which
they knew to a yard. The bombardment steadily increased in
intensity. Woodward of the 27th Battalion, helped by a chum,
had dug well into the wall of the communication trench and
were now glad of it; there was room even for a third man, a
stretcher-bearer. The first casualty was Woodward's rifle, which
he had left in the nearby German gunpit; a falling tree broke
the stock. A ration party of six men, led by Corporal Hill, an
old soldier with twenty years' service in the British Army, were
caught there also by a shell. Corporal Hill, out in front, who had
dropped flat, looked round and saw them all lying dead without
a wound. " The concussion had killed all six instantly; the shell
had passed just over their heads and caused a vacuum, so no
air to breathe," conjectured Woodward.[2] Then a salvo of shells
landed almost on top of them, half-burying the three of them
under clods of earth and heavy lumps of solid chalk strata. " My
chum and I pushed our way out through this, but the stretcher-
bearer was shell shocked and helpless; unable to move or speak
he just laughed loud continuously. The call came for stretcher-
bearers, but he was unable to go, then some casualties came
along who could walk. Private Gifford, another pal of mine,
came past. He had got mixed up with another battalion and had
advanced with them. A German had made a lunge at him with a
bayonet. Gifford grabbed the bayonet, and turned it to one side so

[2] This phenomenon was not understood until the Second World War,
when it became typical, in association with bombs and civilians. Actually,
it was discovered, the impact of blast was like colliding with a motor car
doing thirty m.p.h., but the injuries were internal, often to the kidneys and
spleen, and there was little or no blood. The lesser blast effect of a shell,
together with the protection afforded by heavy equipment, made this type
of injury less common among soldiers, so that it was never properly
investigated during 1914-1918.

that it missed his body, but the German pulled the trigger and the bullet smashed three of his fingers. He told me this while I was bandaging his hand up. The stretcher-bearer had now recovered enough to walk back, but was still laughing and unable to talk. I asked a casualty to help him to the dressing station, which he did. Sergeant Tetherington was helped along by another casualty; a tree trunk had fallen and struck the sergeant across the back, breaking both hips. I heard that Sergeant Rogers was a casualty. Sergeant Whiting was wounded in the jaw by a fragment of shell. Jimmy Sneddon was hit in the leg by falling shrapnel; he was a member of a Lewis gun team in front of our position. Corporal Dokerty came along, wounded just above the left eye, the eye was hanging on the cheek. I bandaged him up, but he did not know it was me. I did not see the Commissioned Officer after we took our objective."

When the battalion came out of the line on 11 April, Woodward's platoon was commanded by Corporal Hill and two lance/corporals; and siege warfare had set in again. But, as Woodward put it, " the German troops that we met on that historic day have every reason to know that the Canadian troops that took Vimy Ridge were the equal of any they could muster."

CHAPTER NINE

EASTER MONDAY MORNING

Advance of the 3rd Division

The 3rd Canadian Division, commanded by Major-General L. J. Lipsett, assaulted on a front of 1,500 yards opposite La Folie with only two brigades, because the distance they had to cover was short. On the right was the 8th Brigade (Brigadier J. H. Elmsley), with three battalions up and one in support. The three battalions in line were, from right to left, 1 C.M.R. (Major B. Laws), 2 C.M.R. (Lieutenant-Colonel G. C. Johnston), and 4 C.M.R. (Lieutenant-Colonel H. D. L. Gordon); 5 C.M.R. (Lieutenant-Colonel D. C. Draper) had the role of support battalion. For obvious reasons, this formation was usually known as the C.M.R. Brigade. On the left was the 7th Brigade (Brigadier A. C. Macdonnell), with three battalions in line—The Royal Canadian Regiment (Lieutenant-Colonel C. H. Hill), the Princess Patricia's Canadian Light Infantry (Lieutenant-Colonel A. S. A. M. Adamson), and the 42nd Battalion (Major B. McLellan); and the 49th Battalion (Lieutenant-Colonel R. H. Palmer) in support.

On the left, the divisional boundary virtually coincided with the northern boundary of Reserve Infantry Regiment No. 262 (Major Freiherr von Rothenhan) holding the fixed defences of Sector Zollern in Group Vimy; but on their left, took in part of the right flank of Regiment 263 and the northern command post of Sector Arnulf deep in the Schwaben Tunnel by the Lens-Arras road, as well as both command posts, North and South, of Sector Zollern. Both regiments were from 79th Division in Group Vimy, and consisted of three battalions of which, at any one time, two were forward in the defence zone, the third resting in rear of the Ridge, but with one company forward as immediate reserve. These companies were down to about sixty men. A German regiment was roughly equivalent to a British brigade, both being up to strength; but, without quibbling, the scale of attack was roughly this: a Major-General's command thrown against a Major's command, after the Major's positions had been shattered by overwhelming artillery. It had taken 60,000 casualties in twenty four hours, to convince the Allied Command that only in this way could the superiority of dug-in fire-power against moving man-power be overcome, in the cramped conditions of the Western Front. The object of a battle being, not to have a good fight, but to win with the least losses possible.

On the front of the 3rd Division, the preparation in places was almost too successful; the assaulting troops walked right over the German trenches without recognising them as trenches, and so ran onto their own barrage, suffering some casualties. But better this than the Somme, with the assaulting lines winnowed by machine-gun and rifle fire so swiftly and efficiently that they lay dead in lines, like heads of corn lopped by a mechanical harvester.

The 2nd Canadian Mounted Rifles were centre unit of the C.M.R. Brigade in the assault. Three witnesses from that battalion tell their story. M. E. Parsons, M.M., was a runner for ' C ' Company. After taking back a message through muck and wire, he rejoined the company five minutes before Zero hour. ' Well done, lads, and good luck ', said the Company Commander, Major Tom Godfrey, as he shook hands with Parsons and Westover, the two runners. " For many of us, this was our fourth time over the top in a major attack," Parsons pointed out. " The previous three were at the Somme, so we were not too fearful of the outcome. ' D ' Company took the lead to take the German front line, but seconds before Zero, ' C ' Company moved up and were with them at the German front line. This was done in order to miss the German ' S.O.S.' barrage. These arrangments were all laid out by our Lieutenant-Colonel G. C. Johnston, D.S.O., M.C., a respected and very clever C.O. The artillery was the greatest. What precision! They and the trench mortars had made the wire quite passable, and the curtain of fire at the time of the attack was par excellent. 18-pounder shells bursting directly overhead, and one could see the shrapnel spraying the earth just yards in front of us. I don't remember hearing any shells falling short that day. On reaching the Hun front line, a Jerry fired a flare at me, at about thirty feet range;

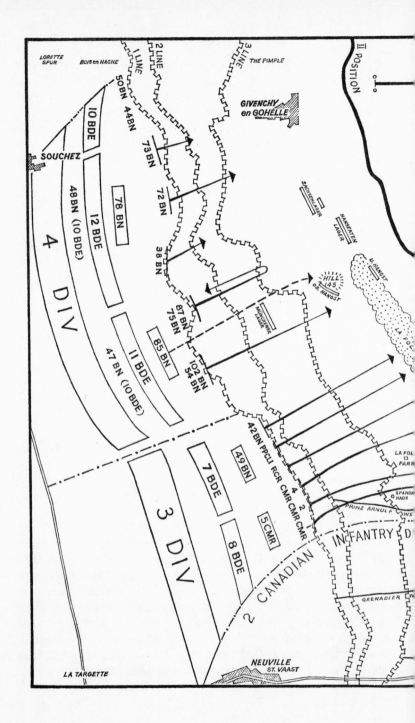

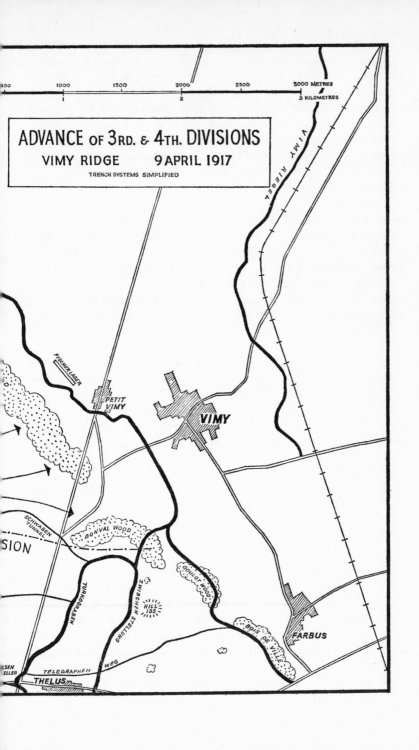

ADVANCE OF 3RD. & 4TH. DIVISIONS
VIMY RIDGE   9 APRIL 1917
TRENCH SYSTEMS SIMPLIFIED

no doubt he was too well shaken up from the barrage to aim straight, poor fellow, he never did get home."

Gus Sivertz had been synchronising watches with his platoon officer, Lieutenant Christie, when the German front lines began to erupt in wreckage, smoke, and the frantic rockets of ' S.O.S.' signals. Three minutes of it. "Then, suddenly, it jumped a hundred yards and we were away. I suppose we must have crossed the German front line, but I have no memory of it at all. Instead of a trench, there was only a wide, muddy depression, stinking of explosives. Then little Lieutenant Christie was hit and just pitched forward, dead. When I straightened up, I tried to hurry to catch up with my group (for the first time, we were attacking in columns of lumps—small, separate groups). I tripped in some snarled barbed wire and fell, just as a big Hun shell screamed into the muck alongside me. I felt that I'd be on the road west in a moment. Instead, I was just knocked over again and, in rising, got a terrific slam on the top of my head. It rammed my tin hat down to my ears. That was a huge chunk of chalk that the shell had blown skyward and was coming down as I came up. Then I ran in a stumbling sort of way to get up with my buddies. It's terrible to be alone . . . one feels that all the enemy guns are pointed at one . . . and naked. You want to touch someone. So I rejoined my group. There wasn't much to shoot at—Heinies were coming back with their hands up, and his counter-barrage wasn't so hot. The man next to me smiled and leaned over to say something . . . I think he meant to say: ' It's going fine ', or something like that. He put his mouth almost in my ear, there was such a helluva noise going on. He never finished the sentence . . . never made a sound, just pitched on his face. A clean shot through the head."

Where the German defences had been, there were no trenches anymore. "The whole thing was flattened," said G. Dorman. "Then I looked back, and it put me in mind of an ant-hill. As far as I could see it was just alive with glittering bayonets, and, boy, did I have courage! I thought, ' Oh, what support I've got, I'm all right.' But before that I thought I was alone, I thought I was the only one in the world there, but when that started, boy! my chest stuck out! But I could see this man going, that man going, and I'll never forget, there was a chap, both his legs shot off, and there he was on his stumps, and he was still using his gun to go forward; you would think he was sitting up in a canoe, trying to paddle with his gun. Oh, Gee! It was terrible."

" There was so little to see except straight ahead," recollected Sivertz. " The smoke and the rain and the sleet obscured our flanks, but I felt—or maybe could hear—trouble on our right towards Thelus where the 28th Battalion was driving up." But it was nearer than that, much nearer. The 1st C.M.R., the unit immediately to the right of 2 C.M.R., had run into heavy machine-gun fire. The hazard of Vimy Ridge lay in the deep tunnels, which could not be touched by artillery. If only a few alert machine-gun crews could manage the climb up in time, with their heavy load, they could halt everything on their immediate front. Sergeant Roland Irwin, D.C.M., recollected: " We were to mop up and gather what prisoners there might still be in dugouts after the barrage. But we were in for a jolt. When the smoke and haze cleared a bit, we found ourselves exposed to a German trench manned by a good number of machine-guns and men with hand grenades. This gave us quite a bad time right then. Those of us who were really active dived into the nearest shell hole to gather our wits on the next best move. We had a volunteer sneak back to contact our signals and explain our situation to the artillery, and in about an hour's time there was the most beautiful sight to see—the artillery dropped their barrage back until that German trench was really being pulverised. During the rest of the day, my chum and I took about forty prisoners, including two German doctors running a dugout hospital in back of Vimy Ridge. That was a long day and more action than enough." An expressive quote from a soldier whose experience ranged from Ypres, 1916, to Mons, 1918.

" Things got a bit warmer as we got nearer to the Zwischen Stellung, the big, heavily-defended trench that was our intermediate objective " (the Black Line), recalled Gus Sivertz. " We swarmed over and cleared it up pretty fast, but then our right was stopped cold by a machine-gun firing from a steel-slotted pill box. Zwischen gave up a lot of prisoners; it also gave up the German regimental commander, and you never saw a madder man. He had started his Easter breakfast of bacon, eggs, toast, cereal and coffee with—if you please, fresh Danish butter and canned cream—'Carnation' brand—from just a 150 miles south of my home in Vancouver. The case was stamped 'Belgian Relief Fund'. Well, he never even got started and Al Swanby really enjoyed it, while Heinie private soldiers laughed their heads off. It was a busy spot as we converted the trench for defence, but Fred Zuehlke lost an arm when he went single-handed down a big dugout. A German officer shot him at a bend in the stair. It was his last shot."

This was a nervy business for both sides, the Canadians going down into deep enemy tunnels and dugouts, not knowing what was down there or whether the defenders were in a mood to surrender or not. And the men down below, helpless against the casually tossed grenade, could have no idea how ruthless the attackers would be, or what their mood was, for that might depend on what casualties they had had, or if just one man up top had had his best friend killed a minute or so before. A wounded German officer's account, from this Sector, survives. "There is a thin, far-away shout: '*The English—get out—get out!*' '*They're coming from the left there, straight through the valley towards Bonval Wood*'. There is the roar of battle—rifle shots—hand-grenades—while, down below, the secret files are being burnt. One man is carried down, whimpering—he is hit in the belly—then silence. Then a burst of shouts and yells: '*They're on top of us!*' But it gets quieter and, finally, a complete silence—broken by a sudden shout in a foreign language: '*Come out!*' The candlelights flicker. A few wild thoughts race through one's head. What will they do? Throw grenades down on us? Shall I hide under the bed I'm lying on? (the witness had been wounded)—no, I'd be done for then, helpless. Will they beat me to death? No!—I'd rather shoot myself first, but my pistol's on the table and I can't reach it from here. Better wait and see—perhaps there'll be a counter-attack to drive them away. But it's very quiet, too quiet . . . A Tommy comes along the tunnel, peers carefully round the corner, a heavy revolver in his hand. '*Officer?*' he asks. Then he examines the dead, and leaves to fetch his comrades."

Dorman took no chances with the first, menacing cellar. " The first dugout we got to was partly blown in, but you could crawl down there, and I could hear them down there. FFUT-PSSS! Down goes a bomb. No, nobody coming up there. So away we go to another one. Finally I come to one where the guys were pretty near the top, you know, I could see them. I ended up with 35 prisoners, some in their stocking feet, some in underwear, some in low shoes and socks, and some in the high boots, others with only a coat, and the odd one had a blanket. They were just knocked out of bed."

" Because our right had been stopped cold by that pillbox," recollected Sivertz, " some of our chaps started more to the left, towards La Folie Farm—which, of course, wasn't a farm, but a well-organised defence set-up with what had once been a wood behind it." At the Zwischen Stellung, which was the Black Line, the two brigades were supposed to halt for twenty minutes while the artillery prepared the way ahead for the next bound; but some men from 2 C.M.R. disobeyed. One of them was M. E. Parsons. " Once the show started, every man was actually his own general," he explained. " I tagged myself onto a well-known sergeant, Sergeant Al Swamby, and we sailed through, and half-way up the barrage stopped. Everybody was supposed to stop and wait till it started again. But in our eagerness, some of ' D ' Company, and Sergeant Swamby, with six men, including my-self, from ' C ' Company, pushed right on to La Folie Farm, down in front of that Ridge. And there we engaged eight Jerries. They gave us a bad time, and we gave them a bad time, but it ended up that Sergeant Swamby and I were the only two alive. How it happened was like this. Our group bumbled into a machine-gun crew, and three of our men were killed. With Mills bombs we stirred them up, and made another try; two fell dead. We separated to about thirty yards and came at them from two directions with bombs flying. There were three live Huns in that trench when we jumped in. When we left there were eight dead ones. I might add, they were good soldiers, they made no attempt to surrender. It sounds like a long time, but actually this little action took about ten minutes. About this moment, we had pre-ceded our barrage, and now we saw it coming. We got back in the trench with our late friends (the Jerries). I don't think it was as severe as at Zero, but it was hot. You could see the whizz-bangs thick as hair on a dog, and Sergeant Swamby was wounded, with a shrapnel ball in the top of his right shoulder. So I'm the only one that came out of there unscathed."

That was on the left of 2 C.M.R. On the right flank, that pill-box with a machine-gun in it was still blocking any attempt to advance from the captured Zwischen Stellung. Recalled Sivertz: " In the meantime we were held up on the right and me—smart as a whip, you know!—figured out that since the pill-box had a steel slot in it, it also had a limited arc of fire; and I would sneak up under cover, until I could get behind him and let the crew share a Mills bomb. It was a good idea, and might have worked, if I hadn't looked up too soon. By the grace of heaven, I had my finger hooked to pull the pin of the bomb, but hadn't done so when his bullet hit me. Of course, I didn't know I was hit . . . I didn't know anything.

" When I woke up, the rain had stopped and it was fairly quiet where I lay. The heavies were pounding our old front line and even there it wasn't too bad. I wondered what had happened. I had no pain, but a salty taste in my mouth, which I kept spitting out until I saw my hand blood-covered. I felt over my head . . . all bandaged. My gas mask container was filled with blood, so I spilled it out. My toes squished in blood. So I sat there and puzzled things out. I felt fine—like being about on a third glass of champagne. What I didn't like, was seeing Fritz prisoners run, look around and then pick up a rifle and start shooting at our chaps from behind. Way off, I spotted Mont. St. Eloi's twin spires, and made a good line towards our trenches.

" I had the feeling that I was taking great seven-foot steps and going over the ground without any effort at all. My left temple artery had been cut. I was so light-headed, that while I was stumbling over the muck I had the sensation of walking over the top of everything and I felt hilarious. I wanted to laugh and talk to the men who were coming up to reinforce, and I asked one for a drink of rum, and he looked at my wound. ' No, nothing doing '. And I didn't know where I was. Nothing looked the same—where trenches had been, there was only some smashed wire. Then I saw a piece of wood, white-painted wood, sticking out of the mud; and I took it out, and wiped it on my pants, and it said on it: ' Ross Street '. That was the point from which we had started that morning before dawn. In a few minutes, I found the big medical trench, and I sat down at the end of the lines of wounded men. A medical sergeant came up every few minutes, looking for haemorrhage cases; every few minutes he would pick someone out, and then he beckoned to me. As we ducked down the big dugout stair, we both heard this bloody 5·9. It sounded like a freight train moving through the sky. And when it had exploded, we looked back, and where I had been sitting, with six other men, there was nothing but tatters of uniform and bits of men. I got through the M.O. fast . . . a ticket and an ' On your way, chum '. I sure felt sorry for those medical people, they were pale with sheer fatigue.

" Soon I was in Neuville St. Vaast on familiar ground . . . with a pleasant fool of a YMCA officer just dancing in excitement; kept trying to push cigarettes into my mouth . . . and they just fell out, because contusion stopped control of my jaws. But I waved and tried to holler at the artillery men of the Lahore Division, who had moved their precious guns as far forward as they could go, and were lobbing the shells over in great glee. They were naked to the waist and their guns' barrels melted the sleet like a hot stove. Man! they were great. So I went back out, and I was stumbling along in the rear area, still happy, still completely punch-drunk, and I found a blind Japanese. He was not a 2nd C.M.R., but he was a Canadian, and by that time I was getting very weak; and he was very strong, but he couldn't see. I got across to the field dressing station at Mont. St. Eloi by being eyes for the blinded Japanese. He provided the legs for the team, mine were rubber. I hope he recovered his sight. At Mont. St. Eloi, I just had no sensation in my knees; I just clattered down on the cobblestones, absolutely inert, like a fish suddenly flung out of a stream. I made C.C.S. and some time next day passed out in the hospital train to wake up at Wimereux with my head in the lap of an angel, who was cutting my blood-matted hair off with a pair of blunt scissors."

4th C.M.R. were assaulting on the left of Gus Sivertz's battalion. With them was Private Thomas Wildridge, from Milford Haven in South Wales, who had gone to Canada in 1912. He went over at Vimy with the second wave, and almost immediately passed a Red Cross man tending a wounded soldier. The Red

Cross man called to Wildridge to help him with the casualty, and Wildridge was hit in the leg by shrapnel almost at once. So he went back as well. " If you really want to know how I felt," he wrote, " I felt very good, as I only had a flesh wound and I was glad to get rid of the Line; and I got bacon and eggs for breakfast at the hospital in England, the first morning. And I looked at it, and turned over in bed, and it was only a few minutes till the nurse came back and asked me if I was hungry? I told her: That breakfast was for officers; but she told me I would get bacon and eggs every morning, so I jumped to it." More than twenty years later, in September, 1939, he again enlisted in the Canadian Army and was once more sent to England, where an army truck put him in hospital for a much longer period than had the Vimy guns.

For A. E. Barker, also of 4 C.M.R., Vimy was his first big battle, and he got left behind at the start. About five a.m., an opening was blown in Goodman Tunnel, where the battalion was waiting, and they all filed out into No-man's-land, deploying right and left in the darkness. Barker had made sure that he would not be going into action on an empty stomach by buying half-a-dozen " nice looking eggs " for ten francs each and frying them just before they moved up. The difference a decent hot meal makes to a soldier in such circumstances is immense, which is why soldiers can always recall in fine detail exactly what they had to eat, even if the battles tend to blur a little. But Barker did not forget the moment of advance at Vimy, for they went forward in semi-darkness lit only by the gun flashes from behind, and he did not see the big, slippery crater until it was under his feet. " The more I wriggled and kicked to get free, the deeper down I went, so I had to wait until it came daylight and I could see what to do. I spotted a piece of barbwire up on a knoll, so I reached out and had to pull it towards me to see if it would get me out. It was OK, so I put my rifle up on the bank, and then my harness and greatcoat, and got myself out and all fixed up again. I could see some of our boys ahead, so I hurried up and caught them and went with them over the crest of Vimy at the edge of La Folie Woods. I still say that in that wood was one of the prettiest sights I ever did see—for the Colonel met up with one of his men going on over who had a bullet wound alongside of his head and half his left ear gone. And just as we got almost to our objective, an over or stray shot burst in the air, and one of our buddies fell to the ground within eight or ten feet from me. I pushed over to him to see what I could do, but he was hit with a piece of twisted shrapnel across his chest and his heart was cut in two. I left the 4th C.M.R. that same year, the 5th of September, from Petit Vimy, with mustard gas and chlorine gas; and I left the Line and never went back. That was 1917, and I am now in my 73rd year and enjoy living without any work attached. Hoping this will help you some." Or, as M. E. Parsons wrote: " I am glad that I was in my teens, and it was a rare privilege to have known all those strong and courageous officers, N.C.Os. and men." That was the one memory which did not fade.

* * *

E. B. Elgood, formerly of 2 C.M.R., but now a signaller with HQ 7th Brigade, was at M.G. Fort in Ross Trench when at thirty seconds before 0530, two small wombat mines were blown at Chassery Crater. " Hundreds of our guns turned the otherwise *un*usually quiet morning into an inferno of flashing leaping flame and red hot shrapnel fragments; the whirring of shells created quite a wind. And over the top went the first wave of infantry (the Pat's pipers played them over), closely following our creeping barrage, the *too* eager men getting some casualties from our own low-firing machine-guns and shell bands; but they were away! The following waves were close behind, to miss if possible Fritz's counter barrage, which began to come down in our old front positions and rear within a minute of our Zero. His trench mortars caused too many flying bits for comfort, so I went down and relieved Grant, who had been on duty for several hours. Our Brigadier-General Macdonnell was driven out of his O.P. in M.G. Fort early, as Fritz's guns began retaliation, which ' amazed ' him and he found a ' better 'ole '. An M.G. crew had seven casualties. Immediately after Zero, speech on the phones in the front area was allowable, as the enemy's forward listening posts were too preoccupied to hear; and that evening I heard General Lipsett of 3rd Canadian Division speaking to our Brigadier-General: ' I have to congratulate you, General, and your splendid troops, on a very successful day!' Old Macdonnell thanked him, and said: 'If I get out of this war alive, I shall spend the rest of my life marvelling how British soldiers remained so eager and cheerful in the appalling, miserable conditions they had to endure in this campaign.'

" As the ration was often short and microscopic, it certainly was not rum that carried them through!" observed Elgood, in his diary. " The density of our barrage was gradually crumbling all his defence and strong points, so that our 7th Brigade—42nd on left, P.P.C.L.I. centre, R.C.R. on the right, with the 49th in support—had taken his front lines in twenty minutes. A pause of another twenty minutes for rest and mop-up, and then on to our second and final objective, a line north of the Ecole Commune along the crest, among the shattered trunks of La Folie Woods, which was mostly gained by 6.45 a.m.—an approximate distance of 1,000 to 1,500 yards. Prisoners, some badly wounded, began dropping into our trench, dazed and glad to get some kind of shelter and first aid, by 6.20 a.m. I went up again about 9 a.m., and found the trench full of our wounded and prisoners; and some Heinies kept slithering down into comparative safety, helping wounded comrades with ' bombardment-grey, pallid, drawn faces ', some looking like imbecilic corpses with staring eyes. Poor devils, they sure had come through hell. But what about us, at Ypres and Loos and a dozen battles, when he had a great preponderance of metal and fire power? 7th Brigade's prisoners and wounded seem to be from the Prussian 262 Regiment, a fairly large, well-set bunch. Many of our wounded coming in, too, but not looking so down in the mouth as Fritz, and getting fixed up by the First Aid men. The dressing station and stretcher-bearers are badly overtaxed, many cases lying for hours waiting to be attended to—it makes you want to help, but we have our own work to do, and I have had no sleep for thirty six hours. It is getting terribly fuggy in our quarters, what with the candles and Primus going day and night, and fumes sifting down from artillery fire, and some gas shells of Fritz's exploding near. I would say that forward Brigade Majors are the hardest worked staff officers, and ours was no exception: no matter what the time is, all messages, in and out,

are O.Kd. by the Brigade Major. By midnight on the 9th, ours
would drop off to sleep standing up, and at 3.30 a.m. on the
10th I took a message to him, and after I had shaken him awake,
he went to sleep holding the telephone in one hand and the
message in the other."

Sergeant Percy Boxall, M.M., was with the support battalion,
the 49th, which spent the night in Le Grange Tunnel. An
extension had been dug towards the German lines, and this was
blown just before the barrage began, to make a direct exit to
No-man's-land which would also be used later as a quick entrance
to safety for the wounded. Many years later, showing his son
over the battlefield, he explained: " The 49th were spread all
over the 7th Brigade front in the attack, working with the other
three Regiments and the Brigade Mortars; acting as mopping-up
parties, reinforcements, and carrying parties. I was with the
Trench Mortars, and we started off from somewhere just over
on the right where the trees are growing now. We were all pretty
well loaded down, and waited quietly for 5.30 a.m. It was still
dark when a Vickers M.G. opened up over our heads, they started
firing about twenty seconds before the artillery. Then, all hell
broke loose. The sky at our back was lit up by the gunfire, and
just in front of us a curtain of shells was bursting, like water
off a tin roof in a heavy thunderstorm. After a short time the
barrage lifted, and came down on the next lot of German
trenches, and so we followed the barrage to the top of the Ridge
at La Folie Wood. Everyone was loaded with extra ammunition,
bombs, etc., and the mud churned up by the shells made the
going hard. Then it started to snow. We heard some planes
overhead as we got near the top of the Ridge, but I don't think
they were able to see much. They were very like the little Tiger
Moths you sometimes used when you learnt to fly. Eventually,
we reached La Folie Wood, and my job with the trench mortar
section was finished. I had to go back to Grange Tunnel for
some supplies, and, on the way there and back again, I several
times helped the stretcher-bearers who sunk deep in the mud
while carrying the wounded. I'd like to be able to take you
over the way we went to La Folie Wood, but it is too overgrown
with trees now. When we knew it, it was a bare hillside covered
with water-filled shell holes. And up there, on the Memorial, are

the names of my old friends and comrades, who did not live to be able to talk about Vimy to their sons."

The 3rd Division was up to the crest and along the edge of the Bois de la Folie by 0730, after the attack of 1st C.M.R. on the extreme right had been stopped for a time by machine-gun fire. The German unit here was from Oberstleutnant von Behr's Regiment 263, with its HQ in the Schwaben Tunnel, Command Post of Sector Arnulf-North. The commander of 1 Battalion, Major Meyer, had no visual observation because of the dense plumes of spurting smoke from the Canadian barrage, but the continual chattering of the machine-guns showed that a severe assault was in progress. At about 0700, the first news from up front came in the form of a badly wounded soldier, Hagemann of the 2nd Company, who was bleeding from three wounds and had his right arm paralysed. He said that the first frontal attack, made by 1st C.M.R. against his company's positions, had broken down in face of the fire from their surviving machine-guns. " Only after another artillery preparation, accompanied by aeroplanes, was it possible for the enemy storm troops lying in front of the German positions to penetrate the completely erased defences," wrote a German official historian. " The battalions retreated from crater to crater, with their surviving men, until they were finally pushed back beyond the 2nd Line." There were only some twenty men available at Schwaben Tunnel, insufficient for a counter-attack, and the tunnel itself was not sited for defence. Meyer therefore decided to retire through the tunnel to the Intermediate Position just in front of Vimy village on the reverse slope of the Ridge. The Canadian tide was now engulfing them from all sides, the heavy Vickers machine-guns being taken forward with the infantry. There were two m.gs. from the 8th Machine Gun Company with 1st C.M.R., and the crew of one of these thrust forward along the Spandauer Weg to the position known to the Germans as the Ruhlebener Haus. From here, its monotonous brrrrr dominated the retreat of Major Meyer and his staff. As they came out of the tunnel on their way to Vimy village, Lieutenant Langelüddecke was hit and had to be carried back into shelter. The staff survivors, the signals officer, two orderlies, and three wireless operators, followed Meyer through the barrage down to Vimy through mud that was nearly knee-deep. But the Intermediate Position also had been erased by the barrage and was no longer defensible, so his Regimental Commander, von Beyr, sent Meyer to the far side of the village to prepare emergency defences on the line of the railway embankment between Vimy and Willerval.

On the right of the 3rd Canadian Division, therefore, the hold up was only temporary; and the two flanking divisions, the 2nd and the 1st, were on their intermediate objectives and ready to continue their much longer advance, while the 3rd Division dug in. On the extreme left of the 3rd Division, however, resistance was heavy and included local counter-attacks. Major Eric B. Finley, who advanced on the extreme left of 7th Brigade with the 42nd Battalion, said: " We had gone, oh, not more than a third of a mile, when I was knocked unconscious through being struck by a flat piece of shell. When I recovered consciousness, I caught up with the line again and came face to face with German resistance, hand-to-hand fighting. I fired the eight shots in my revolver point-blank, and they were hurling potato-masher grenades at us. One hit my helmet and exploded at my back. George Kilpatrick, who was our padre, came out and said, ' Well, they've got you at last, Eric. Can you make home? ' I said, ' I've got to try '. And he said, ' Well, the fire is very, very bad '. I found another chap who was wounded and was coming in, too, and in another shell hole we found a small German who we picked up and brought in between the two of us. And, on the way in, to evidence the fire, this boy was killed right under our noses, while walking in between myself and this other chap. He was dead before he ever hit the ground."

At about 0900, orders reached the 7th Brigade: establish a left defensive flank, from the Bois de la Folie on the crest of the Ridge right back to the original Canadian front line from which they had advanced that morning. The 42nd Battalion extended on their left, and the Princess Pats took over part of their positions, as the brigade thinned out to hold the much longer line. And continual small arms fire swept them throughout the day from the commanding height of Hill 145, the highest point of the German line. The 4th Division had failed.

CHAPTER TEN

EASTER MONDAY MORNING

The 4th Division Hits Hill 145

The 4th Canadian Division, commanded by Major-General David Watson, was to assault the highest (145 metres) point of the Vimy Ridge, which was, for this reason, the most strongly fortified and formidable part of the entire position. The attack arrangements were of comparable complexity, being in successive waves. Two brigades were to assault, their fourth wave being supplied from the third brigade, which was to remain in reserve ready, if all went well, to assault next day the knoll called the 'Pimple' in clear view from Hill 145 on the other side of the Souchez valley. On the right was the 11th Brigade (Brigadier V. W. Odlum), which was to attack with two battalions up—the 102nd (Lieutenant-Colonel J. Warden) on the right and the 87th (Major Shaw) on the left. The next wave, their supports, would consist of the 54th Battalion (Lieutenant-Colonel V. V. Harvey) on the right, following the 102nd, and the 75th Battalion (Lieutenant-Colonel C. Worshop) on the left, following the 87th. As reserve, forming a third wave, was the 85th Battalion (Lieutenant-Colonel A. H. Borden); and the 47th Battalion of the 10th Brigade formed a further reserve. The objective of the 11th Brigade was Hill 145 itself. On its left would be the 12th Brigade (Brigadier J. H. MacBrien), to take the northern slopes overlooked both by the 'Pimple' and Hill 145, with three battalions up and one in support, plus a battalion loaned by the reserve brigade. From right to left, the assaulting battalions were—the 38th (Lieutenant-Colonel C. M. Edwards), the 72nd (Lieutenant-Colonel J. A. Clark), and the 73rd (Lieutenant-Colonel H. C. Sparling); in reserve was the 78th (Lieutenant-Colonel J. Kirkaldy). The 46th Battalion (Lieutenant-Colonel H. J. Dawson), of 10th Brigade was in further reserve. This left 10th Brigade (Brigadier E. Hilliam) with only two battalions— the 44th (Lieutenant-Colonel Davies) and the 50th (Lieutenant-

Colonel L. F. Page); these were intended to assault the ' Pimple '
next day in the ' Northerly Operation ', if the ' Southern Assault '
succeeded.

Hill 145, the objective of the 11th Brigade, was held by
Reserve Infantry Regiment No. 261 (Oberst von Goerne), a unit
of the 79th Division, holding Sector Fischer of Group Vimy. The
especially formidable nature of the fixed defences it was manning
spring to the eye from the German trench maps, which, although
marked *Das Mitnehmen dieser Karten in die vorderen Linien
ist streng verboten!*, doubtless fell into Canadian hands. The
one in front of the present author belongs to Michael Volkheimer. There was the usual triple line of forward trenches,
with a strong tunnel position, the München-Lager, between
the 2nd and 3rd lines. On the hill crest a double trench system
incorporated a deep-tunnel defence, the Obere Hangstellung,
supported on the reverse slope by the Untere Hangstellung, a
twin-tunnel system for sheltering the reserves, plus, further
north, the Hanseaten-Lager.

The northern boundary of this regiment was also the boundary between the Prussian 79th Reserve Division (von Bacmeister) and the 16th Bavarian Infantry Division (Generalmajor
Möhl); between Group Vimy and Group Souchez. This
boundary was more or less in line with Cabaret Rouge in the
4th Canadian Division's area. The opponents of the 12th
Brigade would therefore be the 11th Bavarian Infantry Regiment, in Sector Döberitz, covered by fire from their comrades
on the Giessle-Höhe (the German name for the ' Pimple ') in
Sector Burg. As the left wing only of the Bavarian division would
be engaged, more German reinforcements would be available
here in the north than at any other part of the Ridge; in the
south, the British Army's advance out of Arras would protect
the Canadian right flank to that extent.

Some historians have been able to present a connected,
coherent military picture of the storming of Hill 145 and the
northern extremity of the German positions, which was more
than the witnesses were able to do at the time. For them, it was
a day of complete and utter chaos, a shambles of the first order,
with a great deal of doubt as to who actually, in the end, took
the Hill. Even the meticulous German writers find their units

disappearing in the smoke, some of them forever and without trace, no semblance of a line until halfway through the morning, Canadian units in rear of German troops, and Germans firing on Canadians from behind and from flanks, attack and counter-attack, until in the end, someone, somewhere, somewhen, gave way and an order of sorts was eventually established halfway through the following day, 10 April. Hindsight was not helped, long afterwards, by a tendency (which still persists) to confuse Hill 145 with the 'Pimple', also taken by the 4th Division.

The assault began in exactly the same way as all the others, with a single exception. A German trench almost in the centre of the advance had been left undamaged, at the request of the CO of the 87th (Montreal) Battalion which was to attack it, because he felt that it would be of use to him when captured. The German front lines were only 150 yards away from the Canadian jump-off trenches, and perhaps he felt sure of over-running them all quickly, before the defenders could come up out of their tunnels. This trench was in the German 2nd Line, manned by the 5th Company of Regiment 261; and, when the brief barrage ceased, although the machine-guns on both left and right flanks of the regiment had been destroyed, buried, or rendered unworkable, the nests in the centre were largely intact, as were the infantry sections guarding them. A careful scrutiny of the German histories shows beyond question that this was the first major factor in producing the reverse suffered by the 4th Division; the second was the existence of the reserve machine-guns echeloned further back on Hill 145; and the third, the stubborn fighting skill of this regiment, once it had been allowed time to recover from the bombardment and hit back. But only in the centre did it succeed in restablishing the line, which during the first half of the morning began to form a German salient jutting out into the middle of the 4th Division's advance, affecting the left of the 11th Brigade and the right of the 12th Brigade.

Arthur Farmer of the 11th Brigade M.G. Company had been assigned to go forward with the 102nd (North British Columbia) Battalion on the extreme right of the attack. Here he met his elder brother, Eddie, from whom he had been separated, off and on, throughout their lives—first in the London orphanage, then in Canada, later in the army. For a time, they had been in the same battalion, but this had been broken up; Eddie was posted to the 102nd, part of 11th Brigade, while Arthur joined the M.G. Company of the same Brigade. Even so, they had not met for a long time when, on the morning of 9 April, 1917, they found themselves in the same trench, due to assault Hill 145 side-by-side. They did not mean to be parted again, and managed to stay together during the assault up the hill, all through the morning, and well into the afternoon.

Maurice Bracewell of the 102nd Battalion, together with the rest of those who had survived the digging of the forward ' jump off ' trench a few days previously, went over with the second wave instead of the first; not to assault but to clear up. In the first wave ' Bill ', the man with the smuggled mickey of rye whisky, made the first forty yards; then he went down. Harry Gage, a friend of Bracewell's, had his steel helmet knocked off just before he arrived at the German line, bent down, picked it up, and put it on again; in the excitement quite failing to notice that the crown looked as if it had been excavated with a tin opener—an explosive bullet had penetrated, run round inside, and exploded on top of his head, the force being exerted upwards. The batteries of Sector Fischer, although severely harassed and unable to intervene because of loss of forward observation in the close-quarter fighting which very soon developed on their front, were able to batter the old Canadian front line area, as Bracewell immediately found out. " The creeping barrage of shell-fire that moved ahead of the attacking waves was terrific, but so was the shell-fire coming our way. My partner and I went over with the next wave and started organising stretcher and work parties of prisoners, getting the wounded down to the dressing stations under the Ridge, helping the walking wounded, and marking the location of the more seriously wounded by sticking rifles in the ground by the bayonet. German Red Cross men worked alongside our own. It is not an easy thing to go around among your friends of the day before, lying there face up and in all manner of grotesque shapes. It is not a thing you soon forget. The only good thing that I know to come out of war is learning how much better than you, the other fellow is."

Walter Bapty, M.D., the new medical officer of the 102nd,

wrote down his impressions four days later, when " the sting of battle," as he put it, was still raw. Of the infantry and the barrage, he wrote: " They scarcely waited for it to lift, but commenced their advance almost on the first shot; and almost on the first shot, the walking wounded commenced coming in. Walsh, from Vancouver, the M.O. of the 54th, was with me, besides our staff of dressers, and we were kept busy cutting away clothing, to get at wounds; getting through the dirt and mud; wiping off the blood with solution; or painting with iodine, putting on shell dressings and bandaging. The early cases were chiefly the mild cases—i.e., the walking cases—the stretcher cases not coming in until later. From then onward we were kept busy practically for forty eight hours dressing continuously. I cannot begin to describe all the varieties of cases—rifle wounds, shell wounds, but no bayonet wounds. Fractures of all parts, from depressed fractures of the skull down to the bones of the foot. It was just a bloody jumble, heart breaking because you could not follow your cases through and give them rational treatment, covering the serious as well as the slight with a bandage hiding the dirt in the deeper recesses of the wounds and covering over protruding viscera with pieces of gauze. On the first day too much sniping was taking place to gather in many of the wounded and even the walking cases that struggled in were sniped at. One case told me that he had left with five other cases walking, but a sniper had got busy on them, killing three, the remainder getting into a shell-hole, getting in on hands and knees until they came to their jumping-off trench. Some cases had been dressed by Heinies and these dressings invariably were tied too tight, one man's hand being swollen to double its size; one, a Hun with a wound in his neck, being almost strangled. The most serious cases did not arrive until the next day, that is, they had lain out in the cold and wet and snow for over twenty four hours, so you can understand their condition was deplorable. It is impossible for you to imagine how plastered they were with muck and corruption; cutting through the muddy clothing ruined all our scissors. Many were able to get shelter in the Hun dugouts, but of all the cases we saw it was surprising in what good spirits they were. Victory is in the air and it is a great stimulant."

The 102nd Battalion, and after it the 54th (British Columbia) Battalion, pressed on for the crest. The latter were from Kootenay and had a bear mascot, called 'Koots'. At first, and comparatively, their task was easy. " On the left wing of Regiment 261," wrote a German historian, " the English preparatory fire had destroyed and buried the German machine-guns. Their crews lay dead. Tommy had an easy game, and with no hope of succour, the 9th and 11th Companies under Leutnant Wagner bled to death. The struggle was short and bitter. Five men only succeeded in escaping to the Fischer Weg; few of their comrades were prisoners, for most lay dead in the craters of the 1st Line. By 0600, the enemy storm troops were advancing virtually without resistance."

But in the centre, where the strongpoint had been left unpulverised at the request of the 87th (Montreal) Battalion, the attackers ran into heavy machine-gun and rifle fire, which inflicted losses of fifty per cent. in a minute or so; the attack faded here, and began to fade all along the line. " Suddenly, dense columns of Englishmen were seen toiling across the muck-desert," wrote a German historian. " Now, at last, the fight was to be on equal terms. Everywhere, Germans came up and opened fire, and the bursts from the machine-guns could be heard and seen through the smoky grey of the morning, even among the shell and mortar-bomb explosions that sent streaks of blood-red flame across the mud-fields. Flying hand grenades burst among the advancing masses of the attackers, who were coming on shoulder to shoulder. While the steamroller of the English barrage was storming around the 2nd Line, in order to open a way for the infantry, suddenly the English attack scattered and died in front of the centre of Regiment 261, among the remaining redoubts of the 2nd Line. Heaps of khaki-yellow corpses piled up in front of the 5th Company."

Walter Bapty walked over this area next day. " Not a foot of ground but was churned up by our shell fire. Their wire was torn in all directions and offered but slight obstacle. Their defence was put up at their second line where they had their dugouts. Here at one point was a huge crater, ' Broadmarsh ', at the forward side of which were a number of deep dugouts; out of these they had rushed their machine-guns at the first sign of an attack. It was in front of this part that I saw most of our dead and I was actually glad to see a number of dead Fritzes. Large pools of water in the older shell holes were red with blood in this small area. If those responsible for wars could only be among the dead. If we could only make them fight in such a hole as this the war would soon be over. Two walking cases that came in on the evening of the 9th had stumbled into a little nest of Fritzes after being wounded, and later in the day the Fritzes in turn were captured. Our two boys did not consider that they had been treated any too well. I find our boys are altogether too easy-going and kind-hearted. They will take prisoners after the Hun puts up his hands and cries ' Kamerad ', no matter how much or what he had done previously. In other words, the Hun is a quitter and will never take a hand to hand chance, or fight anything like an equal fight."

To add to the confusion, Germans emerged everywhere from the tunnels, as soon as the barrage passed over, to harass with fire or to counter-attack. Sergeant H. J. Ayris, of 11th Brigade Signals, occupied a forward centre. " Our troops advanced rapidly, but during this activity I spotted German troops coming out of the many tunnels and forming up for a counter-attack behind our forward lines. This I reported, and very shortly Canadian troops came up from our rear and engaged the enemy in hand-to-hand conflict. The threat was soon wiped out, but possibly some of the enemy escaped through the tunnels."

A carrying party following up the 54th Battalion was caught by fire from the undestroyed positions in the German line. " As soon as the 54th had passed the second trench, we started over with this big spool of wire," said Stanley Baker. " It took eight men to carry it. We got halfway between the first and second line, and two or three machine-guns opened up on us. We found out, eventually, that there was about forty Germans that had been over-looked in the dugouts, and had come up after the fighting force had gone over. They pinned us down, and there was firing from both sides behind us. We got back by taking a tin hat and dredging a little passageway between one shell hole and another."

The left wing of Regiment 261 had caved in completely, but the centre held, in some cases; even in the 1st Line trench; and they began to mount counter-attacks on the 11th Brigade, German reserves struggling down the Fischer Weg and Trotha Weg against a tide of German wounded stumbling to the rear. The ' set piece ' battle had suddenly disintegrated. Captain Alex. W. Jack, M.C., of the 54th Battalion, found a confused situation. " Some hours after the action started, reports started coming in as they normally would, but they were all at odds," he said. " Reports from our right flank were to the effect that we had got part way across the Ridge and then gone through the 102nd Battalion, and were held up by a machine-gun sniper fire a considerable distance across the Ridge. Reports from our left flank, on the other hand, were stating that they were pinned down a very few yards out from their starting point by German machine-guns which apparently had been missed by our barrage. But that was not realised, or not known, by the commanding officer and he was very confused with these conflicting reports. He detailed me to go up to the front, see what the situation was, carry out any reorganisation of the battalion which seemed to be necessary, then get them somehow over to their objective which was some five or six hundred yards further on. And finally, I came to the left flank where I found that the 54th and the 102nd, or the remnants of them, were all together. There were about ninety men of the 54th, and there were a few more of the 102nd. The 102nd's officers were all casualties, and so were the 54th's officers. So, as a young fellow of twenty-five, I found myself in command of the remains of two battalions, with our left flank up in the air, and the Germans all around us at the back. I sent in a report on the situation, and then I sorted out the men, getting the 54th to the exposed flank, and the 102nd on our right."

It was here, amid the flurry and confusion of attack and counter-attack, that Arthur and Eddie Farmer parted for the last time. " We were together during the day, until around 4 p.m. my brother was picked off by a sniper and shot through the right wrist. We dropped into a shell hole, where I was able to give him first aid, and after a few hurried goodbyes and words of advice, I realised I could stay no longer, got up and proceeded on my way. I will never know whether my brother got up to watch me go, or whether the shot was meant for me. I had gone only six or eight feet from the shell hole when I heard the shot. I turned, and saw my brother fall. I reached his side in the shell hole, but it was too late. He was beyond help. My thoughts during the next few hours must have been rather confused, but on reaching our objective along towards dark, I obtained permission from my commanding officer to take one man with me and return to the spot; thinking to find my brother and give him a decent burial. But, due to the prompt work of the C.A.M.C., and not because we didn't know the Ridge, we were unable to find any trace of him. But near the spot, a shell hole had been recently filled in and a crude wooden cross erected with this inscription pencilled on it: ' Here Lie the Bodies of 25 Unknown Canadian Soldiers'. Convinced that this was the spot, we returned up front; but the hardest part was yet to come, how to let the people at home know. To make it easier, I told them I had found him and given him a decent burial. But I had a certain amount of apprehension as to whether we had made a mistake and that, sooner or later, he might show up. For some twenty years afterwards this apprehension haunted me to the point where I would wake up at night and imagine I could see him sitting on the foot of the bed. And still I told no one of my doubts. Then, one day I happened to go into an Insurance Office and in conversation with the man he asked me if I had a brother in the 102nd Battalion by the name of Eddie, because he had known him. He said, ' I have here a book on the 102nd Battalion which you might find interesting.' I brought the book home, but for some time it lay around the house; then, coming home one day for lunch, I picked up the book and on opening it, I saw a picture of the Monument at Vimy Ridge, and on closer observation with a magnifying glass I was able to read ' Pte. E. W. Farmer, 126456 ' about halfway up the steps on the right hand side of the wall. Strangely enough, this was the only name I could make out on the whole wall. That made me sure there had been no mistake, that some twenty people, including my wife, had really been told the truth. From then on, I had peace of mind and never another doubt."

When Arthur Farmer died, in 1965, he was a Lieutenant-Colonel in the Militia, with the M.M. and O.B.E., father of a family of four. But at nightfall on the 9th of April, 1917, he was a private soldier lying on the slope of Hill 145, with the ground where the Monument now stands still to take.

*   *   *

The 12th Brigade had an unenviable job; not merely were they on the left of the 11th Brigade, they were the left flank of the entire attack by the Canadian Corps. They had to advance between the still-untaken heights of Hill 145 on their right and the German-held ' Pimple' on their left which was not due to be taken until next day. The only favourable factor was that their attack would fall on the junction of two German divisions —the right wing of Reserve Infantry Regiment No. 261 and the left wing of Bavarian Infantry Regiment No. 11. Such boundaries, under stress, always tend to get out of control.

Although the 12th was to advance with three battalions in line—from right to left, the 38th (Ottawa), the 72nd (Seaforth Highlanders), and the 73rd (Black Watch)—the role of the 73rd was mainly to guard the vulnerable left flank. The 78th (Winnipeg Grenadiers) formed the second wave to the leading battalions. And it must be remembered that, as they advanced, the attack of the neighbouring 11th Brigade on their right broke down, the 87th Battalion's first wave suffering fifty per cent. casualties almost immediately, and part of the 75th Battalion, behind it, being pinned down in their assembly trenches and unable to advance at all. This was Vimy as the French had found it, with Germans popping up everywhere from the tunnels to ruin the assault almost from the start. Also, it must be born in mind, a dashing charge in the schoolboy sense of ' dash ' was out, inconceivable. There were no four-minute miles on Vimy Ridge. As Captain Jack put it, bitterly, " It would have been very difficult just taking a walk across there in normal attire, without the loads we carried." The German picture, of the attackers ' toiling' up the slopes of Hill 145 through ' fields of mud ', is the correct one.

John Cornish, late of Eversley, Hants, who had met his old school chum, Ern Taylor, the night before at Cavalry Rouge, had left him to go up Tottenham Tunnel with his machine-guns. On the 4th Division front alone, 12,000 linear feet of tunnels had been recently constructed, the major ones being Blue Bull,

Vincent, Tottenham, and Cavalier Tunnels. They gave covered access to the jumping off trenches within 150 yards of the German front line. Having brought up sixteen Vickers m.gs., with 20,000 rounds per gun, through the tunnel, on behalf of his unit, the 3rd Canadian M.G. Company, Cornish went up B2 Sap to where the 72nd Battalion was lined up, and had a meal of bread and soup. Twenty machine-gunners, under Captain Hall, were attached to the 72nd for the attack. Initially, they were to occupy a crater—Love Crater—which was to result from the blowing of a mine under the German front line trench at 0530. The Vickers Cornish was with would go left and occupy the right far lip of Love Crater, the other would go right; Captain Hall would go forward in the centre, where he could best control his two guns. A number of these machine-gunners were Americans, whose mother country had officially entered the War one week before, on 3 April. Pete Tabor, No. 1 of Cornish's Vickers, was an American; so was the No. 1 of the third Vickers—he was Monty Mannock, a former United States Marine.

Shortly before 0530, came the order: " Be prepared to go over—fix bayonets." The infantrymen of the 72nd clicked the bayonets home, tested the locking rings to make sure they were secure. In this mud-fouled ground bolt-action rifles were likely to jam; the bayonets were not unwieldy toys. 170,000 men of the Canadian Corps waited quietly. In a sheet of flame, vivid even in the drizzle and drifting snow, the mine blew; a low, rumbling roar. The machine-gun barrage cracked out overhead, the artillery deluge fell on the German front line; stayed; then lifted. The Pimple, jutting forward in the woods on the left, was obscured by the smoke and by a smokescreen put down by the mortars.

Pete Tabor, struggling through the morass under the weight of the Vickers tripod, went down. Captain Hall pitched into a crater 30 yards short of the German front line, hit in the legs by machine-gun bullets. Cornish struggled on with the barrel of the Vickers, his only effective armament a revolver. Then he was in the ruin of the German front line. " The trench itself was chaotic, just bits of wooden wreckage, duckboards and so on, sticking up out of the cratered mud. A few Germans, with their hands up, were coming out. There were a few dead, but not

many Canadian casualties up to now." Cornish set up the gun
to fire with the tiny auxiliary tripod. But besides himself, there
was only one other member of the Vickers' team left, ' Dad '
Davidson, who said: " Look, Jack, what are we going to do now?
You've got the gun, I've got the ammo, but where the hell are
the rest of the gang? "

Overhead roared three spotting planes, only a few hundred
feet up, tooting klaxon horns as a signal to the infantry to let
off smoke bombs and so mark their positions. The one flying
nearest to Cornish was hit by the Canadian barrage, and ended
upon its nose in a shell hole. Both the occupants got out, and
then stood around looking at their machine which, with its
red-white-and-blue painted tail sticking up in the air, made an
inviting target for the Germans. Cornish yelled at them: " Get
in a hole, and stay in it! " Then, after fixing up the Vickers in
what he thought was probably the right spot, Cornish told
' Dad ' Davidson, " I'm going back now, try to organise getting
a few more up." He found Harry Creach, who was wounded
but game to carry on, and Bill Clark, an older, grey-haired man
(Cornish himself was then 19). They began to lug ammunition
forward to the gun and as they did so, another man, Murphy,
of the Montreal Guards, saw what they were doing and joined
them.   That made five men (one of them wounded) to this
Vickers, with Murphy, the senior gunner, as No. 1.

While toiling up with more ammunition, at times up to his
waist in mud and water, Cornish met the other American, Monty
Mannock, on his way back to Tottenham Tunnel to report.
" What's up? " asked Cornish. " Oh, I can't do any good," replied Mannock, " I'm the only one left out of No. 3 gun." The
Vickers, being more or less a light artillery piece, could not be
kept in action by one man, but needed a team, especially for
the ammunition supply. Cornish was now opposite the old
German front line again, and he noticed that there were many
fresh Canadian casualties there, mainly from the 72nd Battalion.
This was puzzling, for they should have been safe there, sheltered
by the lip of the crater from small arms fire in front, and with
the situation too confused for the Germans to bring down
artillery fire which might kill their own men. Then Cornish
noticed that almost all the dead and wounded Canadians had

been hit by bullets—either in the head or in the side of the chest. They were being enfiladed from the ruined trench they were supposed to be holding. "In fact, it was a Bavarian machine-gun battalion," said Cornish. "The devils just wouldn't give up, although everything in their front line was smashed. The Germans loved planks, and these were all broken; it was a hard place to mop up, and I don't really blame those who failed to do it. But it was clear that this was where the casualties were coming from—12 Brigade were being fired at from behind by small arms. I got hold of a Lewis, and fired back down the trench; a lot of others joined in, even Engineers and Pioneers, when they cottoned on. I had a good target that day; got a few down in the trench and forced a few more to give up. They were about seventy-five yards away, at first popping up head and shoulders only, to fire. Then the reserve company of the 72nd saw what I was doing, and came up. They got into this trench and bombed it; and Germans began to come out, several hundred of them in the end."

On going back to the Vickers in Love Crater, 'Dad' Davidson called out to Cornish, "Old Harry's been hit in the forehead with a shell-splinter." That was 'Bill' Clark out of it, temporarily. However, the rest of them turned the gun round and enfiladed along the trench, then, that cleared up, turned the muzzle to the left, to catch in flank any counter-attack coming up from Givenchy-en-Gohelle. They had lugged up with them some 15,000 to 20,000 rounds now. They were still there when, early in the afternoon, Major Pierce, the CO of 3 Canadian M.G. Company, came up with some rum and new orders. Murphy and 'Dad' Davidson were to go back to Tottenham Tunnel to rest and be in reserve in case of counter-attack. "The other two of you must stick this out for God knows how long," said Pierce to Cornish and the newly-wounded Bill Clark, "but I'll see if I can get you some more help." But the German counter-attack had come in, and fizzled out, before Major Pierce got back again, with three men, none of them machine-gunners. "Murphy won't come back to us, nor will 'Dad' Davidson," he said. Of the one officer and twenty men manning the two Vickers of the section, only four lasted until nightfall alive and unwounded. Captain Hall, who was hauled out of the shell hole by German prisoners, recovered to get the M.C.; Mannock, Murphy, and Harry Creach got the M.M. " I got something much better," said Cornish, " I lived to come back again. That was all I wanted and much, much more than I ever expected." Bill Clark survived Vimy, but not Passchendaele. He had been ordered ' permanent base ', due to go out of the line for good. " Vimy Ridge was short and sharp, but a boy scout's affair compared to that. We took in thirty two Vickers, we brought out three. On the way out, we passed rows of dead bodies at Zonnebeke, and the last in the row was Bill Clark. There were rows of long burial trenches to be dug there, and in them, the people you grew up with and knew."

On the right, a V.C. was won. The attack of the 38th (Ottawa) Battalion lagged in the water-logged ground, some of the men died by drowning in the craters; others were held up by fierce resistance, and they lost the barrage. Captain T. W. MacDowell reached the German line alone, crossed it, came on two other Canadian soldiers, and spotted a German tunnel entrance further back. On the way to it, they put out of action two German machine-guns. (Some of the German guns were jamming solid, because the belts had been affected by the mud and damp). MacDowell went down the tunnel alone, and found himself face to face with a milling crowd of Germans—seventy seven of them. Turning to give orders to (totally imaginery) strong forces behind him, MacDowell persuaded the Germans to disarm. Then he sent them up in batches of a dozen at a time, so that his two men up top would cotton on to what was happening, and be able to handle them. It was a fantastic feat of quick and accurate thinking.

On the left, while the Pimple was still shrouded in smoke, the 73rd Battalion drove into the ' seam ' of the German line, the boundary between Regiment 261 and the Bavarians. " Here, the three trenches of the I Position are so close together, one can hardly speak of an intermediate zone," wrote a German historian. " Very soon, the defenders' resistance was broken." William Nicholl, a Lewis gunner on the left flank of the 72nd Battalion, saw it happen. " The 73rd Black Watch from Montreal were left flank of the line, and I remember, when Fritz broke and ran, that my No. 1 was doing pretty good execution. I was in the act of putting on a fresh pan of ammunition, when a sniper clipped me through the slack of my sleeve. That bullet hit the gun then, about the cocking handle, deflected down the barrel and out through the casing, and put our gun out of action. It was rifle and bayonet for us from then on."

The 78th Battalion (Winnipeg Grenadiers), coming on behind, were to drive south-east initially, away from the Pimple, and then angle north-west towards the village of Givenchy-en-Gohelle, establishing a left flank above the Souchez valley. W. I. Fawcett, was then a Private soldier in ' A ' Company. " This battle, the first in which I had the experience of ' Going Over The Top ', was an event that made a deep impression on my memory and I wrote down at a later date my remembrances of that day." He also kept a diary and various documents. The diary entry, after the battle, reads: " On first Parade (under a Sergeant) we mustered seventy five Other Ranks; apparently, every Officer in ' A ' Company was killed or wounded, and only fourteen O.Rs. were unharmed—that is, able to walk out." Gordon A. Mitchell was then a Corporal in ' D ' Company. He too retained some documentation, and was able to state that, of the whole battalion, " At the first roll call after the battle 199 men answered. Approximately 700 men went into the fight."[1] Fawcett noted later that, at a reunion of the 78th Battalion held after the war at Winnipeg, it was stated that, after Vimy, 125 men only were unhurt (this figure including HQ and L. of C. personnel).

Fawcett had slept the night in a tunnel, his pack for a pillow. " About 5 a.m., the Sergeant brought round the rum ration, part of which I returned, as I remember telling him, I wanted to have a clear head. As we left the cave, we had to step over our sentry, now covered with a blanket, as he had been killed by a direct hit on the entrance. Whilst Zero hour was 5.30 a.m., we were told that the blowing of a huge crater to our left front would be our signal to advance. Our instructions were to move forward in a South-Easterly direction for a while and then move

---

[1] Accurate casualty figures are always notoriously difficult to get, from Caesar's time to the Kaiser's. Maurice Bracewell, who lent the present author *Cinquante-Quatre*, Major J. B. Bailey's history of the 54th, says of the casualties listed there (221): " They seem rather unrealistic." The book gives 202 as the number of casualties suffered in the March 1st Gas Raid just before.

North-West. By doing this, we by-passed the Pimple, which, we were told, would be handled by others. In our excitement we moved faster than the regulation two miles an hour and our officer told us to halt to prevent getting caught in our own barrage. I turned round and saw, to our rear, a line of red flame, almost like a prairie fire, field guns popping away like machine guns."

Corporal Mitchell likewise stopped, and made the same observation. "The noise from the Vickers guns and artillery was deafening, and I can remember looking back at the continuous line of gun flashes, and thinking: what an awesome sight. A few minutes after going over the top, two of our mines were blown up under the German lines, throwing up a bright red glare hundreds of feet into the air. Amidst all the noise and chaos, I could not help thinking what a wonderful sight this made, too. We were advancing in artillery formation, which is in groups of twelve men in diamond shape. The ground was terribly cut up, a mass of shell holes filled with water, and our progress was very slow; at every step, we sunk to our knees in the mire. A few shells, mostly whizzbangs, were bursting amongst us; and I saw one large shell make a direct hit on one of the formations near me—all twelve men were blown to bits. I also saw one poor chap hit by a bullet and falling into a shell hole filled with water where he no doubt drowned, if not already dead when he fell. We could not stop to help him, as we were under strict orders to keep moving."

Private Fawcett's observations again kept in step with Corporal Mitchell's. "My experiences, as a Private, would be similar to those of thousands of others. I did not tangle with any Germans in the Vimy attack. Our artillery had subdued their enthusiasm, and in many cases, we were met by men with their hands in the air and the word 'Kamerad'. The shelling had reduced the enemy trenches to nothingness; and the rain changed everything to a quagmire. Our men, who were wounded, slid into the large shell holes and were drowned. When we were relieved, and coming back, we saw many apparently just sitting down at the bottom, and the hole filled with water. On sight, you could imagine them to be still alive and just resting. But as the advance continued, our ranks thinned. The best rifle shot in our battalion became a casualty—a shell landed at his feet and he was lifted into the air. We could not remain to see how badly he was hurt, but were ordered to press forward. It now seems odd that he was wounded at this point whilst I, an indifferent shot, was spared. We strayed too far south, and by this time our own officer was no longer with us—that is, not with those immediately near me. All I know is, that we ended up in a quarry with vertical walls of about thirty to forty feet, where we remained until another officer came along and sorted us out, sending the men of each unit in the way that they should go. There must have been over six different units represented in that crowd."

Corporal Mitchell's narrative still marches in step with that of Private Fawcett, even to the point where he was no longer literally in step. " We did not meet much opposition as we advanced, except increasing machine-gun fire; this principally from our left, as the troops advancing there were held up by stiff German opposition and made our unit open to enfilade fire. The air seemed to be filled with machine-gun bullets, and it appeared a miracle that anyone could escape being hit. After advancing beyond the German first and second lines, our unit was pretty well scattered, and myself and a pal of mine named Avery ended up separated from the rest of our outfit. We kept going until we met increasing fire from German snipers. We then took cover in a deep shell hole, where we were joined later that day by two chaps from other units. A short time after, I saw one poor chap climb out of a shell hole near us and attempt to come into ours, but he was no sooner above ground, when he was shot through the head by a German sniper."

By this time, the 78th was no longer a battalion. Lieutenant-Colonel S. Scott, at that time a junior officer, said: " I must confess that the situation that first day was terribly confused. Where my sergeant was, I couldn't tell you, where my company commander was, I don't know, and he certainly didn't know where I was. Not knowing, either, whether we had overshot our objective, but suspecting we had, because we were getting some of our own stuff. There seemed no way of communicating back, so we just sat it out in a big shell hole, and took a fair amount of punishment."

It would be reckless to hazard just where the 78th Battalion and the units it was supporting had got to, but there is a clue in one of the German official histories, the detailed *Die Oster-schlacht bei Arras*. Describing how the right flank of Regiment 261 was rapidly overwhelmed and the defences broken at the junction with the Bavarian Regiment to the North, it says: " While the main thrust of the attacker was aimed to penetrate further East, strong forces swung round to the South and moved against the flank of the 1st and 3rd Companies. Here, too, no machine-guns remained in working order. Not until near the Berliner Riegel were the attackers checked, and then by the fire of two machine-guns. Of the enemy's first three waves, hardly anything remained." With the defences coming to life, suddenly one of the two German machine-guns jammed, after firing only 250 rounds. Belt trouble, from mud and damp. The surviving Canadians pressed on, killed the crew and most of the covering riflemen, but were unable to get the machine-gun, which was withdrawn to a better position. " In front of this m.g., the enemy thrust sharply forward, but his attacks sizzled out in face of the fire of the surviving German infantry and got stuck in the mud of the craters." Obviously, many incidents of the battle will forever remain untold, because the witnesses did not survive. The German accounts are just as confused and scanty as the Canadian. " The remnants of the 3rd Company, under Leutnant Klabisch, held on. They fought desperately against the enemy, who was advancing nearer and nearer. Private Siefert, from the rim of a shell crater, was picking off the Englishmen one by one, as they rose up out of the holes where they had sought cover and attempted to throw hand grenades. After each shot, came his report: ' Got another one! ' But the brave handful of men became fewer and fewer from minute to minute. A last shot, a final hand grenade, then Leutnant Klabisch and his few faithful went forward in impotent fury with their bayonets, staggering shadows which soon vanished like ghosts in the muddy, smoke-wreathed battlefield. And of the machine-gun post in the front line by Prince Heinrich Weg, no one knew its fate, for not one of its crew ever returned."

Near the boundary between the Prussian and the Bavarian divisions, the Canadian attack had penetrated already one kilometre deep, according to the German account, and was coming on towards the Potsdamer Riegel. They were counter-attacked by Leutnant Hoppe of the 2nd Company of Regiment 261, supported by a few guns from M.G. Sharpshooter Unit 20. They virtually wiped them out and took the surviving Canadians prisoner—one officer and three men. According to the Canadian official history, these were the leading companies of the 78th Battalion, trying for their final objective just outside the village of Givenchy-en-Gohelle. Then, state the Germans, Leutnant Hoppe's force joined with the 4th Company under Leutnant Ketzlick for further counter-attacks " against the enemy lying in the crater field at the right wing of the 2nd and 3rd Line " at around 0830. This attack was partially successful, but a similarly improvised attempt from the Canadian side prevented the Germans from regaining their lost 2nd Line. It was then that the officer entered the quarry where Private Fawcett was, with a mixture of disorganised soldiers, and sorted out what Fawcett thought was " over six different units," or remnants of them. " We crossed the skyline and descended on the East side of the Ridge," wrote Fawcett. " As all signs had been obliterated by the fire of our artillery, and we had no maps to guide us, we just figured that we had reached our objective. We looked for, and found, what looked like the largest shellhole in our immediate vicinity, and started to tidy it up; digging a firing-step and levelling the base. Again, an officer intervened and told us we still had some distance to go yet. He directed us to a spot North West of where we were, about 200 yards further downhill. About this time, the enemy machine-gunners were enfilading our front, so we were told to move out of our cosy hole one by one, about ten yards apart. I was near the middle of the group, and, when I was told to go, I took a deep breath and ran as fast as I could, although encumbered by all my equipment, double ammunition, double iron rations, and two waterbottles. Luckily, we all reached the spot unharmed; possibly the background helped us, seeing that we were going downhill, towards Givenchy-en-Gohelle. We were now quite exposed, and we worked like beavers to deepen our shellholes and again dig firing-steps. As my equipment was interfering with this, I took it off and laid it to the rear (as all the dirt we moved, we threw to the front of our position). At this time, the Germans were seen jumping into a trench to our right front. Word was sent to our artillery, and they did a good job in shelling the enemy, so that, soon after, they jumped out of their trench and disappeared to their rear. We went on digging, and a German shell, luckily a dud, picked up my equipment and gave my back a real wallop. This would be after 11 a.m. and before 1 p.m. The time is approximate, for I attached little significance to this incident, and, naturally, we were also, at all times, under strain. When our shellhole was shipshape, we started digging laterally to join up with the other holes on either side. I also gathered about six rifles, as I figured that each would only fire once, if needed, on account of the mud."

The Germans opposite the 4th Canadian Division were doing exactly the same thing: linking up the scattered units and small groups which had survived among the wreckage of their trenches and in the mass of craters. "The paralysis of despair, the feeling of insecurity, the cautious probing, had ceased," wrote their official historian. "Once again a continuous front had been established, and they could look forward with more confidence to a renewal of the enemy attacks." The Germans, of course, had the same difficulties and the same methods of dealing with the location of their units during a battle. The first German 'infantry' aircraft droned out of the clouds over Zollern Haus, behind La Folie Wood, near the junction of the 3rd and 4th Canadian Divisions, fairly early. It was from Flying-Squadron 233, flown by Sergeant Schultz, with Leutnant Hansing as observer, and it repeatedly dived and circled over Zollern Haus until the German troops put out panels and Hansing could see just how much of the Vimy Ridge, at this point, had been lost. Then Schultz turned South to fly over the area where the 2nd and 1st Canadian Divisions were advancing rapidly and to plan. But he was never able to observe their advance: cloud kept him low and three 'spotting' aircraft from No. 16 Squadron turned to harass him; with machine-gun bullets in his engine, Schultz went down to a bumpy forced landing just over the railway embankment beyond Vimy village on the 3 Division front. At 1000, with the second stage of the advance by the 1st and 2nd Division under way, Leutnant von Knilling turned up in another aeroplane; but he, too, had to make a negative report. No contact at all with the German ground troops, no panels, no flares, nothing. He put it down to the difficulty of observing such things, when the ground was largely covered by the drifting smoke of the barrage. In fact, here the German line had been completely broken; and their front was wide open. There were no formed units left to signal to him.

But, at the same time, 1000 hours, a German plane which dived out of the clouds over Hill 145, was able to get encouraging signals almost all along the line of the front where the 4th Division was attacking. The observer wirelessed back the hopeful message: "We are holding the line." By 1030, the remnants of Regiment 261 were holding a deep salient: the northern flank being the Berliner Riegel, as far as the 2nd Line, then the Hanseaten Weg as far as the original 1st Line in the centre, and the southern flank bent back south of the Trotha Weg, up to La Folie on the crest. Uncomfortable and exposed, but the defences of Hill 145 were still jutting out into the centre of the 4th Canadian Division, where the left wing of Brigadier-General V. W. Odlum's 11th Brigade had been cut to ribbons from the start.

The Brigadier called on his immediate reserve, a new, untried battalion—the 85th Nova Scotia Highlanders—to go in and take the Hill for him. Early in the afternoon, two of the 85th's company commanders, Captains Anderson and Crowell, reported to his HQ in Tottenham Tunnel. Recalled Crowell: " I never saw a more worried man. The only information available from him was that the 11th Brigade had attacked that morning with five battalions, but no message had been received from any of them, or contact made with them, for several hours. All scouts and runners had failed to return . . ." It looked like a forlorn hope.

But, at the same time as this desperate venture was being planned, on the left of the Canadian Corps, the entire right wing had burst clean through to Farbus; and the cavalry were about to be put in.

CHAPTER ELEVEN

EASTER MONDAY AFTERNOON

'Swords in Line'

"We fired at increasing ranges from 0530 to about 1100, then the range was too far for effective shrapnel," recollected Sergeant W. G. Smith of the 2nd Division's field artillery. "When the shoot was over, just for curiosity, I counted the empty shell cases back of my gun. There were nearly six hundred, and some of the other guns in the battery did even better. My gun was awful hot, and I was sparing with the water on the heated barrel; the 18-pounder was such a good piece of machinery, I hated to abuse it. An artillery piece requires care and attention. For example, an 18-pounder threw a 13-foot gun flash, consequently you required that, and more, height (ridge, trees, houses, hedges) between you and enemy observers. If not, he spotted you, and at the very time the infantry needed you most, you would be out of action. I have seen a whole division of artillery placed on a flat plain under direct observation. Result: wire not cut, machine-guns not kept down, infantry got nowhere with their attack, and useless, unnecessary casualties. Who was to blame? Certainly not the enemy. In the 1914-1918 War I am not sure that commanders ever learned to use artillery properly; the staff in most cases did not know even the rudiments of battle requirements, for they never saw it. They were safe themselves, and most of them too yellow to go forward with the troops and learn their trade. At Vimy, we were in close touch with our immediate front, for we had sent an officer and three signalmen forward with the first wave of infantry; they carried telephone equipment and wire; and the officer was killed soon after they started. Imagine sending a man in officer's uniform against snipers hidden in the cellars and holes of that Ridge. Even a private's tunic would have been some insurance. I wonder of those red-tabbed creatures ever felt responsible for that man's death?

"At noon on the 9th we received orders to move to the top

of the Ridge. The horses and limbers came up from the wagon lines and we started East on the La Targette-Thelus road. The road to, and a short distance beyond, Neuville St. Vaast was passable; but about where the front lines had been, we became hopelessly bogged. After floundering and half-killing ourselves in that morass, we got turned around and regained the Arras road; then South to a junction near Arras, where we turned left and North. About where the road crossed the front line, again we were bogged. This time for good, and it was now blowing, snowing, and getting dark. I noticed both times it was nearly on the site of the front line trenches the mud was the worst. Possibly the two years of shelling caused that spot to be softer than others. Despite peremptory orders from the safe and comfortable division and corps billets, we just could not move, and none of those red-tabbed beauties came to help us. We waited in the mud all night, no rations, nor water, for a soldier is a funny fellow. He will not carry the extra weight of iron rations or water unless made to do so. He will carry wine or rum in his water bottle, but not water in winter. The next day, I had eighteen horses and a hundred men with drag ropes pulling my gun through the mud. The shield acted as a snow plough. It took all that day and most of the next day, to get the gun, and our battery, in action. Most of that time we had neither rations nor water. But one of the cooks got forward with tea rations in a sandbag that night, the night of the 11th. In one of the old cellars of Thelus, he managed to make some hot tea. Next morning, I saw the water hole where he had filled his tea dixies, for no water cart ever got to us at that time. This water hole was an enlarged shell hole, with a dead German in one end of it and several piles of human excreta in the water at the sides; it must have been a German latrine. Now it was the 12th. Is it any wonder the German reserves got to the break in their line and stopped the penetration? Mind you, all this time those brass bound creatures were sitting in warm chateaus eating off silver and linen table services, keeping away from all misery. Is it any wonder they did not know what was going on? "

W. N. Nickle, an infantryman of the 21st Battalion, in the 2nd Division also, was in Thelus on the 9th. " We took a tremendous number of prisoners," he said, " and, not only that,

ABOVE: Aerial photograph of Vimy Ridge taken on 17 March, 1917. BELOW, LEFT: A B.E. tries to escape from the Richthofen Circus by diving for the British Lines—a contemporary sketch by Captain Routh. BELOW, RIGHT: For the Royal Flying Corps, April 1917 was the worst month of the War . . .

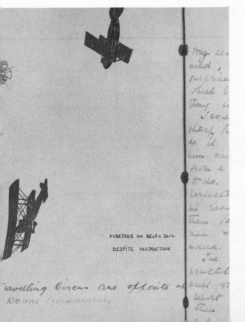

Canadian soldiers looking out over Vimy village and the Douai Plain after the capture of the Ridge, a view they described as that of the 'Promised Land'.

What Price Vimy? G. R. Alliston (with rifle, *right*) escorting low-grade prisoners taken on 15 August, 1917, at Hill 70, Loos.

A long column of German prisoners being marched back to a concentration camp.

we took four guns; and the Canadian gunners came, and in a matter of hours, while I was lying there, I saw the guns turned round and fired by the Canadian artillery. The piles of ammunition were there like cordwood and, in no time flat, they were using the German guns to fire on the Germans who were retiring on the plains of Douai. Then I saw our own guns coming up, and the limbers got stuck in the mud, so they had to take the ammunition up saddlewise on horses and mules. You just couldn't get wheels through. It was just a quagmire." Brigadier R. J. Leach, of the corps artillery, said briefly: " As far as the 60-pounder is concerned, on the afternoon of the first day I tried for six hours with eight heavy draught horses and a hundred men, and I got one gun moved about a quarter of a mile."

The 60-pounders of 145 (East Cheshire) Heavy Battery had better luck; there was a road they could use. " Between 11 and 12 noon the field artillery guns began to move on and the weather brightened," wrote Lieutenant Iveson. " During the afternoon we were ordered to pull the guns out and move forward. I remember riding alongside the gun teams on our way forward to a position on the Bethune Road, near where our observation post had formerly been situated. We passed a number of German prisoners. My diary calls them ' a miserable lot '. They looked with surprised gaze upon the forward advance of the guns. Like all German prisoners I saw in France, they appeared a dirty and unpleasant crowd, and I am afraid one did not feel quite so sorry for such unhappiness as they experienced when one saw what a very hard and cruel type of man most of them seemed to be. As we were getting the guns into their new positions the weather broke, as it generally did upon the occasion of a British offensive, and after the improvement of the afternoon we began to experience a cruel storm of hail and sleet—my diary states: ' a foul night, wet and miserable '. The terrain, which was already scarified and ploughed up by the intense shell fire, became a muddy morass. The days following were, unfortunately, no better, and conditions were really appalling. Nevertheless, the men's spirit never failed them; they would joke and remain cheery and bright as if they were not experiencing trials and tribulations. At tea-time on the 10th April, I took my first spell of observation post work, going over the Ridge to relieve Bradshaw. On the way forward, I saw efforts being made to pull out tanks which had stuck in the mud of 'No-man's-land' during the attack and were left derelict. It was raining as I crossed the old German trenches on my way forward. There were heaps of shell holes full of water, coloured red in most places, and the mud was so frightful that we had to pull out one of our men who became stuck in it. I did not reach the Ridge itself until 7 p.m., so difficult was the travelling. On the 13th April the enemy retired to Willerval and Givenchy, and had conditions been normal we should have moved our battery positions forward, but we could not move the guns forward owing to the mud. My diary records that many field artillery horses and transport horses were shot daily through being stuck in the mud. But our Engineers made considerable progress in laying tramway and railway lines to ease the situation." And in a note, inserted later, Iveson commented: "But for the plank roads transport would have been impossible."

The plank roads were simply wood and timber laid down in the mud; they were supposed to be an adequate answer to the barrier of the morass which any heavy artillery barrage automatically laid down in front of its own advance. 5,000 men were slaving to build them; without them, there was no way of getting the heavy guns and ammunition forward; and this was to take days yet. Said D. C. Higgins, of the 4th Division's artillery: "The Third Brigade of Artillery had specially allocated one battery commander to this job, and he had a large working party. This battery commander was Major Crerar, the same gentleman who commanded the Canadian army in the Second War. They worked at nights, and pushed forward what was called the Plank Road, and it succeeded up to a point. But from the time you got past the German front line, you were still bogged down, because it was a long way from there to the crest of the Ridge; so that, in fact, the whole attack, artillery-wise, couldn't have gone beyond the Ridge that day."

Some Canadian artillerymen had been specially trained in the working of German guns, so that captured pieces could be brought into action at the critical moment when the battle on the front of the 1st and 2nd Divisions moved beyond the range of the light field artillery; but few German guns were taken in immediate working order, precisely because the Canadian gun-fire had been so heavy and well-directed. " One thing that struck me when going over the newly captured ground," recalled Maurice Bracewell, " was that the majority of German forward artillery emplacements had been literally ' burned out ', which would seem to suggest that our artillery fire must have been ' dead on '."

" No doubt your thesis will be to assess the value of various units in their contribution to the success of the Battle of Vimy Ridge," wrote the Reverend G. H. Hambley, B.A., at the time a member of the Canadian Light Horse who fought in the battle dismounted, manning a Vickers machine-gun. " In this connection I would have to state that our regiment of horses were of little or no value whatever in the actual victory over the enemy. Certainly in your study of the battle you will have come on the fact that all the old-time soldiers, including General Haig and many others, thought of this war in terms of the one before, namely the South African affair. That is why we had such a tremendous array of cavalry, all through the war, at the cost of untold millions, yet the horses were of no value to us, except for sentimental purposes. Every cavalryman loves his horse, you know. So it turned out that we who were just a ' working party ' on the machine-guns, certainly had a more successful go at the enemy." The more critical outside observers, such as Sergeant W. G. Smith, of 2 Division artillery, made precisely the same point, and took it further: " Can anyone believe that if Haig, Plumer, Gough, Byng, had led that cavalry patrol under those conditions, they would continue to tie up 20 to 30,000 horses and men, only to clutter up the back areas and dog communications? Can anyone believe that if Haig, Plumer, Rawlinson, Allenby, and the juniors like Alanbrook had pulled on the drag ropes trying to manhandle guns through two feet of mud, that they would ever have expected material and supplies to advance over country pocked with holes and water, which they themselves had previously ordered to be made? To do it once, was excusable; to do it time and again, was purely criminal. In your time, you would know the German 88, and have a healthy respect for it in all its forms. With us, the worst German weapon was the 5·9 howitzer. Whenever a man had withstood the effects of a concentrated barrage of 'five nines', he was never the same afterwards. Later, at Passchendaele, the Australian battery that we relieved were so broken they were completely unnerved, and it was not long before we were the same. Hitler or Himmler never punished their prisoners worse than that, but it was our own people who did that to us, and then the British Government gave Haig and his cronies huge gratuities; and, worse, they took them. If our leaders had known even the fundamentals of combat conditions, they would have realised this fact about the 5·9, and then doubled or tripled our supply of 6-inch howitzer. They already had the horses and men in the useless cavalry, but such a piece of intelligence did not occur to them."

The staff were not unintelligent; merely of limited intelligence. And, except in some of the technical arms, the tanks and the artillery, for instance, their ideas had solidified years ago. The only new idea they were capable of grasping, was last year's French or German model. To find out what they were thinking, when last capable of original thought, it is necessary to go back long before the war. Almost all the typical trends, which led directly to the appalling infantry slaughter in the First World War, are implicit in a single issue of *The Cavalry Journal*, that for July, 1911. Published by the Royal United Service Institution, from Whitehall, S.W., this issue is admirably international in scope, containing articles by Lieutenant-Colonel Matkovski (Russia), Captain Kamozawa (Japan), lengthy reviews of works by Captain Niemann (Austria-Hungary) and others, plus reviews of the French, German and Austro-Hungarian journals devoted to the mounted arm. Some of the targets offered are too easy: Major-General Buxbaum (Austria-Hungary) was advocating that the dismounted cavalryman ought to carry his lance as well as his carbine; Rittemeister von Galli was making the revolutionary suggestion that the mounted despatch rider ought to be armed with a pistol instead of a sword. But, underneath them, there is a note of dissatisfaction with the cavalry in the 20th Century, best illustrated by the article, " Pack-Maxim Guns for the Use of Cavalry." Not being completely stupid, they had realised the obvious, that a man on a horse offers a large target which cannot instantly merge with the ground, as a foot soldier can; and that the advantage of cavalry, its ability to move over the ground faster than the foot soldier, was partly thrown away by the time it took him to bring his fire-power into action. The Maxim-gun, for instance, had to be carried on the horse, dismantled, and what the author was really searching for was a horse from which a Maxim-gun could be fired or, alternatively, a Maxim-gun which could be fired from a horse. But what got in his way was the horse. Its military history, its romance, the excitement which it must have lent to the participants in a cavalry charge. In short, the cavalrymen were in the cavalry for 'kicks'. Otherwise, they could not have failed to follow the logic of their own thinking: if the horse is an unsuitable vehicle for a Maxim-gun, find another vehicle—an elephant, say, or a motor-car, or a tractor. They would be costly, of course, but so too was cavalry. The Russian author attacked " the threadbare idea that cavalry is an expensive arm, and must be coddled. No; cavalry is too expensive an arm not to be used. It must not be spared, and it must be worked so that it repays with interest the sums that have been spent upon it."

Yet Haig maintained a Cavalry Corps in idleness throughout the war. Why? His pre-war ideas, here quoted, explain. " Whereas the ruling maxim for the employment of fire by Infantry may be said to be that fire should only be opened when it is considered likely to be effective; in the case of cavalry the importance of securing the highest results by fire has to be considered in connection with the retention of the power to break off the action whenever it may be advisable to do so. Moreover, a prolonged fire combat will be the exception for the cavalry. Its action must be swift and decisive, and the object will usually be attained by means of accurate and highly concentrated rapid fire." This idle dream is part-explained by the wide open spaces of South Africa, and the fact that in the Austro-Hungarian army, likely to be engaged on the endless Russian plain, the front of a Cavalry Division when operating in a reconnaissance role was sixty kilometres. But the actual conditions on the Western Front are illustrated by Vimy: a 1,500 yard front for an infantry division in the attack, the result of the congestion caused by the use of mass armies in Europe in the 20th Century. Spiritually, Haig was thinking in terms of Napoleonic Europe, when the population of England, for instance, was eight million, and a mass army raised by conscription numbered 500,000 men instead of five million. Above all, the Napoleonic spectre lay behind that revealing phrase, " swift and decisive," regarding the blow to be struck by cavalry. Very rarely indeed had this been so; all too often, long before Napoleon, cavalry had been repulsed by infantry equipped with anything from primitive fire-arms to pikes. The cavalry did not, and could not, become a decisive arm until it took to the petrol or diesel engine, tracks, armour-plate, and the high-velocity gun. In Haig's dreams, his cavalry were roaring Panzer Divisions, not high-perched unarmoured men and poor, blind animals.

But behind this romantic dream of unlimited power lay another idea: the thought that eventually was to drain the blood of Europe's youth into the morass of the Western Front. But it is all there, back in 1911. There is Colonel Cordonnier with his study of *la puissance morale dans le guerre,* illustrated by examples from the pre-Napoleonic battle of Valmy. More apt still is the article by Captain T. Kamozama, an infantryman, entitled: " The Value of the ' Arme-Blanche ', from Actual Instances in the Russo-Japanese Campaign." This was the Korean War of 1904-05, and it is apt because what the Japanese author is advocating, as the secret of victory always, is Cold Steel and the spirit of Hari-Kari. It is also important, because it is a sharp reminder that some thinkers in the British army had drawn the right lessons from the Boer War. " At this distance—600 or 700 yards—it was assumed that the result of an action was practically decided by fire effect, and that any subsequent charge was limited to driving off the remnants of the enemy. In short, the value of the *arme blanche* (i.e., cold steel) seems to have been temporarily forgotten by everyone at this period. In the South African War the British army failed to realise the right times and places for using cold steel, the reason being that study of this mode of attack had been neglected, and the use of the *arme blanche* almost disparaged. Looking at instances in the recent Russo-Japanese War, where the combatants fought with the very latest firearms, one is convinced that the advocates of fire effect alone are mistaken in their arguments. Victory always attended the side which, with martial spirit roused and naked sword in hand, absolutely refused to yield; which fought on resolutely to the end, in combat after combat, and which had the grim determination of attacking and annihilating the enemy. The final result in each case depends absolutely on the charge with cold steel. Before the recent war with Russia, those debaters who were obsessed with the study of the South African War leant too much towards theory, and put too much reliance on the effect of artillery and rifle fire, so much so that it was enunciated that a bayonet charge should never be attempted in daylight." The author then goes on to quote chilling examples from Banzai Charge after Banzai Charge, to show that the Japanese always won, just, with forces reduced in a few minutes to a handful. (He also quotes a Russian red herring, still used, to the effect that: If soldiers are not trained in bayonet work, their rifle fire, as the enemy approaches, will become shaky, and they will eventually run away.) But, again, an idea with some element of truth hidden in it, had been blown up to over-riding importance; and there had been a failure to think out thoroughly the implications. The Russo-Japanese Korean War, like the American-Chinese Korean War of the 1950s, was a limited colonial affair on the perimeter, with limited objectives. But what if great nations were fighting for their lives, on their own borders, and were equally matched? The doctrines of Hari-Kari, the Banzai Charge—not natural, even to the Japanese—must lead to an orgy of mutual destruction ruinous to the best interests of all the combatants. Those who had learnt the real lessons of South Africa—the effect of artillery and small arms —lost the war of ideas, before the Great War began. The Hari-Kari men were in charge.

Vimy, with its immense and careful artillery preparation, represented a pause in the process of Hari-Kari, shortly to be resumed at Passchendaele; but it represented also yet another failure to follow through mentally: to think out the implications to the end. The Cavalry Corps which waited behind Arras, spent the battle listening pleasantly to the guns, as it had done before and would always do in the future. A Cavalry Division was not a Panzer Division. It had no hitting power. Having no armour, it was frighteningly vulnerable to every form of fire-power, from bows-and-arrows to shrapnel (unless it abandoned its horses, went to ground, and became an infantry division without the supporting weapons which made this a division rather than a rabble of riflemen). And it had no mobility, without the railway train. The amount of fodder consumed by the Cavalry (and also by the immense number of horses used by the artillery of the infantry divisions), could not be supplied by ' living off the country ', even when the season was appropriate. Without railways, no army of 1914-18 could advance any worthwhile distance, even if opposed merely by ghosts. But if the enemy should prove to be more substantial, that enemy would have railways, too; and not railways abruptly disconnected by the morass of the fighting zone. To any threatened point, the railway train would bring up his reinforcements; while the attacker toiled through the mire of his own making, like a motorist on a cold morning trying to move off to work after having first applied the handbrake, and then made quite sure by firmly—and in the full spirit of Hari-Kari—standing sharply on the footbrake. This, in essence, was the strategy of Field-Marshal Haig. But even the Germans, who did not make the mistake of applying all brakes before beginning an offensive, were to fail in 1918; because more still was required. What they had in 1940, but did not have in 1914-18, may be defined as: Tempo-tempo-tempo. The attacker moving forward faster than the defender can cope. And the ' interdiction ' (from the air) of his rail and road system was an essential ingredient. These considerations are elementary—any schoolboy can grasp them in an instant—but they are also fundamental. The generals of the First World War could not see them, firstly because the technical means to a decisive campaign were in a rudimentary (but still, comparatively effective) stage of development, but fundamentally, because they had their noses firmly to the grindstone of out-dated techniques, maintained there by an out-moded, emotional, and basically romantic and sentimental conception of war. Bonaparte, whose artillery-based blitz-kriegs still obsessed them, being nothing if not a revolutionary general, would have been highly amused.

Further, by a most unhappy irony, the Vimy sector of the Arras offensive gave the lie to the comfortable belief (among the English) that the English are efficient and flexible, whereas the Germans are methodical to the point of rigidity. The German offensive, when it came in 1918, was fluid, inventive, with the emphasis on initiative at the very lowest levels. Whereas Haig's Arras offensive of 1917 turned Major-Generals into Sergeant-Majors. Indeed, it suffered from lock-jaw. There was his Cavalry Corps, brought up for the umpteenth time to listen to the music of the battle from afar, with one Cavalry Division theoretically allocated to the Canadian Corps; a clean breakthrough is achieved within 105 minutes from Zero hour; nothing standing in the way of his cavalry, in which he believes to the point of fanaticism, but the retreating backsides of a broken remnant of a German regiment; and what happens? Damn all. He had forgotten to allow for this possibility, and once the levers have been set for the battle to begin, nothing on God's earth can alter them by one fraction of a millimetre, let alone Field-Marshal Haig.

The official historians subsequently perceived it, although they did not appear to grasp that the opportunity for cavalry was for limited gains only; for a few hours, until—by boot and train—the German reinforcements arrived. However, considering that they were prepared to pay with the blood of thousands, in the month after Vimy, for the few miles beyond, this methodical inflexibility of the British High Command takes on the aspect of a high tragedy. In the view of the British official historian, with which the Canadian official historian concurs, " Only by immediate exploitation of the situation on the Ridge at 7.15 a.m. could such action on the part of the Cavalry have been brought within the realms of possibility." This he thought, was the critical moment of the Battle of Vimy Ridge: the German resistance broken on the Canadian right; the prisoners demoralised; and a swift pursuit on the front of the 1st and 2nd Canadian Divisions both possible and advisable, before time was given to the Germans to bring up their reserves. But the time table did not allow it, and therefore the brilliant and staggeringly complete success of Canadian arms could never be exploited, but must be written off instead as a limited action, of no particular consequence to the war. The idea that this could ever have been is, of course, a military illusion, but nevertheless it represented the thinking at the time, and on the German side, too. Michael Volkheimer, serving in one of the units which broke and dissolved under the devastating artillery fire and the long lines of Canadian bayonets, considered that: " Had the enemy used faster troops, such as

Cavalry, or even motorised units, our front would have been torn open even wider." But what actually happened, in the battle launched by the apostle of " swiftness and decision " by Cavalry, was that the 3rd Troop of ' C ' Squadron, Canadian Light Horse, charged a battalion of munitous Chinese early in the morning, and, late in the afternoon, a riderless horse of this Troop led the 4th Troop into Willerval, where it was wiped out. Not many saw this action. One of those who did was Albert C. Woodward of the 27th Battalion, 2 Division. " We saw the German troops advancing in open formation; one or two Lewis guns fired a few rounds and word was passed along to be prepared to ' open up ' if the German troops advanced any nearer than the railway embankment. They did *not* advance beyond the railway tracks, but we now knew we had a solid line of fresh troops in front of us. It was about this time that the Cavalry was noticed on the plain to the right of the ruins of the town of Vimy. It was low-down barb-wire entanglements that prevented the horses from operating properly. We heard the German machine-gun firing, and did see the Cavalry was unable to advance and was in trouble." Fred Walker, of the 3 Division artillery, had only a brief, but fatally significant, recollection : " I was stood to when the patrol of Cavalry was waiting orders just in front of my battery. Then off they went. They were only spare horses and stragglers that came back. That is all I can tell you, except my wife's brother was in one lot of Cavalry later, and they got cut up bad."

*　　*　　*

The Cavalry were being used in the reconnaissance role, for which in any case aircraft were far more suitable and efficient, and in this particular case, was perfectly pointless, because, as the 1st and 2nd Divisions now held all the high ground at the south end of the Ridge, the view was superb and all necessary information could be obtained through field glasses. Two troops from ' C ' Squadron of the Canadian Light Horse were involved. A troop at full strength consisted of one officer, two sergeants, and thirty two men. The 3rd Troop led by Lieutenant Greenlay, with D. H. (' Steve ') Keay as Troop Sergeant, was to reconnoitre Farbus Wood; while the 4th Troop led by Lieutenant Murray, with Thomas (' Tam ') Smith, D.C.M., as Troop Sergeant, was to pass through onto the plain towards the villages of Willerval, one mile to the east, and Oppy. Early on the morning of 9 April, the Canadian Light Horse were brought up to Neuville St. Vaast, and finally 3rd and 4th Troops were ordered forward to newly-captured Thelus, where they received their final orders. At 2.40 p.m. Lieutenant-General Sir J. H. G. Byng, commanding the Canadian Corps, telephoned his superiors at HQ First Army (General Sir Henry S. Horne) that the capture of the Brown Line now seemed assured and that his two right-hand divisions, the 1st and the 2nd, had succeeded to such an extent as to warrant the use of a Cavalry Regiment. Originally, the 1st Cavalry Division had been allocated to the task of securing rail and road crossings out on the Douai Plain, but this had been cancelled on 5 April, because of the rigid time-table for the Vimy attack. Therefore, Byng had now to secure permission from G.H.Q. (Field Marshal Sir Douglas Haig) before he could obtain part of the great mass of Cavalry milling about behind Arras in readiness for an unexpected breakthrough on the British front of attack; but it was not until late in the afternoon that the 9th Cavalry Brigade was allocated to him. By that time, the brief but bloody saga of ' C ' Squadron of the Canadian Light Horse had signalled that the lights were ' Red ' for Cavalry, for all time.

As the regiment rode up towards Neuville St. Vaast, they were stopped and the two troops at the tail, 3rd and 4th of ' C ' Squadron, told off for urgent duty. A labour battalion of Chinese nearby had mutinied and disarmed their white officers and N.C.Os. Sergeant ' Steve ' Keay heard that they had killed a couple of the officers and some of the N.C.Os. Anyway, the Cavalrymen were in the mood to quell the riot when they rode into the labour camp compound and formed line at the western end of it. The horsemen galloped down on the mass of armed and yelling Chinese, and, as they thundered through, a good friend of Sergeant Keay's lent down and grabbed a mutineer firmly by the pig-tail. " Believe me, he was making jumps of twenty feet or more," commented Keay. " They were very glad to give up their arms and turn them over to their officers."

From Neuville St. Vaast the two troops moved in single file up to newly-taken Thelus, where Lieutenant Murray's 4th Troop was told to charge down the road to Willerval and Lieutenant

Greenlay's 3rd Troop was ordered to cut away to the right towards Farbus Wood. Both officers gave the command: " Draw swords! " 3rd Troop moved away at the trot. Within minutes, it was apparent that by no means all of Farbus Wood was in Canadian hands, and that the attack by the 51st Highland Division on the extreme right of the Canadian Corps had not gone according to plan. Briefly, the sun came out and shone brightly in the valley beyond the Ridge, as the machine-guns hammered at the advancing horsemen. Lieutenant Greenlay gave the order to charge, " with swords in line," and the Cavalry opened out, the horses beginning to plunge heavily over the ploughed up ground, the glittering sword points held forward with stiff menace as the attackers gathered speed, charging into the whine and whipcrack of the bullets. Trooper Gee pitched from the saddle, his foot catching in a stirrup, so that he was dragged down the road beside the pounding horse. " I wished with all my heart that he had been killed outright, for he took an awful beating," too vividly remembered Sergeant Keay. The rising whine of an approaching shell cut through the noise and a fountain of earth and smoke flashed up beside Lieutenant Greenlay's mount. The horse turned a complete somersault, the troop officer parting company with it in mid-air. Both man and horse got to their feet again, but the terrified animal bolted down the road after the 4th Troop. Keay swung over to his troop officer, and Greenlay pointed to Farbus Wood, gesturing him to go on. Gathering most of the survivors with him, Keay carried on the charge, but as they swung into the shelter of the wood, they numbered only about fifteen or sixteen mounted men. Half the 3rd Troop had been killed, wounded, or unhorsed already.

It was clearly impossible to charge through the splintered trees, so Keay gave the order to dismount and sheath swords. The horse-holders (the Number 3s of each section of eight men) took charge of the horses at the edge of the wood, the pack machine gun was set up, and the troop advanced into the wood on foot, with rifles. " We met very little resistance, as the enemy was scooting out the far side of the wood," recalled Keay. " I think our infantry had gone as far as Farbus wood in the morning, but had retired to the Ridge around Thelus to consolidate; hence the reason the wood was held so lightly by the enemy, although the few machine-guns they had raised havoc with our troop while advancing." After clearing the wood, they returned to where the horses were being held and decided to wait, in the hope that some of the 4th Troop might come back from Willerval, just down the road.

Trooper F. M. Morton was with this troop, which consisted of born horsemen, mostly farmers, ranchers, and cowboys from Saskatchewan. "The approach to the Ridge was a quagmire," he recalled. "There was considerable difficulty in getting the horses over the low ground and some of them just about foundered. Then we crossed the Ridge and went down to Farbus Wood, where our troop leader, Lieutenant Murray, an American veteran, and a very fine soldier, gave us the order: 'Draw your swords and follow me'. This we did, at the gallop. The enemy opened up on us with machine guns and a number of men and horses went down on the road. Approximately ten mounted men out of thirty or so arrived in Willerval. We turned left into the village and the Boche, seeing the Cavalry charging at them with drawn swords, thought 'This is it', and started running for cover. We caught up with them and a considerable number dropped weapons and put up their hands."

"They did a good job on the Germans," commented Thomas Smith, the Troop Sergeant, who received the D.C.M. for his part in this action. "But our casualties in men and horses was heavy, as the Germans had rushed up fresh troops to prepare for a counter-attack on the Ridge." Almost immediately, a hidden machine-gun opened up, scything down the street, hitting Germans as well as Canadians. "Get back, boys, back!" yelled Murray, a moment or two before he was killed, leaving Sergeant Smith in command. Trooper Morton was one of the casualties.

"We were forced to leave in a hurry and went down the street on the gallop," he recalled. "On making the right turn onto the highway, Lieutenant Murray was killed, and my horse went down, falling on top of me and breaking my leg. However, the break was a minor one and in the excitement I did not feel it too much. One member of the troop offered to take me back on his horse, but owing to my injury I could not mount behind him. I also tried to catch Murray's horse, but he evaded me and followed the remains of the troop back to our lines. I started walking west.

My sword had gone flying when my horse fell, my rifle was on the saddle, the bullets were knocking sparks out of the cobblestones, and as I could not retrieve either my sword or my rifle, the only weapon I had was a bayonet. I kept on walking, aware that once I stopped the leg would stiffen and I would not be able to proceed. Horses and men were lying in the road. I pulled a horse off one man, who apparently was not injured, and he helped me pull the horse off another man. Just then the Germans started shooting at us, and we dived into the ditch. I kept on walking after that, but both my companions were captured and remained prisoners until the armistice. I finally arrived at our line, where the Squadron was entrenched expecting a counter-attack, and was sent back to the dressing station, where I received a ticket to Blighty. The effect of the injury is catching up on me now, my hip joint is worn out and I am becoming crippled. I never did learn why we were sent out on that patrol, but believe that our infantry had lost contact with the enemy and we were to locate him. If this was the objective, it was accomplished, and little else. While the enemy had been pushed back so fast and was disorganised and confused, I do not believe that a large-scale cavalry break-through was possible then. The enemy held the ' Pimple ', a very strong point north of the Ridge, and he had a heavily fortified line with much barbed wire to fall back on." Trooper Morton had actually seen this line being built, during the winter of 1916/17, when he was on O.P. duty on Notre Dame de Lorette Ridge. " This was the highest point west of the Ridge, and we could see as far as Douai, into Avion and other villages in front, and we used to watch a German observing from the face of Lens' town clock, from which he had removed a tile. The enemy was working on these fortifications and when a number of them were observed, we called up the Lahore batteries and watched the shells exploding and Fritz diving for cover."

While the unhorsed and wounded men of the 4th Troop were straggling back from Willerval, Sergeant Keay held on at Farbus. Only two or three came in, according to Sergeant Keay's recollection, although others got back later under cover of darkness. As the survivors of Keay's troop waited with their vulnerable horses in the shelter of Farbus Wood, a small red aeroplane came over, saw them, and dived to the attack. " It was one of the Flying

Circus ' Red Devils '," recalled Keay. " He swooped down and raked our horses, and it wasn't long after he left, when all hell broke loose. No doubt the pilot had notified the German artillery of our position. In the meantime, only two or three of the other troop had joined us, and I couldn't see any sense in waiting longer. I gave the order to retire, every man for himself. I can see my mount yet. When I got up to her, her eyes were almost crying with fright, but she never made a move until I got mounted. I remember, I had just taken the bridle reins from the fellow holding my section horses, when a junk of shrapnel almost cut his head off. Well, we headed back to Thelus, and I may say, just as fast as we had gone in. We didn't accomplish much, although we gave our infantry a tremendous lift. They cheered when we went over. But they weren't so happy when they saw so few return."

What came back from Farbus was a dozen riderless, mostly wounded, terrified horses, and two mounted men. One of the men was ' Steve ' Keay, whose mount, ' Countess ', fell at Thelus. There were eighteen bullet holes in the poor beast's neck. The other man was the trumpeter. " I'll never forget the trumpeter when we stopped at Thelus," wrote Keay. " I looked around— he was picking horse's guts from around his neck and face, and the only white part of him was teeth. I asked if he was badly hurt, and he said he didn't know. As it turned out, he wasn't hurt at all. A shell had landed under a horse running beside him and blew its guts up in his face. No doubt that poor horse saved his life. We lost a lot of good men, although a few found their way back to our lines after dark. Of the dozen or so riderless horses that came back with the trumpeter and myself, most were very badly wounded and had to be destroyed right there, at Thelus. Only three were unwounded."

There is a postscript. " A few days later the regiment had a muster parade," recalled Keay. " I was an a remount I had never ridden before, so when the Colonel and his Adjutant came galloping up, my mount took the bit in his teeth and ploughed right through the regiment up to beside the Colonel, while all the boys kept shouting, ' Hold her, Steve, I held her for you '. So I called my remount Steve, and I got the nickname of Steve, too; all my old buddies still call me Steve, and even my wife."

The Germans had broken at 0715, the timing coinciding almost exactly with the compulsory ninety minute pause laid down in the artillery plan. The Cavalry action at Willerval at about four in the afternoon merely confirmed that German reserves were beginning to come up. But this could be perceived with the naked eye from the crest of the Ridge, and was in fact noted by many an infantryman, and not in Willerval only. All along the front, from Vimy village to Givenchy, that afternoon, the infantry were preparing to resist counter-attacks which they could plainly see forming up on the plain below them. The Cavalry had been sacrificed to a romantic gesture from out of the past; its unworldliness rubbed home by the attack on the horsemen from the air.

But even the more modern means of observation were vulnerable also to the fighter aircraft. Lieutenant W. G. Dreschfield was observing that day over the Ridge from north of Arras, his balloon one of a long line of static aerial observation posts. Three balloons began to glow red, then collapse, then wriggle slowly down the sky in irregular zig-zags. Dreschfield jumped, followed by his companion, Captain Sansom, their parachutes opening clear of the glowing, smoking remnants of the slowly falling balloon. They hit the ground heavily, among the wire, and were in danger of being dragged bodily across it, when the canopies too caught up in the entanglements.

The burning balloons, the diving aircraft of the Richthofen Circus, the red ruin of the Cavalry: there were lessons, and a portent here, for anyone with open eyes to see. A pity that the minds had closed, at Aldershot, so many years before.

CHAPTER TWELVE

EASTER MONDAY AFTERNOON AND NIGHT

The Fight for Hill 145

On the morning of 9 April, the line up of the German Sixth Army was:—Gruppe Loos (HQ IV Armeekorps), Generalleutnant von Kraewel: the 7th and 8th Infantry Divisions in the line; the 3rd Bavarian Infantry Division and 111th Infantry Division in reserve. Gruppe Souchez (HQ VIII Reservekorps), General der Infanterie Wichura: 56th Infantry Division, 80th Reserve Division, and 16th Bavarian Infantry Division in the line; the Garde-Reservekorps in reserve. Gruppe Vimy (HQ I Bavarian Reservekorps), General der Infanterie Ritter von Fassbender: 79th Reserve Division, 1st Bavarian Reserve Division, and 14th Bavarian Infantry Division in the line; the 18th and one-third of the 17th Infantry Divisions in reserve. Gruppe Arras (HQ IX Reservekorps), Generalleutnant Dieffenbach: the 11th Infantry Division, the 17th Reserve Division, the 18th Reserve Division, and the 220th Infantry Division in the line; the 26th Wurttemburg Infantry Division in reserve. There were also several formations from the First Army in the rear, working on the new fortifications.

The German Sixth Army (General Freiherr von Falkenhausen) was being attacked by, reading from north to south, the First Army (General Sir H. S. Horne), the Third Army (General Sir E. H. Allenby), and the Fifth Army (General Sir H. Gough), on a front of twelve miles, with initially overwhelming forces, backed by a gunpower immensely greater than that used on the much longer Somme front the previous year. There was, of course, not a vestige of surprise. The Germans expected the attack to run from north to south, with Vimy perhaps being followed by Arras, rather than a simultaneous assault, and with the attack by much greater French forces under General Nivelle coming later, about 17th or 18th April, in Champagne, according to information from prisoners, nearly two weeks in advance. When the attack came in, actually on the 16th, the Germans were very ready to meet it. At Vimy, too, the Germans were able to assess the date of attack fairly accurately, but they were not able to reach this assessment in time to do much about it. But they were able to bring forward some of the reserve divisions to positions about twelve miles behind the lines, where they would be able to intervene on the second day of the anticipated attack; by Somme standards, they thought, this should be ample, although the Vimy and Arras front defences, unlike those opposite the French, were technically out-moded and of Somme standard. Therefore, when the barrage broke out at 0530, from the Vimy heights down to south of Arras, some of the reserve formations were actually moving up to the front, to meet the offensive. They were the 111th Infantry Division, coming up to support Group Loos, where a spoiling attack of some kind was always possible (but did not materialise); the entire Guard Reserve Corps, coming up in support of Group Souchez (the extreme left wing only of which was to be attacked); and the 26th Würrtemberg Infantry Division, coming up in support of Group Arras. The reserves to Group Vimy, the 18th Infantry Division, and one-third of the 17th, were not in motion.

The fact that the offensive fell on the southern part of the German Sixth Army, along a comparatively narrow front, meant that some of the formations held well back in reserve behind the northern front, and some of the units in immediate reserve, too, could be shifted south. This would be particularly menacing for the left wing of the British offensive, the 4th Canadian Division, already in trouble. But matters would be easier on the right of the Canadian Corps, because, although the 51st Highland Division had failed to keep up,[1] the British attack in general had also secured a momentary breakthrough, apparently more threatening than that of the Canadians, and German reserve

---

[1] Less one platoon of 4th Gordons, which, when the rest of their Brigade went the wrong way, stayed with the Canadians. For one complete day, this Brigade was in the wrong trench, facing the wrong way, and doggedly insisting that it was in the right trench, facing the right way.— see *The Shadow of Vimy Ridge*, pp 77/78.

units allocated to counter-attack opposite Thelus, were diverted further south.

The position on the afternoon of the 9th, from the German side, was as follows: opposite the 4th Canadian Division, a reserve battalion of the 16th Bavarian Infantry Division was being marched up for counter-attack and a battalion from the adjoining 80th Reserve Division was put in at 4 p.m. to plug the hole on the Bavarian Division's boundary; opposite the 3rd and 2nd Canadian Divisions, three reserve battalions (one each from the 80th, 56th, and 79th Divisions) were being assembled by General von Bacmeister for a combined attack to re-take Telegraph Hill, north of Thelus; opposite the 1st Canadian Division, three reserve battalions brought down by rail from the extreme right wing of the German Sixth Army, were to counter-attack towards Farbus, but were arriving at intervals, and were put into action separately. As we shall see, none of these attacks got anywhere, but the danger of a breakthrough was over, for the Germans signified by the ruin of the Canadian Light Horse. Their official historian wrote: "In the afternoon, the enemy quietened down. English cavalry, which had turned up in the afternoon near Willerval, suffered heavy losses from the fire of our infantry and artillery, and made a hasty retreat. The critical hours, of waiting until the reserves arrived, were over." The railway train, and not the horse, had proved decisive.

Not that the battle of Vimy had gone the way the Germans expected it to: far from it. They had expected to lose parts only of their front line trench, and then to retake them. Instead, they had lost at one fell swoop virtually all of Vimy Ridge, except Hill 145 and the ' Pimple '; in one morning, the German Gibraltar had largely fallen into Canadian hands. And then their immediate counter-attacks, which in the past had almost invariably proved successful, driving out at small cost the disorganised attacker from positions for which he had paid in full measure for what proved to be but a momentary occupation; these counter-attacks, launched now against the Canadians, stalled and foundered before they had hardly started. This was not the least important feature of the Vimy battle. Not only was it a successful attack, carried out very rapidly and with comparatively small loss (the Somme being the criterion for heavy loss), but the gains were held; and held for good.

*   *   *

When the 27th (Winnipeg) Battalion, of the 2nd Division, took their final objective and began to dig in early that afternoon, Dickie Green paced along the length of the captured German communication trench, playing *Colonel Bogey* on the flute. An hour or so later, no one was getting out of that trench to play the flute, or do anything else. Very heavy and accurate shellfire was falling. However, a strong patrol had already gone out to the ruins of Vimy village, as an advance shield and to probe what remained of the German defences. Later, from the Ridge, heavy machine-gun fire was heard from out on the plain some distance to the right, the Canadian Cavalry were noticed, and seen to be held up. "About this same time," recollected Albert C. Woodward, " German troops were seen advancing towards us in open formation, and one or two Lewis guns fired a few rounds. This looked like the counter-attack that was expected, and we were told to ' open up ' if they advanced beyond the railway track which runs from Lens to Arras, roughly 3,000 yards in front of our position. They did *not* advance beyond the railway tracks, but we now knew we had a solid line of fresh troops in front of us." The three German battalions involved had been at Loos, in the north, that morning, and their move to the Vimy front by rail had been ordered at 0800 by von Falkenhausen. An excellent illustration of the tempo which would have to be achieved by an attacker, in order to convert a breakthrough into a breakout.

While increasingly heavy shellfire fell on Woodward's unit, with a continual toll of casualties, Sergeant Roland Irwin, of 1st C.M.R., in the 3rd Division, had a more mobile time of it. All the forward units had been ordered to send out patrols onto the plain in front, once the Ridge was taken, and he was ordered by his company commander to take part in a two-man patrol, the other fifty per cent. of which was Lieutenant John Mathieson, a very fine soldier from the ranks who collected, while he was at it, the M.M. and Bar, the D.C.M. and Bar, and the M.C. If *all* the medals came up with the rations, then he was taking more than his fair share. This patrol was on the extreme right of the 3rd Division, the neighbouring unit to 1 C.M.R. being the K.O.S.Bs. of the 13th Imperial Brigade. "We were ordered to search our immediate front to establish the location of the German's new front line," stated Sergeant Irwin, briefly. "We made contact with the Hun by way of their machine-gun post on the outskirts of Petit Vimy, and the first burst of bullets sees one through my officer's neck. It went clean through the side of his neck, and I put a shell dressing on to stem the blood—but we had no idea how serious the wound was. The machine-gun made it impossible for us to return to our unit by the original route. We found better cover by working our way in a large circle to our right and, when we judged we were beyond the Hun gun range, we walked openly on top to reach our own front line; and not knowing what unit was in the trenches we were approaching until four soldiers came at us with fixed bayonets and took us prisoners, seeing we were coming from No-man's-land. They were the King's Own Scottish Borderers, and told us we were prisoners until they could confirm our claim that we were Canadians. Of course, there were lots of uniforms that could be picked up and used, but Lieutenant Mathieson was in severe pain, and he had no shortage of words when riled—he expressed what he thought of soldiers who did not recognise two Canadian soldiers when they saw them. After a little better than one hour, a K.O.S.B. officer came to where we were sitting in their trench to say that we were in the clear and could return to our own unit. They said they were sorry to detain us, and offered cigarettes and a generous tot of rum—which I enjoyed—but Mr. Mathieson, very impatient, said: 'How in hell can I drink a damn thing with two holes in my neck?'"

John Cornish, with the machine-gunners attached to the 72 Battalion, in the 4th Division, saw red flares and two green parachute flares go up at about 2.50 p.m. These were Canadian, calling up artillery support against a counter-attack. At 3.10, German shelling began, and then he saw the counter-attack forming up in the red-brickfields of Petit Vimy, to the right of his position. "They showed themselves for a bit, but they never came out of Petit Vimy." On the extreme left of the 4th Division, where the scattered, mixed-up units of 12th Brigade were holding craters and shellholes short of their objectives, Corporal Gordon A. Mitchell and his pal, Avery, of the 78th Battalion, were sharing a shellhole with two strangers from other units. They started to dig out cubby-holes in the sides of the crater, and, as they did so, there was a sharp explosion and one of the strangers called out that he was hit, and could not see. While digging, he had struck a buried German hand grenade, which had exploded into his face, blinding him. There was no question of his being evacuated to hospital. The last man who had moved above ground (in an attempt to get into their shellhole) had been shot through the head the moment he showed himself. Mitchell decided that he would try to get the blind man back, as soon as it got dark. So they lay there all through the afternoon. " The German long-range guns kept up a steady bombardment with the shells which we called ' coal boxes ' because they emitted a black smoke when they exploded. I lay there in the shellhole most of the day, watching those shells hit all around us, and wondering if the next one would have our number on it. One shell landed about twenty five yards from me, and the next thing I saw was a man's body, completely severed at the waist, flying through the air. I will never forget this, as it turned out to be one of our boys whom I knew quite well. Then, while the three of us were digging, one of these ' heavies ' hit quite close, and we heard a large fragment coming toward us. We crouched low, and waited. The fragment of metal, weighing about fifteen lbs., struck the middle one of us, Avery, right in the back. The only thing that saved his life was the fact that he wore on his back his haversack containing mess tin and other articles."

All afternoon, the position on the 4th Division's front was confused. Only the 102nd Battalion, on the extreme right, had got up to the crest of the Ridge, and two of their companies, having lost all officers and senior NCOs, were commanded by a corporal. They were out of touch with the 7th Brigade's 42nd Battalion on their right. On their left, the 54th Battalion had also suffered severely. But so had the Germans. Although a continuous line had been re-established in Sector Fisher by about 1030 in the morning, this made such a deep and exposed salient into the centre of the 4th Canadian Division, that for the Germans to hold it in its entirety for long was impossible. Nevertheless, the position was potentially dangerous to the Canadians for, with most of Hill 145 still in German hands, they were open to a counter-attack which could form up, out of sight (and fire) behind it. A deliberate attack, behind another barrage, could have been mounted; but, inevitably, it would have slaughtered many Canadians, simply because there was no straight line. The decision taken by General Watson was to send in the 85th Battalion to restore the situation for the 11th Brigade—without a barrage; then, next day, halt the impending assault on the Pimple (Hill 120) by the 10th Brigade, which instead would take the final objectives assigned to the 11th and 12th Brigades the day before. It was a decision poised on a razor's edge of doubt, probably the only decision of any importance taken by a divisional commander during the battle. And it had to be made on very little evidence, very hastily.

How hastily, Major Harvey E. Crowell, then a Captain commanding 'C' Company of the 85th Battalion, found out when at 2.50 p.m. he was ordered to report to Tottenham Tunnel. The 85th, the Nova Scotia Highlanders, was a proud battalion. "Strong, big men, never been in action before, but did wonderfully well," was the sober comment of John Cornish, who witnessed their attack. Praise from a soldier is not lightly won; only war correspondents are automatically compelled to lay it on thick, regardless. But, so far, their only experience of action had consisted of carrying picks and shovels and digging holes for other people, as if they were elderly or unfit Pioneer Corps. "Not having a place in any Brigade, we were only recognised when working parties were wanted," wrote Captain Crowell resentfully in a detailed narrative written shortly after. "Always reminded of 'Down on the Somme' by other units to whom we were detailed. Laughed at, because we were Highlanders without kilts. Questioned, because we had three Lieutenant-Colonels and five Majors. We simply had to dig in and make a place in order to survive." The veterans always twit the rookies in this manner, and even elderly progressive pacifists have been known to boast that their bombs were the biggest and/or nearest; but things were getting beyond a joke on the morning of 9 April, when it really seemed as if the 4th Division could well do without their services in the matter of Vimy Ridge. " The 85th's instructions were to be ready at Zero plus two hours, which meant 0730," wrote Captain Crowell. " By 0600 prisoners and wounded commenced to straggle along down through our area. At 0730 our men were all in their place ready to move forward, but no orders were received. The whole morning passed. The roar of battle had gone beyond the Ridge and we were in comparative calm and apparently of no use—in fact, we figured that the Hun had been driven off the Ridge, although the objective for the whole attack was only the crest."

Then, at 2.50 p.m., came sudden orders: Captain Anderson, commanding 'D' (Cape Breton) Company, to report to OC 102nd Battalion at Cavalier Tunnel; Captain Crowell, acting commander of 'C' (Halifax) Company, to report to OC 87th Battalion at Tottenham Tunnel. The 87th was that battalion which had unwisely requested that a German second line trench should not be destroyed by artillery fire, as they themselves wished to use it after capture. At the HQ of the 87th, Captain Crowell was told that " since early morning, every party, sniper or scout that had gone up through the tunnel into No-man's land to ascertain the situation, had failed to return, with one exception. He reported that the enemy were still holding their old 2nd Line on the left 11th Brigade front." Both Crowell and Anderson were then taken to see Brigadier Odlum, commanding the 11th Brigade, together with their own OC, Colonel Borden, and the OC of the 87th (now Major Shaw). Brigadier-General Victor Wentworth Odlum, C.B., C.M.G., D.S.O. and Bar, was then aged 36. The son of a college professor, he was in real life a bond and insurance broker in Vancouver, where he also published a newspaper (having begun professional life as a reporter). He went to war as a major with the 7th Battalion, was wounded eight or nine times and, apart from decorations, was seven times mentioned in despatches. Colonel Harwood Steele wrote of him: " At the time of Vimy, a strict teetotaller, he was very like ' Stonewall ' Jackson in austerity as well as ability, and even while a brigade commander would lead small raids to capture isolated Germans." While discussing the matter with Colonel J. L. Ralston in 1939, Crowell was subsequently to write: " I never saw an officer quite so worried as Brigadier Odlum was that day." He had every reason to be. Three of his own battalions, plus an-

other lent to him by the 10th Brigade, had gone up the Ridge;
and vanished. He had no news of any of them. And, by the inflexible army rule, that the senior carries the can, he was responsible for the decision made by the former OC of the 87th Battalion. If a sentry falls asleep, he may or may not be shot, but
his company commander must, and will be, held responsible.
Putting in the 85th Battalion was a gamble. Brigadier Odlum's
gamble. How many Germans were out there in front, and how
game were they? As so often in war, there was no answer except:
' suck it and see '. Somewhere, however, some item of co-ordina-
tion went wrong. After the quick conference, Colonel Borden of
the 85th wrote out Battalion Orders for the attack.

Under the heading INFORMATION, they stated that:
" BATTER trench from BLACK to BAUBLE is held by the
enemy, who have come up from under the ground. The 87th
Battalion is holding crater near Junction of BASSO and
BATTER. The 102nd Battalion is at Junction of BLEARY and
BATTER." Translated into English from the marked map, this
meant that there was a gap between these two battalions, on the
enemy 2nd Line, which was held by German machine-gunners
who had come up from their safe dugouts in time and were still
holding up the advance. The information might, or might not,
be accurate. It was, in fact, roughly accurate, but incomplete.
Under the heading TASK, it was ordered that: " The 85th
Battalion will capture and hold BATTER trench and will get
in contact with battalions on the flanks. This operation is in
conjunction with 12th Infantry Brigade Operation. After Zero
hour which will be notified later, an intense artillery barrage
will rest on BATTER for twelve minutes." This meant: close
the gap. The rest of the order simply divided the objective into
a right flank for ' D ' Company and a left flank for ' C ' Company.
The reference to 12th Brigade is not clear, but two companies
of the 46th Battalion, 10th Brigade, did come forward to the
attack further left. This is typical of orders issued very hurriedly
to meet a confused situation.

Crowell's ' C ' Company filed out of Tottenham Tunnel and
the three platoons extended in one long, spaced line to the left.
Anderson's ' D ' Company formed to the right, with the three
platoons in close rank. And there they waited, for about an hour,

some of the men up to their waists in muddy water, the jumping off trenches being " simply small brooks." It was unpleasant
waiting in more ways than one. Thirty scouts had been sent out
up to now, and one only had returned; as Brigadier Odlum had
concluded, there must be many strongpoints and machine-guns
out there, capable of picking off anyone who moved. " Just before Zero hour I remember looking back and seeing the brassy
setting sun hanging just over the broken spires of the old tower
at Mont. St. Eloi, and this same sun was blazing in the eyes of
the Germans while we were advancing, and I think this saved·
us a considerable number of casualties," was Captain Crowell's
afterthought. " From my position I could see when ' D ' Company
first came out and turned to the right, and from then we waited
about one-quarter hour, for Zero, which was set for 5.45 p.m.,
to make a daylight attack under a barrage (although it will be
noted that the instructions were to advance at Zero hour and
the question of a barrage was incidental). At 5.45 there was no
barrage! Watches had been synchronised. My runner, George
Colley, checked up with me, and half a minute went by—still
no barrage! forty five seconds—no barrage. I had then to decide
that when one minute was up, barrage or no barrage, we were
to advance. Mr. Manning on the left (9 Platoon), stood up so
that I could see him. Apparently he was worrying about the
same situation. I signalled to him with the hand to advance
and immediately led off myself at the centre of the company.
As soon as we stood up, the machine-guns opened fire on us, and
my runner, Colley, was hit. Flares were sent up by the Hun
which brought instant response from his artillery, a shell landing in our line, before we had advanced twenty five yards. To
my horror ' D ' Company were not advancing with us, and then
it flashed across my mind that perhaps, after all, I had made a
mistake in advancing without waiting for the barrage, but it was
too late to stop. (I saw Captain Anderson later and he told me
that he was waiting in his trenches for the barrage without respect to time and would not have gone forward if ' C ' Company
had not.)

" Our line went along just as steadily as in Aldershot, Nova
Scotia, or training on Thursely Common in Surrey. The situation was not anything like as exciting as it was at 0530, when

we were down in the valley and out of it all. Sergeant Nelson
had been wearing long rubber waders; I still recall seeing him
with his platoon, in bare feet, amidst the stringy wire and pieces
of shell. The surface was a regular ' Bay of Fundy ' in the winter-
time. We had nearly fifteen minutes of it, under steady fire from
five machine-guns in a short trench dead ahead of us. About
five minutes after starting, word came along the line from the
right that ' D ' Company was advancing and, shortly after, word
from the left, that Mr. Manning had been killed. We were expecting a Hun barrage but none came—only regular shellfire
every half minute. No assisting barrage, and no rum issue to
start off, and yet the effect of such exposure to machine-gun fire
was ' stimulating ', even afterwards. It was worthwhile to get
cheers from a section of our troops who were hanging on to an
exposed flank at a large crater, as we advanced. But when we
could make out the groups of enemy where fire was coming from,
at about 100 to 150 yards, the machine-gun fire was getting real
unpleasant. Our rifle bombers started their work at that distance,
and the result was instantly effective.

" Corporal H. M. Curll started the rifle bombs. I watched
his first one land within five yards of a machine-gun crew and
they quit right then. Up to that time we were steadily advancing
and making no effort at fighting our way along. As I recall, it
was my endeavour to keep the company advancing without taking any cover, fearing that once the men were allowed down it
would be hard to get them going again. I had never drawn my
own revolver and no man was even thinking of Mills bombs,
or even attempting to pause for a moment and shoot. It was
Curll's action in sending off a rifle bomb from the hip that was
more than anything else responsible for the success of the attack.
Other rifle bombers got the idea, and by the time our company
was within fifty yards of the German 2nd Line, where they still
operated five machine-guns at the top of undemolished dugout
entrances, they turned and ran. And then the ordinary man was
overcome with the lust to kill. At this point I was shot down,
hit by an explosive bullet near the top of my right arm while
I was leaning slightly forward, with arm extended; but was able
to carry on at once, and found the next situation something to
sweat over. I don't think I was twenty yards away from one of

those guns, when the gunners started to race back to go down over the hill. They had to climb up out of their slippery trenches, and I can see three Germans now. The top man started to slide, and he slid down and whacked into the face of the man behind him, and the three of them came right down hill, right there at our feet. I was almost on the point of laughing, when I followed, and went down myself, and I couldn't stop my boys going beyond the objective. We had been trained to death about not going past objectives, and here was ' C ' Company chasing Huns towards the ' Fatherland '. It occurred to me that, as we had had no barrage to help us advance, perhaps it was the intention to put up a ' box barrage ' later, to enable us to dig in and keep the enemy off. It had been just like another of our hundreds of practice attacks, but after capturing the trench and listening to the cries of the wounded, expecting counter-attacks and the Hun barrage, the situation seemed unreal. As I was hardly able to speak, let alone shout any orders, I had great difficulty in getting ' C ' Company back on its objective. The men had been chasing Germans in all directions, and I found that ' D ' Company had gone way behind its objective, and my right flank was accordingly ' in the air '.

" Mr. Manning had been reported killed and definite information as to Mr. Crawley was not available. I left Sergeant Nelson in charge of the company, and with one of the scouts, Private Porter, I pushed out to my right front to look over the situation, at about 9 p.m. To the right and forward of Hill 145, we ran into Major Ralston and reported to him. Instructions were given to have ' C ' Company brought up on the left and then for me personally to report back to the M.O. The weather turned extremely cold that night, but clear, and such conditions were very trying on men who were wounded, wet, and shivering, and unable to walk to dressing stations. On the way back, I located Lieutenant Manning half frozen in a shell hole, and understood from him that his leg was broken. His batman, Cooke, was with him. A party of us brought him back to the Tottenham Tunnel dressing station, but it appears that he was also shot through the head, and he died next day. There has been no fighting since the night of April 9th on Hill 145, the exact spot where the Canadian War Memorial has now been erected," added Major

Crowell later, a claim borne out by the 4th Divisional History.

Corporal Gordon A. Mitchell, of the 78th Battalion over on the left, had started back with the grenade-blinded soldier as soon as it got completely dark. " I left my rifle stuck in the ground and led him by the hand, threading our way through shellholes filled with water. The moon was full, and it was almost as bright as day; I expected every minute to be shot at by a German sniper, but nothing happened. I was just taking chances, as I was not sure of my direction; every minute, I would call out my battalion number in a low voice, in case I should come near any of the support outposts. I learned later that we had passed about thirty feet from one of these outposts, without seeing it, and that one of the men there had his rifle trained on us and was about to pull the trigger, thinking we were Germans, when his partner told him not to shoot. But I finally came to the support lines, where I handed over the blinded man. I then tried to find my way back to the shellhole I had left and was walking fairly fast in what I thought was the right direction, when a German flare went up about twenty yards in front of me. I did not lose any time in reversing my direction, and was going along an old German communication trench when I heard the command, ' Halt! Who goes there? '—and found myself looking into the business end of an automatic revolver. All I could think of, was to shout, ' 78th Battalion! ' It turned out that the man behind the revolver was an officer of the support unit which was coming in to relieve us; he was reconnoitring the ground. I was directed back to the supports and did not rejoin my unit until Friday, when I found that I had been reported ' Missing in Action ', and my parents notified to this effect. At first roll call after the battle, 199 men answered out of the approximately 700 men who went into the fight."

One of the officers who came up, further to the right, was Brigadier Odlum, intent on sorting out his 11th Brigade. " In the end, towards the middle of the night, or towards morning, I went forward myself to see what the position was," he said. " I had two or three officers with me, and as I got up on top of the hill, I could see that we had not got over. We were bent back on the top. There were Germans still up there, and I went around and I started on the left flank of my brigade and, unit by unit, I'd take them forward and place them in position. I went along the line and took the last one up and right over the crest of the hill, just as daylight was coming."

The 4th Division was nevertheless still short of its final objectives, long after all the other divisions had attained theirs. In the neighbouring 3rd Division, M. E. Parsons, a runner of 2nd C.M.R., recalled: " Organisation in all departments must have been perfect. Late that night, the rations came up. The welcome rum jars were delivered to CSM Hewlett, from whom Westover and myself gathered the platoon sergeant's bottles, and the CSM filled them to the brim. The runner's privilege was to neck the bottle, to make room for the cork, plus our own ration. It truly was a great anti-freeze. With the rations, came the mail. I received a letter from home, with the words:

' We do hope you are not near that dreadful fighting '.

I replied that night with an issue postcard, known as a ' Whizz Bang ', on which I ticked off the two lines:

' I am quite well '.

' I hope to be home soon '.

I was with the unit two-and-a-half years, missed only one tour of front line duty, and was never wounded. My one big disappointment that day, was that I had procured two eggs to cook on Easter Monday and had packed them in my mess-tin. Monday afternoon, while I was resting on the dugout steps, a chap behind me said, ' Fat, you're wounded '. A hunk of shrapnel had gone straight through the mess-tin. It took a day or two to laugh off those egg yoke stains down my pant leg."

CHAPTER THIRTEEN

ASSAULT IN THE SNOWSTORM

The Pimple

Tuesday, 10 April, was a messy day, in more senses than one. While barrage attacks went in against the railway embankment by Vimy village, George R. Alliston of the 7th Battalion, having spent most of the 9th working with the wounded, spent most of the 10th working with the dead. This sort of thing happens if your name begins with 'A'. "The same party who had carried all the wounded now had to dig a long grave at Nine Elms, four feet deep. All we could do, but long enough, too long in fact. Then, with the attacking people getting on, we were detailed to bring up Mills grenades, small arms, anything, to a new headquarters in a trench in Thelus. I remember, I was carrying a stretcher and the leading men had just got to this headquarters. The leading men—five of them—got blown to blazes at the doorway. As for me, I found a hole like a rabbit. It was the beginnings of a new dugout. Yes, the Germans had dug down about twenty five feet, no stairway yet, just a plank skidway to pull the earth up, and a bare wall which I hit bang. But then about six canny 7th Canadian soldiers slid down the plank, with yours truly at the bottom of the heap. All because Heinie had the range on that trench and was letting us know it. And from where we were, we could see the 2nd Canadian Division taking a lashing."

Arthur Baguley was with the 1st Cheshire Regiment, of 15th Imperial Brigade, which was acting as reserve to Canadian Corps. "On Easter Monday the Canadians simply blew the Germans from the top of the Ridge, but what a toll of casualties on both sides! The following day, we got over the Lens side of the Ridge towards La Collette, where we found strong barbed wire defences. At first sight we thought the enemy had vanished, it was so quiet. Until we started to get through the wire, then the Germans opened terrible machine-gun fire on us, and we had to withdraw in disorder like a lot of lost sheep. No one took proper charge, and I think if the Germans had made an attack on us he would have taken a lot of us prisoners. We took shelter in a deep dugout under a railway embankment; a number of our men fell asleep and were not wakened by other men, and when they came out later a party of Germans captured them. We were held there for days, because the Canadians went back for rest and refit and the atrocious weather prevented the artillery getting the guns over the Ridge to give us support; then we made a further attack, as it was going dusk one night. I was going along as cautiously as I could when—wouff—a coal-box shell dropped a few yards to my left, damaging my left hand and leg and dropping me in a shellhole, where I lay for hours, after everybody had disappeared. After shouting a long time, I was very lucky indeed to be seen by a stretcher party. I was put in a dugout until next morning, when the stretcher-bearers took me to the casualty station. My hand healed, but I had my leg amputated later in Mosley Hill War Pensions Hospital Liverpool."

Bitter wind and snow blew over the battlefield on the 10th, carpeting alike the faces of the dead and the forgotten wounded. It was a bad day for flying, but two machines at least from No. 16 Squadron went up in the evening, when the 4th Canadian Division was to take its final objectives of the previous day. Both were caught over the lines by a snowstorm, and forced down. Captain Routh ducked underneath, and at fifty feet, hedge-hopped back to friendly soil, where he landed in a field to wait for the storm to cease. The other pilot tried the same trick, but was not so lucky. He flew straight into two lots of field telegraph wires, which tended to arrest his progress, which was finally stopped by some barbed wire. The two men got out of the wreck to find that they had actually been lucky; if they had missed the telegraph wires, nothing could have stopped them from flying head on into Mont. St. Eloi. One of their opposite numbers, an NCO pilot, who had been forced down by a Sopwith, was interrogated on this day, and was equally bitter about Sopwiths and his own observer. " We don't like Sopwiths," he explained, " but we don't worry about B.Es., unless they get in our way, and that is the end of them." Asked to explain why his observer, when

One of the machine-gun pill-boxes in the preserved part of the German front line. The neat-looking 'sandbags' are actually concrete replicas, 1965.

A heavy mortar which threw the projectiles known as 'rum jars'. Knocked out by the bombardment in 1917, photographed 1965.

The Canadian line on the 'crater front', looking towards the German line, 1965. Note how 'No-Man's-Land' is still a maze of depressions, although the trees have grown again.

ABOVE: A party of Canadian veterans approaching the Monument on Hill 145 during the Battlefield Tour of 1965. BELOW, LEFT: Mr. and Mrs. Boxall looking at the names on the Monument, 1965. BELOW, RIGHT: View out over the Douai Plain towards the coalfields of Lens, from the War Memorial on Hill 145. The brooding figure with bowed head represents the spirit of Canada mourning over her dead.

captured, was wearing full mess kit, with spurs, the N.C.O. complained that the officers had had a large dinner the evening before, which had lasted from 10 p.m. to 6 a.m. His own officer, failing to find anyone to take his place, had reluctantly climbed into the machine and then fallen into a drunken sleep which even the Sopwith had failed to disturb.

In order to complete the 'Southern Operation', the two battalions which had been briefed to assault the Pimple were committed now to take the 4th Division's line over the crest and down the other side. They were the 50th Battalion (Lieutenant-Colonel L. F. Page) and the 44th Battalion (Lieutenant-Colonel Davies), from Brigadier-General E. Hilliam's 10th Brigade. Hilliam, an ex-Lancer and North-West Mounted Police Brigadier, was a terrific martinet in the best sense of the word, who eventually went as Major-General to restore a shaken British division. Colonel Harwood Steele once heard him reprimand a Brigade-Major who had committed the unforgivable sin of 'ticking off' a battalion commander in front of his men, with the rebuke: " So-and-so, I knew your father, and many a time I've spanked your little bottom. So now shut up!" Hilliam had been given plenty of time to prepare this attack, which was really to go in behind a barrage at 4 p.m.

" The most beautiful barrage opened up," said D. M. Marshall of the 44th Battalion, " and we looked out to our left and saw the 50th Battalion going over the top, just like in the book. It wasn't half-an-hour after, that my company commander came running along and said, ' Look, we've got to go over the top of this hill '. I said, ' When do we go? ' He said, ' Right now '. Well, right now—and there were the fellows all sitting along the trench, their rifles leaning up against the parapet. Anyway, we went. We bounced over from shellhole to shellhole, in and out, and up and down, and finally we got over to the bottom of the Ridge without any opposition, but we did run into a bunch of dugouts in the side of the hill, and there were all these Germans. They thought the battle was over, apparently, because they were just sitting around in the entrances to their shelters. So I bang a couple of pistol shots, and that wakened them up, and they all came out with their hands up and were quite willing to quit. But that wasn't the finish, for pretty soon the Germans that had gone over into the flat started to shoot at us, and they were getting a few, because we didn't have much shelter. We were on the down side of the hill. We did stick it, then that night we were relieved and moved off towards the bottom of the Pimple for the next show."

By nightfall, the ' Southern Operation ' had been completed; of Vimy Ridge, only the Pimple remained. It had cost the Canadian Corps 7,707 casualties (including nearly 3,000 killed), plus some 400 casualties in the brigades of the 5th Imperial Division. 8,000 killed and wounded, approximately, in two days' fighting. Light losses by the standards of the time. But, as George Alliston put it, " By the 11th, we had been reinforced twice to bring us up to strength, and I'm telling you we lost a few of the best boys a mother could have—all of them A·1 kids—all in a few days. The flower of the land, you might say. Just a big loss to us." Some 4,000 German prisoners had been taken (3,400 had been counted by midnight on the 9th). But prisoners live to return home, in the end.

During the 10th and the 11th of April, German reinforce-ments continued to come in, and the remnants of the battered 79th Reserve Division were finally withdrawn. They were re-placed by the 111th Infantry Division. South of them, the 17th Infantry Division came into the line near the junction of the Canadian Corps with the British near Arras. North of them, around the Pimple, the 4th Guards Infantry Division came in to help the Bavarians of Group Souchez, already reinforced by the 80th Reserve Division. Nevertheless, the Germans had been terribly mauled along the entire front of the attack, and shaken by the loss of the Ridge, together with Monchy and Hill 102, which had been in the path of the British advance from Arras. On hearing the latter news, during the afternoon of the 10th, von Falkenhausen called a conference with the commanders of Groups Souchez, Vimy and Arras. General von Fasbender sug-gested that the troops be withdrawn well back onto the plain in front of Vimy on the line of the fortified villages of Mericourt —Arleux-en-Gohelle—Gavrelle. Von Falkenhausen not merely rejected this, but called for artillery reinforcements from Army Group in order to carry out a planned counter-offensive to retake the lost ground. This was squashed by his superiors at Army

Group, who pointed out over the telephone that he might well be caught by the next enemy attack, while forming up for his own—which would mean disaster. Reluctantly, von Falkenhausen gave the order for the threatened parts of his Sixth Army to withdraw during the night of 12th/13th April, as secretly as possible.

The German official historian was to write: " In general, during those three days of attack, from the 9th to the 11th of April, the English had achieved a purely tactical but nevertheless quite remarkable success. They had put a dent into the German lines approximately eighteen kilometres long and six kilometres deep. The right wing of the Siegfried Position had been affected, and seven divisions had suffered to such an extent that they had to be relieved immediately. Losses were 23,000 men, of whom no less than 16,000 were reported ' missing ' (the German troops were in many cases cut off in their dugouts by the shellfire and had to surrender in large masses). Furthermore, 233 guns (ninety eight of them heavy), and many mortars, machine-guns and weapons of all kinds had been lost. This was all the more serious as both men and material were becoming short. Also, the French offensive, still to come, was expected to prove far more powerful than the English one. In detail, losses by the British Third Army had been more than 8,000 men. The losses of their First and Fifth Armies amounted to a further 17,000 men, which may be compared to losses of 57,000 men by an equivalent number of British divisions on the first day only of the Somme battle. British artillery ammunition expenditure had amounted to 89,000 tons of high explosive in six days, compared to only 25,000 tons during the first eight days on the Somme." This growing strength in artillery was ominous for the Germans, but they could still afford to be amused by Field Marshal Haig's order of 10th April to " keep the Germans on the run "; and by Allenby's assumption that all that was now required was the " pursuit of a defeated enemy." As soon as the timely German retirement took effect, then " the enemy would be forced to move his batteries and the essential masses of ammunition further forward. He would also have to get his reserves across a completely mud-and-water-logged, crater-torn battlefield. All this would have to be done before he could think of a further thrust against the

German front, which day by day became stronger." The British were learning (from their enemies and from their allies); they were becoming less bunglingly amateur, more professional; but the basic facts of life still had not occurred to them; and they were utterly without originality.

* * *

" The Pimple was an isolated knoll in front of the 4th Division. It had been strengthened by concrete pill-boxes bristling with machine-guns. The original bombardment passed over it without doing much damage. Consequently, it had to be by-passed as it could not be approached. However, heavier guns were brought to bear on it and fresh troops were brought up and the Pimple was taken in a snow storm two days later. I have heard it said many times, and even read, that the main battle was fought in a snow storm. Not so; I have no recollection of snow on the 9th," wrote Donald Patrick. " But there definitely was snow on the 11th." In fact, diaries do record snow flurries on 9 April, but mixed with sleet, hail, rain, and brief bursts of bright sunshine; it was not a snowstorm proper, in which the snow lies and gathers in a deep carpet. E. B. Elgood, who kept an informed diary (because he was serving, like Patrick, at a brigade HQ), wrote: " The 44th and the 50th Battalions, assisted by the 46th, attacked at 5.30 a.m. on 12th April in the dark, with a gale of snow, in knee-deep mud and slush; the wind and snow, however, helped the men along, and blinded the German machine-gunners, so that our men came on them suddenly, and fought it out with the Prussian Guard, and by 9 a.m. had taken all their objectives. The whole Ridge was now in our hands." Snow had fallen already on the previous day and was lying; as Captain Routh's log makes clear—he noted how plainly the trains, railway tracks, and used roads showed up on the frozen landscape below him.[1] But on the 12th, the weather was far

---

[1] Vimy was such a small-scale affair in area, that witnesses far apart frequently corroborate each other. e.g., Routh noted that because two German kite balloons had been brought down, none were up on the 11th, and that a British balloon had lost its string a few days before, and blew into the German lines, the occupants parachuting out. Elgood had this entered in his diary for the 9th: " One of our balloons got loose and was shot down by our guns, the crew parachuting down safely."

too bad for flying. Considering that machines from the squadron had been hedge-hopping at fifty feet on the 10th, this is a plain indication that visibility was near Zero and that a real blizzard must have been raging.

Major Crowell once wrote to Colonel Ralston: " I met two officers who served with the 44th Battalion and who were claiming the capture of Hill 145 by their battalion, and it turned out that they did not know the difference between Hill 145 and the ' Pimple '." The present author met this same error, actually on Vimy Ridge in 1965, and Colonel E. S. Russenholt, formerly of the 44th Battalion, said in the course of the elaborate C.B.C. programme series, *Flanders' Fields*: " The Pimple was just a little raise of ground, on the very left of our positions on the Ridge, and this is the raise of ground on which the Canadian Cross of Sacrifice is raised, at the very north end of Vimy Ridge." It is easy to see how the confusion arose. Two hills, both near the north end of Vimy Ridge, both taken later than planned, the 44th Battalion participating in both attacks, and, not to mince matters, neither of them a feature of striking visible importance in peacetime. Hill 145 was not really a hill at all, merely the invisible contour line marking 145 metres on the slow, gradual upswelling of the hogsbacked Ridge. The 85th Battalion had gone somewhere across the top on the night of the 9th, and the 44th Battalion had gone across to the north and down the other side to the Untere Hangstellung on the afternoon of the 10th. Where the hill began, or where it ended, would be hard to say; but it is today marked by the majestic twin white pylons of the Vimy Memorial unveiled in 1936 by King Edward VIII and President Lebrun, and perhaps the most moving war monument in Europe. The Pimple on the other hand was a little, wooded knoll jutting out into, and commanding, the valley of the Souchez; it was also known as Hill 120; and it was called by the Germans the Giessler Height.

The operation in which this was taken was backed by very heavy artillery support, and was launched in conjunction with an attack by the 73rd Imperial Brigade from the Bois en Hache to complete the clearance of the Lorette Spur. When it ended, all the higher ground would be in the hands of the British and Canadians; ground which uncounted Frenchmen had died trying to take. From right to left, the 44th, 50th, and 46th Battalions attacked in line, lost the barrage because of the hopelessly cratered ground, but stumbled on over obliterated trenches and were among the shaken and half-blinded German defenders. " With the gale and the snow behind us, there seemed to be not much trouble," said T. H. Hewitt of 46th Battalion. " It went right into their eyes, you see, and we were fortunate to get in on this storm. It kind of covered our movements." That was understatement, the 46th on the left took over a hundred casualties. " I don't think the Germans expected the attack, because they'd brought in a bunch of fresh troops, and they were all shined up and shaved and everything," said C. K. McDonald of the 50th. It was the 44th Battalion which actually took the Pimple. " It started to snow like the dickens, a regular blizzard," said D. M. Marshall. " I went maybe 100 yards past our objective, because you couldn't recognise anything. The mud was so bad that you couldn't stand still in any place. You'd have to move or you'd sink." Allen Hart, also of the 44th, has the last word: " We were very much annoyed that we couldn't go further, that arrangements hadn't been made for moving up the artillery and so on, because we felt that we had them on the run, that we could have moved a lot farther than we did, and we weren't in a particularly good position. That was the wrong side of the slope to be when it comes to facing an enemy."

In fact, the same old story. Having actually got the Ridge, with casualties now approaching 10,000, the staff couldn't leave well alone. They had to get down on the plain on the exposed side of the Ridge—or rather, the troops they were organising had to get down—and there, of course, the inevitable heavy continual drain of casualties began again, as bad as they had ever been when the troops had been sitting at the western foot of the Ridge. But worse still was to follow. If the plan had been more flexible, they could have had the defences of the Avion-Mericourt-Arleux line on the afternoon of the 9th, just by allowing the troops to walk forward. As it was, the Germans withdrew to this line on the night of the 12th/13th, and settled down in prepared defences in the fortified villages, at a density of one man to every six feet of ground. They, at any rate, did not intend to sit at the foot of enemy-occupied high ground and pay a heavy toll in lives for the sheer pleasure of doing so. The reaction of the British staff was to knock them out of those strongpoints and they therefore immediately began to unprepare a major attack. The careful arrangements which had made a success of Vimy were not made; the lessons learned five minutes before, forgotten.

But, at the time, the troops did not know that they were due for the slaughter, with the newly-captured Ridge as a springboard for it. They knew merely that it was going to be harder. " The Germans fooled them a few days later, by deciding that there was no use trying to hang on to the bottom of the hill and they pulled way back across the plain," said Elmore Philpott of 2 Division artillery. " And then we were left in the position of having to chase them out onto the flat plain, which was a much less advantageous position. I happened to be there the day that the Germans pulled back, and I was trying to convince my own Colonel and he wouldn't believe me, so I went down into the village of Vimy and came back and told him I'd been down myself and so I know they're gone. Then they did believe." It was, of course, the deadly obsession with ' ground ' which caused the disbelief. If an Admiral had claimed to have captured some sea, complete with several hundred waves on it, he would have been ridiculed; but no less ridiculous was the romantic (surely it came out of some adventure book for schoolboys?) fixation with the importance of territory, even when it was merely miles and miles of muck-all, and foreign muck at that.

Not that all the military mistakes were on the Allied side. Vimy and Arras cost von Falkenhausen his job, and rightly so. The Germans applied a ' British ' solution to the problem of firing him; he was kicked upstairs to become Military Governor of Belgium.

The taking of the Pimple was important for two members of No. 16 Squadron. They were found lying wounded in a German dugout in Givenchy, having been shot down on the 9th. Richthofen was still around, and it may have been on the 11th that, as George Alliston was advancing with the 7th Battalion, a single red plane came roaring over. The nearest officer shouted: " Now, if you want to do something for your country, *shoot*! " As there were only two Lewis guns per company, few did. Then, about the sixth and last (official) day of the battle, from their positions by the railway embankment, by now dazed and numb, not merely with the exhausting strain of battle, but of living in the open under appalling conditions, they witnessed a different kind of combat. The machines had such a poor performance, and flew so low and so slow, that the men on the ground could, and did, take a personal interest in these battles. This, far more than propaganda, was responsible for the wide fame of Richthofen. "Make no mistake, he was really something as a flyer," wrote Bracewell of the 102nd Battalion. "That whole group of flyers were so skilful and audacious, in both their defensive and aggressive tactics and manoeuvres, that our own troops on more than one occasion stood up and cheered them for their audacity. Our own flyers, due to their slow machines, were helpless against them, unless they waited upstairs and came down out of the sun on top of one." On this occasion, the fight was brief. Alliston recalled: "Soon after we got to the embankment that Red Devil Baron Richthofen drove one of our fighters down across the track from us. A young lad was the pilot, the observer was about thirty. Talk about guts. Those two were full of slugs and chirpie as they come. But it was a devil of a job getting them out and down to the ground. You must understand that we were without sleep and had very little food, so our limbs were moving with very second hand instruction by this time. We were relieved on Monday following the battle, 16th April. I went out at dawn, put up markers where I was to guide the boys to turn, and I passed one marker at night with all those tired men; some could hardly walk! They didn't have strength enough to swear at me; but we got out and for two days laid around too tired to sleep."

"We were a sorry sight, for filth and vermin," recalled James Gordon MacArthur of the 13th Battalion, as they marched out. "On the 13th we were relieved by the Cheshires," wrote Fawcett of the 78th Battalion. "We returned to our first cave under the Ridge, and there I took off my boots. My feet swelled so much, that when I tried to put them on again, I could not do so." Bracewell of the 102nd came out on the 13th, too. "After five days of attacking, counter-attacking and digging in, our battalion was relieved by a British regiment and we made our way back to rest billets. We did not stop for eats or anything else, we just hit the blankets! But next morning about eleven a.m., we had dinner in our blankets. Yes, Sir! we had dinner in bed and some of the boys cried a little, they could not take that sort of thing. And what a dinner it was, what a wonderful meal. By God, we could have kissed the dirty old cooks, that day! The cooks were always dirty, they couldn't be anything else, but they were a real bunch of white men all the way through."

*　　*　　*

By 14th April, the Canadians had moved as far forward as the Germans were willing to go back, and casualties had now topped the 10,000 mark officially. The line they now held was to be final, until late in 1918; but Haig was planning to advance it within weeks, in order to keep up British pressure in aid of Nivelle's offensive in Champagne, which had begun behind an immense barrage on 16 April and ended in the mutiny of the French army on 3 May, which was the date the Canadians once more went forward to the attack. This time, not against outdated defences, but the new 1917-style German model which had just ruined the French army for 1917, 1918, and 1940. Pétain was called in both times to try to repair the damage, and unfairly blamed on the last occasion (he was merely sorting out the pieces left over from other people's botched butchery).

One of Captain Routh's machines, flown by Mackenzie and Everingham, had been shot down by four Halberstadts on the 8th, while spotting for the artillery behind the German lines. On the 14th, their bodies were found on the captured ground close to the wreck of their machine, and on the 16th they were buried. Routh wrote soon after: " Mac was looking most peaceful and normal, being shot through the back and arm, but Everingham looked as though the end had not come quite so peaceably. He was not shot, but badly broken by the fall, some 4,000 or more feet. All around were hundreds of dead bodies, our own and Huns. One dead man was leaning up against a tree, another had a cigarette in his mouth, with a box of matches in his hand, and looked very much alive. Burying parties were at work, but it was a lengthy and tedious undertaking. ' Boom ' Trenchard (the R.F.C. General) came to inspect us on this day also. He told us that all the work we had done previous to the 9th had been the cause of the successful attack on the Vimy

Ridge. This was stale news, as we knew it. He also complimented
us on the amount of flying, especially in the rain and snow. He
told us he was sorry we had had casualties, and that our machines
were not quite all that could be desired, but a working machine
will never have a chance against a fighting scout, a subject upon
which we were all agreed." Talking to the author, Wing Commander Routh added: "You had to keep a good lookout for
hun fighters, because you had no protection. A B.E.2c had one
gun only, which fired ahead at a thirty degree angle from your
course. If you saw a hun, all you could do was try to keep him
off your tail. It was a mistake to try to escape by diving away."
On the 20th, Captain Routh was in a brief dogfight, diving onto
a German machine attacking a Sopwith, but his gun jammed
after ten rounds. On the following day, in his inadequate machine
with its inadequate and awkwardly placed armament, he was
supposed to act as fighter escort to a photographic B.E.2c from
'C' Flight flown by Jock Mitchell. Coming back from Lens,
they were jumped by the Richthofen Circus. Routh never had
the chance to identify his attacker, but saw two Albatros 'destroyers' go for Jock Mitchell and shoot him down in flames.
As it fell, a man jumped clear. There were no parachutes then
for pilots and observers, only for 'balloonatics.'. The first warning Routh had was the sound of bullets whipcracking into the
cockpit; one of them hit and smashed his hand. With his un-
injured hand, Routh twisted and turned to throw off this
obviously expert marksman, while his observer, Mackenzie, fired
burst after burst at the German, who wheeled with them until
he hit the engine, the petrol tank, and the camera of the wretched
B.E. Routh went down to a forced landing by the railway embankment at Vimy village, bouncing crazily over the shellholes,
but not overturning his machine. The gun could still fire, so
he told his observer to carry on firing, even if it was from the
ground. But his attacker sheered off and went for yet another
B.E., flown by Saunders; while the two Germans who had got
Jock Mitchell ganged up on an F.E. The F.E. went down, but
Saunders drove off his assailant, who was later shot down by a
British fighter. Routh saw this, while waiting in a shellhole.
After six months in the trenches with the 60th Rifles, and nine
months over the line with the R.F.C., it was his last fight; so he

had leisure to write down his account of it very shortly afterwards.

It was a very public affair, and as widely witnessed as a bullfight. But the present author was very pleased to see, after interviewing Wing Commander Routh in July, 1965, that ex-Sergeant-Major W. G. Smith, of 2 Division field artillery, had described what undoubtedly was this battle, in letters written previously, in March and April, describing from memory events which had taken place exactly forty eight years before. And only on one point—the number of German fighters—did his account disagree with Routh's, which was written at the time, within days in fact.

"It could not have been April 13th,[2] for that was only four days after Vimy, it must have been towards the end of the month," wrote Smith, correctly, for this dogfight was on the 21st. "He caught three of our old R.E.8 observation planes in front of the Ridge close by the ruins of Willerval, and he downed those three planes in minutes, even seconds. I happened to be almost underneath at the time. I had been walking from our wagon lines at Mont St. Eloi to our gun position on the plain east of Vimy Ridge. The dogfight took place at a slight angle, but almost above me, and the passing bullets were hitting the ground like wasps. It happened too fast to be scared, but afterwards I thought how foolish it was to have hugged the ground, for I was a bigger target prone than upright. I remember seeing three planes go down, but remember only one red plane. At the time I did not know of Richthofen, but I distinctly remember two bursts from that red plane after the R.E.8 was afire and the pilot out of the plane. The fight was about 1,000 feet up, and he made that pass at the pilot who had jumped from his burning plane, and the pilot already was a dead duck, for those wonderful people at headquarters refused to allow pilots to wear parachutes for fear they might jump out instead of fight (but made sure they were perfectly safe themselves). But don't let anyone tell you Richthofen was a Sir Galahad. In 1935 I spent some weeks with a German aviator who flew two-seater observation planes on the French front. He gave me the current German

___
[2] 13th April was the day that Richthofen with four companions attacked six of the new R.E.8s and shot down the complete formation in less than a minute.—see the 'Bloody April' chapter in *The Friendless Sky*, by Alexander McKee (Souvenir Press, 1962).

pilot gossip. Richthofen was much disliked by other pilots. He only wanted to build up his score and insisted on being the trigger man while others in his squadron must and did supply him with tail protection. What I saw that day verified that story."

As a feat of memory, an extraordinary achievement, as in the first place a dogfight is hard to follow, especially in its entirety. The confusion of three B.E.2cs with three R.E.8s is understandable; only an expert could tell them apart; but there were three, though only two of them were shot down, the third victim being an F.E. There were, however, three Albatross 'destroyers', not one, involved (probably an error of observation, for a scattered dogfight cannot be covered simultaneously by a single pair of human eyes). The German scout was shot down later, by which time Routh had been evacuated back as far as Thelus, which explains why Smith did not see it. But the vivid picture of the man jumping from the burning plane and the red air fighter making a firing pass had lasted intact down the years.

The judgment on Richthofen's methods is a harsh one, but the facts are correct. He was driven by the competitive spirit, and admitted it; and although he had begun by regarding war flying as a sport, he did so no longer, and indeed of a fight with a Spad which he had in the last week of April, 1917, admitted : " My man was the first who fell. I suppose I had smashed up his engine. At any rate, he made up his mind to land. I no longer give pardon to anyone. Therefore, I attacked him a second time and the consequence was that his whole machine went to pieces. His wings dropped off like pieces of paper and the body fell like a stone, burning fiercely."[3] Yet only a few months earlier, he had stopped firing as soon as his British opponent, a Vickers Gunbus, began smoking. " I felt some human pity for my opponent and had resolved not to shoot him down but merely to compel him to land. I did so particularly because I had the impression that my opponent was wounded." Even as late as 2 April, 1917, when he shot down an opponent behind the British front by Arras, he showed mercy. " I flew over him at an altitude of about thirty feet in order to ascertain whether I had killed him or not. What did the rascal do? He took his machine-gun and shot holes in my machine. Afterwards Voss told me that

[3] *The Red Air Fighter*, by Manfred von Richthofen, 1918.

if that had happened to him he would have shot the aviator on the ground. As a matter of fact I ought to have done so, for he had not surrendered." But after Vimy, Richthofen's attitude changed. Iveson was at the battery position over the Ridge when, he wrote, " The Red plane brought down one of the unfortunate boys and the German aviator, not content with having crashed the British plane, came down to a very low altitude and sprayed it with machine-gun bullets as it lay wrecked on the ground. This I thought was far from being a sporting action and particularly did I not appreciate it, as I myself had to take cover behind some sandbags to dodge the bullets." It was true, too, that Richthofen did have an organised squadron, which flew in stepped up layers and with rudimentary use of the concept which became standard in World War II, when all fighter formations became based on pairs, in which the No. 1 did the hunting and killing, while the No. 2 protected his tail. This, of course, was Richthofen's value precisely: that he was not a lonewolf hero like the British Albert Ball, but a leader of efficient fighter units. Vimy Ridge marked the point in his career when he ceased finally to be an amateur sportsman and became a professional fighter leader. The great odds he was facing probably had something to do with it. The odds also indicated the common sense policy of fighting mainly over the German lines and destroying the enemy artillery observation planes which were essential to the success of ground operations. The parallel is exactly with Keith Park, commanding the vital 11 Group in the Battle of Britain, who reprimanded a Polish squadron for pursuing German bombers across the Channel to France, with the comment: " This practice is not economical or sound now that there is such good shooting within sight of London."[4] Richthofen was shot down or forced down several times while fighting over his own lines, and survived to return to his squadron; had he fought over the British lines always, he would long ago have been out of the war.

This policy, virtually a ' must ' for the numerically weaker side in air warfare, served to enrage less level-headed men. One of these was the fiery and ruthless Welshman, Ira Jones, who

[4] *Strike From The Sky*, by Alexander McKee (Souvenir Press, 1960), p. 201.

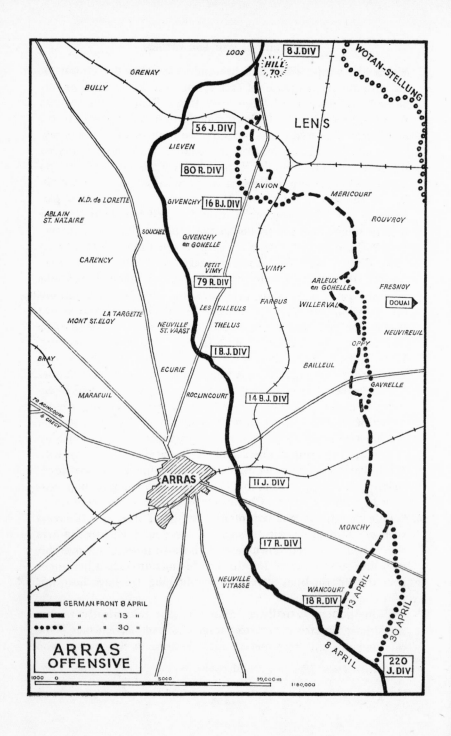

LOOS

8 J. DIV

HILL 70

WOTAN-STELLUNG

GRENAY

BULLY

LENS

56 J. DIV

LIEVEN

80 R. DIV

MERICOURT

N.D. de LORETTE

GIVENCHY

16 B.J. DIV

AVION

ROUVROY

ABLAIN
ST. NAZAIRE

SOUCHEZ

GIVENCHY
en GOHELLE

CARENCY

PETIT
VIMY

VIMY

ARLEUX
en GOHELLE

FRESNOY

79 R. DIV

FARBUS

WILLERVAL

DOUAI

LA TARGETTE
MONT ST. ELOY

LES TILLEULS

THELUS

NEUVIREUIL

NEUVILLE
ST. VAAST

OPPY

BRAY

1 B.J. DIV

BAILLEUL

ECURIE

GAVRELLE

MARAEUIL

ROCLINCOURT

14 B.J. DIV

TO AGINCOURT
& CRECY

ARRAS

11 J. DIV

MONCHY

17 R. DIV

NEUVILLE
VITASSE

13 APRIL

30 APRIL

GERMAN FRONT 8 APRIL

"   "   13   "

WANCOURT

"   "   30   "

18 R. DIV

ARRAS
OFFENSIVE

8 APRIL

220
J. DIV

1000   0   5000   10,000 m
1:80,000

was to become a leading fighter pilot claiming forty victories (half Richthofen's total), but at the time of Vimy was a humble observer in a B.E.2c of No. 16 Squadron. His first contact with Richthofen was over Vimy Ridge on 13 April, 1917, when " three red Halberstadt and Albatross machines " attacked in the blind spot from below and behind and put the B.E., upside down, into the British rear trenches. " Blimey, what would your muvvers say if they saw you naw! " was the greeting they got from the infantry. Jones, in his narrative,[5] attacks Richthofen's markmanship, courage, veracity, ability, and lack of sportsmanship. But a more balanced view is that of the Canadian, William Bishop, V.C., D.S.O., M.C., D.F.C., who came to England in 1915 with the Canadian Mounted Rifles, and, gaining his M.C. over Vimy Ridge on 7 April, 1917, by shooting down a German balloon, went on to be officially credited with seventy two victories. On 30 April, 1917, when still on the Vimy front, where the most spectacular battles of the aerial war were still taking place, he and his Major saw five Albatross scouts some distance away, then four more much nearer, and, " feeling rather bored with doing nothing," and believing them to be " Baron von Richthofen and three of his best men," attacked.[6] " Immediately the leader of the scouts did a lightning turn and came back at the Major, firing at him and passing within two or three feet of his machine. In my turn I opened fire on the Baron, and in another half-moment found myself in the midst of what seemed to be a stampede of bloodthirsty animals. Everywhere I turned smoking bullets were jumping at me, and although I got in two or three good bursts at the Baron's ' red devil ' I was rather bewildered for two or three minutes, as I could not see what was happening to the Major and was not at all certain as to what was going to happen to me. It was a decided difference from the fighting of the morning. The Germans seemed to be out to avenge their losses, and certainly were in fighting trim. It was a lightning fight, and I had never been in anything just like it before." When four Sopwith triplanes came in to help the two Nieuports, the four Germans broke off the combat. Their policy was to inflict losses, not take them. But both Bishop and the Major got

---

[5] *An Air Fighter's Scrapbook* (Nicholson & Watson, 1938), pp. 51-54.
[6] *Winged Warfare*, by W. A. Bishop, 1918.

back, although examining his Nieuport afterwards, Bishop found that his machine " had been very badly shot about, one group of seven bullets having passed within an inch of me in one place." The markmanship was so different to that described by Ira Jones, that one doubts whether his attackers really were from Richthofen's units, especially as he identified some as Halberstadts, whereas Richthofen at this time was using the Albatross DIII. In any event, as a leader in a fighter force outnumbered seven to one, where only discreetly timed aggression could pay, Richthofen more than earned his keep. Thirty victories in the thirty days of ' Bloody April ', over Vimy, Lens and Arras, the highpoint of his own personal score; plus the leadership of a highly efficient and high scoring unit. And most of their victories were real ones, confirmed beyond doubt, unlike the claims of less professional and experienced killers.

CHAPTER FOURTEEN

FRESNOY

The Assault From The Ridge

The British troops, in spite of undeniable bravery and endurance on the part of the men, have proved so clumsy in action that they offer no prospect of accomplishing anything decisive against the German Army in the immediate future. *General Erich von Falkenhayn.*

The 30th of April was also a day to remember in the ' Admiral's Battery ', 145 Heavy. " About the end of April we were in position just on the right of Thelus village with our guns a few yards from the road," wrote Iveson. " For some reason, probably arising from his naval training, the Admiral declined to camouflage his guns and there they stood in their pits, bright and gleaming, the Admiral caring nothing so long as they were in good order to give the Bosche occasional broadsides. Between our battery position and the village (on the left flank of the battery) the Admiral collected a considerable amount of ammunition at the end of the track of the light railway which had delivered it. This dump comprised from 3,000 to 4,000 rounds and was not covered up or concealed—in any way. The Admiral was far from well, but the most we could persuade him to do was to go to Wagon Lines for a few days rest. On the morning of April 30th, therefore, Captain Forbes was in command at the guns. Shortly after breakfast a German aeroplane came over and seeing, no doubt with delight, such an inviting target of guns and ammunition, he did not hesitate to call up one of his batteries with the result that shortly after the aeroplane's appearance, a 5·9 shell exploded a little distance from the dump. Forbes immediately asked the two Royal Flying Corps wireless men, who were attached to us for co-operation in aeroplane shoots, as to the nature of the signal given by wireless by the German 'plane to its battery and, on being informed that the 'plane had signalled that the round was about 100 yards from the target, Forbes immediately and very wisely ordered the gunners into their ' funk ' trench, about six feet deep, which we had dug behind the guns. Scarcely had the men got under cover than a second round burst in the middle of the dump, and this time the Flying Corps men informed us that the 'plane had signalled ' Z.M.' to its battery, which was the German for ' O.K.'

" The dump of course commenced to explode, and we therefore worked our way round to a position higher up Vimy Ridge, and some 200 or 300 yards away, from which point of vantage we watched the show. Immediately the Bosche saw smoke coming up over the Ridge he re-doubled his efforts and it was not long before an 8-in. battery joined the 5·9 battery in the work of destruction, and shells began to pour into the dump, which now commenced to explode in no uncertain fashion. When the strafe began, Bradshaw was in his canvas bath after a night's Observation Post duty, and whilst in nature's costume he was dumbfounded and very much annoyed, to see the roof of his shelter blown across the trench. As we were moving away from the dump, some of the chaps laughed at something which was happening behind me, and told me with great gusto that I had only just missed being knocked down by a piece of light railway line, about eight feet long, which had pursued me but missed its mark. Bradshaw, after hastily dressing, was called to the temporary command post in the ' funk ' trench to answer a telephone call from Brigade. The message was from the Adjutant: ' How many men of Jewish faith have you on your strength? The return must be sent off immediately.'

" With interest, and I suppose a good deal of dismay, we watched the show from a position of comparative safety. The whole neighbourhood became deserted, as no troops for a considerable distance liked to approach the dump. A 4·5 Howitzer Battery near us suffered the loss of one of its guns, which was blown out of its pit; whilst the 6-in. Howitzer Battery behind us, having opened fire in an endeavour to silence the Bosche guns, suffered the loss of an officer, who was killed by a shell while giving orders. It was under these circumstances that we were amazed to see an officer in a cloth cap walking about our battery position. We enquired from each other who the perfect idiot (or some stronger term) could really be, but on the figure being identified as that of the Admiral, Forbes and Bradshaw ran up to him to give him warning. Personally, I did not see the fun of exposing myself for his benefit, as clearly considerable danger existed, but Forbes and Bradshaw were both cool customers and thought it their duty. They met with a very different reception from what they expected.

" Their entreaties to the Admiral, that he should come away at once, were met by a calm and collected enquiry to Forbes, as to whether the gun which had just come from ordnance had been duly calibrated. Forbes replied, ' Come away, sir, come away—the dump's going up again ', but the Admiral persisted in his question, and would not move. It was under these circumstances that the dump exploded once more. Forbes told me that Bradshaw jumped into a shellhole, and that he himself squatted down on his heels in an endeavour to make himself as small as possible, almost wishing the earth would swallow him up. But whilst whole shells came raining down near by, he looked up to see that the Admiral, with his riding crop on his hip, was gazing upwards and coolly watching the shower descend. Miraculously, none of them were hit, and the Admiral was eventually persuaded to come away. This is only one instance of his extraordinary powers of self-command and his entirely reckless disregard of shellfire."

But the Admiral was not the only one. " Some of the field artillery drivers, either out of sheer bravado, or because they did not like going over the Ridge at night towards the batteries, passed our guns near Thelus one evening on their way over the Ridge in broad daylight. The inevitable happened and, after being greeted by showers of shell—it must have been a delightful target for brother Bosche—they ignominiously galloped back over the Ridge, being not only badly scared but having learnt a lesson which I do not suppose they ever forgot. Such tactics might have been safely employed in the old days of the Zulu campaigns, but are sheer madness in modern warfare against a European state. We were equally fatuous in our visits to the Observation Post in the early days following the capture of the Ridge, for each day about the same time either myself, or one of the subalterns, would walk towards the summit, followed by two telephonists laden with rations and gear and then, after appearing on the skyline for a moment, would walk down the reverse slope in full view of the enemy; and jump into the trench immediately adjoining the place from which the observation work was carried on. About ten minutes later, the officer from whom we took over duty would jump out of the trench—at the same point where we had jumped into it—followed by his two telephonists, and would return to the battery in the same way and by the same route; and then, when the Observation Post was badly strafed, we would solemnly announce, ' They must have found out our position '.

" From the post one could see Douai cathedral. I could see the clock on the tower but could never make out the time from it (although I tried to do so), and I have seen, perfectly clearly, German horse batteries manoeuvering in a distant field, possibly twelve to fifteen miles away and well out of range of our guns. I remember sending some shells after a German wagon which moved very rapidly out of sight. Apparently the wagon driver, having reached safety himself, informed a horseman who was about to cross the small portion of the road over which we had observation, for, when he appeared, that horseman rode like John Gilpin with head down on his horse's neck, and at such a speed, that I laughed so much I could not get a round off at him before he was out of sight. He might have been riding a Derby winner and, no doubt, imagined that for once he was riding for his life. Actually, he was reasonably safe, because at that range it would have been a lucky shell which would have caused him any damage."

The most revealing incident concerning the Admiral happened later, when Iveson was ordered to take two guns forward to Vimy village and emplace them by the railway embankment. Being on the reverse slope of the Ridge, this was a notorious hotspot, and Iveson had frequently seen 4·5 Howitzer batteries, and also 18-pounder field batteries, having a very warm time there. It was, in fact, asking for trouble, damage, and unnecessary casualties; and, to cap it all, Iveson got only one of his guns emplaced before daylight—the other bogged down hopelessly where the road had been most hurriedly reconstructed over the carcase of a dead horse. By daylight, it was still there, hurriedly camouflaged in the open. Then the Admiral came up, " I expected a very considerable strafe, and thought I was acting tactfully, when I expressed my regret at the unfortunate incident.

The Admiral, however, took another and entirely different line but managed, of course, quite naturally to retain very complete command of the situation. ' You must take me, Iveson ', he said, ' for an unjust Commanding Officer '. I said, ' Not at all, sir, not at all '. Whereupon he somewhat severely insisted that that must be the case, or I should not have thought of apologising for something which would have happened had he been in charge of the guns himself. Then he went on to say, ' Bombardier Grimes was killed at the rear position this morning, Iveson '. I replied, ' I am very sorry ', whereupon the Admiral responded, ' Sorry, why are you sorry? Probably he is better off than either you or I. I don't mind if I am killed today ', (I thought to myself: No, but you are old enough to be my father,) ' The only thing I should like to live for, would be to see what happens in Europe after the war. It will be a very interesting situation '. Since the war, I have often thought how true were the Admiral's comments, but at that time post-war days seemed remote indeed.

" Life in Vimy village was not very pleasant. There was no proper flash cover for the guns, with the result that our position was soon spotted, and practically every time we opened fire, it was only a matter of minutes before fire was opened on us. Moreover, mosquitoes abounded, and bit one. It was under these circumstances that we were visited by a Church of England Padre whom we nicknamed ' Splendid ', on account of his frequent use of that adjective. I remember being tickled when, on his first visit, he drawled, ' Splendid, splendid, and the men are *so* happy '. This Padre, however, was a wonderfully good plucked one. Later in the war, he became attached to the staff for a time, and when Albert was badly bombed in the great retreat of March, 1918, he was one of the few of the staff who emerged from the cellars to attempt to rescue the horses. Later, at his own request, he became attached to an infantry unit with whom he went over the top no fewer than three times in one day and, on being attacked by a Bosche officer, succeeded in shooting the Bosche first, as well as taking part in the capture of some German prisoners.

" We were often ordered to fire in the evening, in an attempt to silence a battery which was firing shrapnel with clockwork fuses at our balloon over Neuville St. Vaast. The occupant of the balloon was no less a person than Captain F., a well-known character in that part of the line." (This was the Captain F. with the undying hatred for the staff, who used to say that the best sight he saw on the Somme was two Brigadier-Generals lying dead in the same shellhole.) "The Germans had invented a wonderful clockwork fuse which permitted of extraordinary accuracy in firing at long range, and regularly at 6 p.m. the battery opened fire on the balloon with remarkable success. Practically once a week one could see shrapnel burst closer and closer to the balloon from which F. would make a hasty exit in his parachute. It would not be long before the balloon came down in flames, but fortunately without ever enveloping F. therein. F., however, was entirely undaunted and immediately went up once again in a new balloon, only to suffer the same fate a little later."

The fate of the infantry was even more uncomfortable, stuck out on the miserable plain, for no particular good reason, hard up against the ruined villages held and heavily fortified previously by the Germans. "From the 29th April to May 6th we were in the line, halfway between the Ridge and Avion," wrote Private Fawcett of the 78th Battalion. "This was where our line was only about sixty yards from the German front line and we had to enter our trench on hands and feet, again downhill, and Heinie was using machine-guns and rifle grenades. In this trench was a dead German on the parapet to the rear and, when the wind was right, the smell was pretty bad. We occupied a German dugout and the first night, when I tried to sleep, I was awakened by being bitten in my ear by a rat. Thereafter we had to sleep with our groundsheets over our heads, being lulled to sleep by the patter of their little feet." They ate the living, and they ate the dead. It was a time when history favoured rats. And, far away from the sight of the staff (and the newspapers and the politicians) men came to an understanding with each other. "We were told, when going into the line on the outskirts of Lens, that we could go into No-man's-land and go to a certain house (either before or after midnight—I don't remember which), where there was a pump; and we could replenish our water and no one would bother us. We on our part allowed the Germans to do the same—if we went before midnight, then they would go after midnight. Otherwise, both had a long trip to the rear of several miles. The arrangement worked fine when we were there, and when their turn came, we could hear the Germans talking as they went to get their supplies. When we took prisoners we generally stripped them of watches, etc. We did the same to the dead—revolvers, telescopic sights, binoculars, all were taken and traded, if and when a shortage of money occurred; but we did turn over Identification, so it was a two-way street. In the main, except for robbing them, we did not abuse any prisoners we took. We were not good and we were not all bad. Our feelings were those of countless others who participated: the inward conflict of those who were called on to fight and yet who had previously shunned the idea of killing, feeling that it was repugnant to their natures."

Maurice Bracewell, private in the 102nd Battalion, was also stuck out on that desolate plain. " We advanced (later in May) to the next sizable height of land, which in our case was a triangle of railway embankments. It was known as the Triangle Front. Such a position was naturally a very uncomfortable and miserable one for infantrymen, as they were constantly under enfilading fire from the sides as well as to points well in the rear of their positions. We looked down into the rubble of the outskirts of Lens, a sizable French town; the Power House was just behind the German front positions and was used as a strong-point and as a sniping and observation post. One Canadian battalion that had strong political affiliations had made two sorties against it, but were turned back each time by the German defenders." Then occurred an incident in some ways typical of the Canadian Army. " A member of our battalion called Kelly went missing, as did three other men while in the line on that front. Kelly was notorious for the time he spent in detention and for his lust for rum, his own or anybody else's. Finally, he showed up again, scrounging along the trench looking for rations. When asked where the hell he had been, he floored his questioner with the reply: ' We're over in the Power House, but we've got no rations '. They had captured it on their own, and put in sand-bag blocks to keep the Germans out. These blocks were officially known as Kelly's blocks from then on, but poor Kelly was killed the next trip in on that front."

For some odd reason, GHQ had thought the Germans were about to retire behind Lens and earlier staged an attack by the British 46th Division which was north of the Canadian Corps. This was the division which had helped hold Vimy Ridge in 1916, and the 5th Sherwood Foresters were sent over on 23 April to encourage the Germans to leave. They were stopped dead, in both senses of the word. All along their new front line (their old III Position), the Germans had one man to every six feet of contested ground, and had heavily reinforced their artillery. For the usual muddy reasons, no breakthrough was possible, and merely to advance a short distance must require a long and heavy artillery preparation, such as had just ' blown ' the Germans off Vimy Ridge. Even this was unlikely to succeed, for the Germans had now set up their new ' defence in depth ' system on this front also; and its effect in blunting any conventional attack could well be judged, for copies of the two German textbooks concerning it had already fallen into British hands. Furthermore, Nivelle's offensive was failing, and known to be failing, so that ample German reserves would shortly be available. And lastly, because Haig had no grip on the forthcoming battle, by a series of muddled and confused arrangements and compromises, the assault was to be neither a true night attack (in which, in any case, the British were thoroughly untrained), nor yet an attack at dawn, but a shambles at 3.45 a.m. with the full moon well behind the troops so as to light them up as targets for the German machine-gunners and riflemen. The battle was to engage the attention of the Germans for two weeks, from 3 May to about mid-May, or so it was planned. On the south of the fourteen mile front, where General Gough's Fifth Army was engaged, it did so; and this particular affair was to be used afterwards by instructors as a shining example of how a battle ought *not* to be conducted; the Australians, who took the brunt of it at Bullecourt, never forgave Gough and his airy-faery staffwork. In the north, what was called the Third Battle of the Scarpe, lasted twenty-four hours, during which the Canadian Corps momentarily captured Fresnoy. All the British official historian could find to say about that, was that it was " the relieving feature of a day which many who witnessed it considered the blackest of the War."

Albert C. Woodward, private of the 27th Battalion, witnessed it; but he did not witness it long. " The troops at Arras were to make the longest advance. The 27th Battalion, being on the extreme left, was the pivot; we only had 200 yards to go. Zero hour—and out in the open, immediate heavy barrage from both sides, and subjected to angle fire as well as fire from directly in front. I was wounded in the leg, and with other casualties got back to the trench; eventually out over Vimy Ridge, in a light railway car hand-pushed by Canadians and German prisoners; later that day, field hospital; then Calais, Dover, various hospitals; and returned to Canada, December, 1917; honourable discharge, February, 1918. That battle on the 3rd of May was fierce. The 27th Battalion was able to advance only a very short distance. We went in the line roughly 850 men; less than 250 answered ' Roll Call ' when they came out."

Captain Nisbet, writing for the *Ypres Times* in 1936, commented : " In the month following Vimy the division was engaged in heavy local fighting in the Douai Plain, its terrible casualties being out of all proportion to the results obtained. The vital necessity of careful preparations before attacks were launched did not seem to be appreciated by those who controlled our destinies. After the lesson of April 9th one may well demand why? For ' Vimy ' was from first to last an outstanding example of the way to win a battle. As such it should have been regarded. As such it cannot fail to interest future students on the Art of War."

Ex-Battery Sergeant-Major W. G. Smith, of the 2nd Division's field artillery, remembered everything about it except the exact date. " There was another foolish, senseless exposure of troops somewhere around May, at Oppy and Fresnoy. I know, because some stupid jackass placed the entire 2nd Division field guns on a flat plain a mile east of the Ridge. German observers in the buildings across the line could see what was in your mess-tin. They knocked us to pieces when the attack started. This was not unexpected, but the poor bloody infantry did not get the barrage nor were the machine-guns kept down. They got nowhere and took awful casualties. Properly handled, our troops could have beaten the enemy almost from the beginning. Our regimental and junior officers were splendid men, and early in the war—

before too many casualties had occurred—I believe the British and Commonwealth armies had the best regimental officers in the world, and the poorest high commanders. It is not fair that Haig should take all the blame. His army, corps, and division commanders were little better, for the security of their appointments, of their promotion, rested entirely on their agreement with Haig's ideas. The battle arrangements were purely criminal, time and time again, perpetually the same mistakes. We who had long service, became similar to dumb animals, obeyed orders, no longer caring what happened. Don't you ever believe those lying bastards who are still trying to put a good face on four years' stupidity. As near as I can gather, from reading as many military accounts as I have been able to get, the real good men of the B.E.F. were mostly killed or incapacitated at Le Cateau, First Ypres, and in particular that awful winter of 1914-1915, those remaining got it at the Second Ypres, Loos, Givenchy and the Somme. (I refer you to Montgomery's Memoirs, p. 72). It was the free-loaders and the foxy boys, the toadies and the flunkeys who mostly made up the staffs, and they had caution and self-preservation ingrained in their very souls. If the commanders had been any good, they would not have accepted the false information fed them by staffs who were never near the battle. The value of the commanding high ground at Vimy was largely wasted by putting the infantry out on the Douai Plain and against a row of fortified villages. No combat man could ever understand such antics. The Battle of Arras was lost when Nivelle's French army failed. The continued pressure of the British at Arras only hurt themselves."

Iveson, having been on observation post duty the day before, slept right through the Canadian attack on Fresnoy on 3 May. But he quite failed to manage this on the 8th, when the Germans retook it. The 5th Bavarian Division was supported by seventeen batteries of heavy guns and twenty seven batteries of field guns, plus the fire of neighbouring German divisions. The British field artillery, having already been sacrificed, could make only inadequate reply to the torrent of fire which raged for two days before the attack. " At 3.45 I was awakened by a noise and the feeling that the whole world was coming on top of me. The

Hun had commenced a counter-attack on Fresnoy and was firing on our battery in the hope of silencing us. A 5·9 shell had fallen—with the rim of the shell hole about a foot from edge of the trench opposite where I was sleeping, throwing down upon me a large quantity of soil from the side of the trench. The command post was, of course, wrecked. My diary records: ' I got my limbs free and crawled out through the hole made by the shell, in my shirt, trousers and socks, through the mud and rain. My boots and blankets were buried. A nasty experience but very thankful to be still alive. Anyhow, I carried on and fired 140 lyddite into him before being relieved at 8 a.m.' The whole business was an unfortunate one, for the Germans re-took Fresnoy that night, being assisted by the fact that the blow was struck during the slight confusion which resulted from the taking over of that part of the line, that same night, by a new division; and by a mist which prevented the infantry S.O.S. rockets from being seen by many of the artillery observation posts. The telephone communications had been interrupted by repeated breakages of the lines by shell fire, and although the linesmen did their best to effect repairs, the German artillery was too active to allow communication to be restored. A young machine-gunner, who rested at the battery observation post on his return from the fight, sobbed bitterly when he described the slaughter of his two friends, both wounded, who raised both hands in vain and were bayoneted in cold blood."

The line was back where it had started from, with heavy losses to both sides, in a scramble of attack and counter-attack, of which 3rd and 8th May were merely the highlights. Although the new Sopwith Camels, S.E.5s, and Spads were beginning to replace the obsolescent Nieuports and Pups, the German fighter squadrons were still, in the early half of May, maintaining their aggressive defensive, and, in spite of anything said to the contrary, boldly crossing the line to cover their own artillery observation planes. The Canadian infantry units, who were there all the time, and suffered the results, complained that the Germans were able to work unmolested in the air. In fact, they did more than complain: they opened accurate fire from the ground and knocked down some of the fast German fighters, including one flown by the ' Red Devil's ' brother, Lothar von Richthofen. The Baron himself, Manfred von Richthofen, was on leave in Germany, being feted by the Kaiserin, von Hindenburg, and von Ludendorf, in what he dryly referred to as the ' Holiest of Holies ', and being allowed to shoot a bison by the Prince of Pless. Which forced the comment: " The Bialowicz forest has suffered terribly through the war. Many a magnificent bison, which ought to have been shot either by the Czar or by some other monarch, has been eaten by German musketeers."[1] However, he noted: " I had not yet passed eight days of my leave when I received the telegram: ' Lothar is wounded, but not mortally '. That was all. Inquiries showed that he had been very rash." Manfred did not approve of his brother's methods; by now, from a sloppy start with the cavalry and a lot of chivalrous larking about in antique aeroplanes, he had developed into a drilled, ice-cold killer during the actual operations for which he received his wages. " My father discriminates between a sportsman and a butcher," he wrote. " The latter shoots for fun. When I have shot down an Englishman, my hunting passion is satisfied for a quarter of an hour. Therefore I do not succeed in shooting two Englishmen in succession. If one of them comes down I have the feeling of complete satisfaction. Only much, much later I have overcome my instinct, and have become a butcher. My brother was differently constituted." And less successful. The month he paid for his lack of professional care was May and the place was over the Canadian lines near Fresnoy. Flying a ' pair ' with Allmenröder, he picked on " a lonely Englishman crawling about, one of those hostile infantry fliers who make themselves particularly disagreeable to our troops. We molest them a great deal. The Englishman thought he would avoid a duel, and he disappeared likewise by a plunge. My brother, without hesitation, plunged after. He didn't care at all whether he was on one side of the lines or the other. He was

---

[1] The custom continues. In Germany, in 1945, the present author was denied a shot, because the boar was a (British) Major-General's boar, and could be shot only by a marksman of that rank. He had to content himself with a Sergeant's boar (300 lbs.).

animated by a single thought: ' I must down that fellow!'[2] That
is, of course, the correct way of managing things. Now and then
I have myself acted that way. However, if my brother does not
have at least one success on every flight he gets tired of the whole
thing. When very low, he obtained the right position, and could
shoot into his shop window. The Englishman falls. After such
a struggle, especially at low altitude, the average mortal has no
longer the slightest notion of his position. On that day it happened that the air was somewhat misty. My brother quickly
took his bearings, and only then discovered that he was a long
way behind the front. He was behind the Ridge of Vimy. The
top of that hill is about 300 feet higher than the country around.
My brother, so the observers on the ground reported, had disappeared behind the Vimy height. It is not a particularly pleasant
feeling to fly home over enemy country. One is shot at and
cannot shoot back. It is true, a hit is rare. My brother approached
the line. Low down, one can hear every shot that is fired, and
it sounds then very much like the noise made by chestnuts which
are being roasted. Suddenly, he felt that he had been hit. That
was queer to him. My brother is one of those men who cannot
bear to see their own blood. Somebody else bleeding would not
impress him very greatly, but the sight of his own blood upsets
him. He felt how his blood was running down his right leg in
a warm stream. He noticed pain in his hip. The shooting continued, but at last gradually ceased. Now he had to be quick, for
his strength was rapidly ebbing away. He saw a wood and next
to it a meadow. He made straight for the meadow and switched
off the engine. At the same moment he lost consciousness. My
brother was in a single-seater. No one could help him. It is a
miracle how he came to ground. He recovered consciousness only
in hospital." Another irony, Lothar was to be credited with killing Captain Albert Ball on 7 May, just before he himself was
to be shot down from the ground; and the proof that the pilot

[2] The irony here is that Richthofen was writing for a popular German
wartime audience, most of whom would not know what he was talking
about; but Ira Jones would have known. To screw up his courage to
sticking point by reference to his hero, Albert Ball, he had this notice, on
cardboard pinned to his cockpit instrument board:
" He must fall.
Remember
Ball."

he engaged was not Captain Ball (who was flying an S.E.5) but an unknown in a Sopwith triplane, is contained in Manfred's own book. The claim was not dishonest, for after the S.E.5 had hit the ground, the wreckage was unidentifiable; only the pilot's identity disc and battered cigarette-case showed that this particular airman was Ball, from what Richthofen called 'The Anti-Richthofen Circus', No. 56 Squadron, R.F.C., which had in fact been sent to the Arras front, with the latest type of fighter, to counter Richthofen's 'Flying Circus'.

Originally, only Manfred von Richthofen painted his machine all-red; but as this made him too conspicuous, around this period the other machines of his squadron were painted mainly red, but with some other colour jazzed in. His command at this time was a squadron only; there were many other German fighter units concentrated also on the Vimy front, many of them equally aggressive and skilful. It may have been one of these, rather than a member of the 'Circus', that Maurice Bracewell, private in the 102nd Battalion, helped to shoot down behind Vimy Ridge about mid-May. "We were in the old pre-Vimy artillery positions, halfway between the old reserve lines and the Ridge. The 'plane had a 'spade tail' (probably Albatross DIII); it was camouflaged with wide brown marking on a khaki background; there was no red on the plane that I noticed, but I understood it was one of the planes of the famous 'Red Knight' German fighter squadron, the only one of that squadron I ever saw brought down, and I have a small piece of the fuel line still. That pilot had shot down all the observation balloons along the Ridge, five of them, one after the other. They all burned, and the observers in the baskets under them had to jump for it. After shooting down the balloons, he turned and flew back along the Ridge, gunning the observers as they swung in their parachutes. He apparently thought it was a lot of 'Fun'![3] That is where we troops got busy and grabbed anything we could lay our hands on, chiefly Lewis machine-guns, resting them on the shoulders

[3] Strictly speaking, he may have thought it was his duty. Balloons were cheap, trained artillery observers were expensive, and as they were parachuting down on their own side of the lines, could be presumed not to have surrendered. In 1944 and 1945, the R.A.F. over Germany did a lot of 'popping off of pilots on parachutes'. Unpleasant, but logical, it made military sense.

of a man in front and blazing away at the German 'plane as it flew up and down the Ridge machine-gunning the balloon observers. He was flying so low, that the anti-aircraft batteries were helpless. No one knew who knocked him down, and it must have been sheer luck, but *we did knock him down.* He came down awful fast, but managed to straighten out, and crash-landed but did not burn; that machine was quite shot up. When we swarmed around the 'plane on the ground, all our interest was centred in *who* was inside. I was not one of those who actually seized the 'plane, but I was well up among those who surrounded it. There was some heated conversation going on, and the German pilot was very cocky. Among the first words he uttered, was a demand as to where was the nearest Officers' Mess? One of our boys was so incensed at the brazen conduct of the man, that he hit him in the mouth with his fist—and was promptly arrested for his trouble." To be fair, there was no future in shooting down balloons; they were too well protected by anti-aircraft guns; and William Bishop had got the M.C. just for shooting down a single German balloon, an indication of the magnitude of the feat performed by this man.

After that, Maurice Bracewell went up to the Triangle Front, where the Canadian Corps made a small advance towards Avion, over the ground where the British had failed on 23 April. And there the line settled down more or less for good, apart from the attack on Hill 70 in August. Then, as Bracewell recollected, " We went out for divisional rest, following which we set off north. When we had marched far enough to shake off any possible local interest in our movements, we were picked up by a convoy of London buses, and headed for Ypres and an exceedingly grim affair that was known as ' Passchendaele '. Our ranks were very considerably thinned when we returned." The secrecy was because Canadian Corps had now established such a reputation that the Germans, too, regarded them as ' storm troops '. Where the Canadians went, there was trouble; there the British meant business.

CHAPTER FIFTEEN

POST MORTEM

What Price Vimy?

A journalist once asked: "What price Vimy?" He meant, how many lives did it cost. The question can be asked in another sense; and answered many times, at different levels, in varying perspectives. The immediate reaction is contained on the front page of the Continental Edition of the *Daily Mail* for Tuesday, 10 April, 1917. Vimy Ridge beat Arras in type size and prominence; it was the story of the day. Column two was devoted to quotes from the *Petit Parisien,* under the headlines: FRENCH PRAISE : HANDSOME TRIBUTES TO BRITISH TROOPS : VIMY RIDGE THE KEY TO LENS AND DOUAI. The French military commentator had written: "The British Army Corps were ordered to attack at dawn. Our Allies formed up and started to storm the formidable line before which so many attacking waves had died since 1914. The strongest position was the first, the Vimy Ridge, and those who know the ground will understand the reason. The Ridge, which runs from the south of Givenchy to the fringe of Farbus, dominates the whole plain of Lens and Douai. The Germans were bent on holding it. Since the days when their armies after the Marne and after the Yser took to trench warfare many engagements, many battles indeed, were fought by the French with the express object of taking this position, considered as the key to Lens and Douai. It was on December 17, 1914, that the French troops under the command of General Maud'huy dashed for the first time against the Vimy Ridge. They were unable to get beyond the approaches to Carency. Five months later, on May 9, 1915, General Pétain led his famous 70th Division against the German positions. This was the first great attack supported by a strong artillery force. General Pétain's division succeeded in a very short time in capturing a whole series of positions. It climbed the slopes of Hill 119. Some patrols went as far as Vimy. At the end of the battle we kept Notre-Dame-de-

Lorette and the fringe of the white road. A month afterwards, on June 16, a new attack took place on a longer front. We occupied Ablain-Saint-Nazaire. But the coveted Vimy Ridge was not reached. Further operations were necessary. Preparations went on actively for three months and on September 25 a great offensive began under the direction of General Foch on a fifteen mile front. The battle was extremely hot. An appreciable advance was made, Souchez fell and even the small fort of Givenchy. But still the Vimy Ridge was strongly held by the enemy. This fighting taught the need of strong artillery. The great battle of Artois in September 1915 was prepared by heavy artillery, numbering in all no more than 400 guns. For the present offensive, thousands of heavy guns for several days prepared the tremendous operation which began yesterday. What the French troops could not succeed in doing, because their artillery was inadequate, the British have accomplished. The Vimy Ridge has been snatched from the Germans, and this a great success, indeed a splendid victory, of which our Allies have the right to be proud and on which they are to be heartily congratulated."

In the next column was a British war correspondent's report, headlined: FLOWER OF GERMAN ARMY BEATEN : MAIN BRITISH WEIGHT THROWN IN : SOMME BATTLE SCENES ECLIPSED : 130 MILES AN HOUR AEROPLANE ATTACKS. Underneath, W. Beach Thomas wrote phrases calculated to please Sir Douglas Haig and impress the British public. " At 5.30 this morning Sir Douglas Haig, by deliberate choice, threw the weight of the British army against, perhaps, the strongest force of the enemy ever yet concentrated in such a fortress. Near Arras our troops leapt to the attack in the midst of such an artillery fire as the world had never seen. It was accompanied by an onslaught of strange weapons of war (i.e., tanks), while overhead, as soon as the clouds allowed, our aeroplanes, moving at 130 miles an hour (sic), rushed to tackle any German machines they could find. I saw all the Somme battle, but never such a scene as this. The shock was beyond all grasp of mind or senses, though I saw it only as a panorama from the neighbourhood of the guns and not the trenches. We attacked in order to wreck the flower of the German army, who fled, in fear of rout, from the Somme battlefield. Would they, or would they not, face us here and put it to the touch? Would

Rupprecht of Bavaria take the challenge of General Allenby and General Horne, Sir Douglas Haig's chief lieutenants in the battle . . . The men whistled, cheered, and jested up to the end. ' Make Bank Holiday of it', was their form of encouragement to one another. A wild west wind blew a frozen rain, and they charged as strong an earth fortress as Europe holds, but they went merrily on their charge to adventure all the same."

One must not blame Mr. Beach Thomas, he would not have long held his job had he not presented a cheery and efficient picture; and correspondents were not then allowed in the front line. For the matter of that, the tone and arrangement of the report are identical to those used by the British press throughout the Second World War also; there is a drill for it, just as there is for forming fours. And, it must be wryly admitted, perhaps the British propaganda machine's greatest admirer was then serving on the opposite side of the lines—L/Corporal Hitler, A. Later, he determined to have an equally efficient apparatus himself. Nor was the French press one whit behind. The working journalists (as opposed to the military commentator quoted, whose assessment was sober and accurate enough) were writing in superlatives also: " Not merely an immense number of prisoners—more than 6,000—but also a gain of ground which recalls the glorious days of the beginning of the Somme offensive, or of the French offensive in Champagne in September, 1915." Yet, even under the barrage of cheer and hate, some of the too-trustful public of 1914-1918 could still keep their heads, as a letter in the same edition of the *Daily Mail* showed:

Sir,—In your issue of Saturday you publish a letter signed " F.H.C." and headed " Denounce the Criminals," in which " F.H.C." tells your readers that " the blood of Edith Cavell still cries for the avenger's heavy hand." Edith Cavell—of noble memory—in her last words said: " This I would say, standing as I do before God and eternity: I realise that patriotism is not enough. I must have no hatred or bitterness towards anyone." I cannot agree with " F.H.C." that these dying words constitute a cry for vengeance.

Paris.   A. A. WARDEN, M.D.

When the soldiers came home, in 1918 and 1919, with their tales of what the reality had been like, there was a change in pub-

lic opinion; a violent reaction to having been fooled. The
Generals and the politicians wrote their memoirs. The lid came
off. Lloyd George wrote of the generals ". . . inexhaustible vanity
that will never admit a mistake . . . individuals who would
rather the million perish than that they as leaders should own
—even to themselves—that they were blunderers . . . a narrow and
stubborn egotism, unsurpassed among the records of disaster
wrought by human complacency . . . this insane enterprise . . ."
Churchill likened Haig to a " great surgeon before the days of
anaesthetics, versed in every detail of such science as was known
to him; knife in hand, intent upon the operation; entirely removed in his professional capacity from the agony of the patient,
the anguish of relations, or the doctrines of rival schools . . . If
the patient died, he would not reproach himself." When, in
1952, an edited version of Haig's *Private Papers* was published,
Lord Beaverbrook judged that Haig had committed professional
suicide a quarter of a century after his death. Others, such as
Montgomery, who had been junior officers at the time but became
Field Marshals themselves, determined never to make the same
mistakes; above all, never to fail to admit a failure or a half-
success in time, and pull out; they were to be very cautious with
their infantry. And the next generation, whose fathers and
grandfathers had fallen in Hari-Kari assault after Hari-Kari
assault, became cynically determined never to be so used themselves. If the only way out of the army was through Berlin
well all right, but they were going to see Berlin personally, if it
could be managed at all.

As a military achievement, the battle of Vimy Ridge became
lost in the general revulsion against the Great War, as it was
then called. Wrote W. G. Smith: " Vimy Ridge, as part of the
greater Battle of Arras, was primarily an artillery battle. But the
lesson of Vimy was lost on the High Command. The artillery
so smashed the country that communication was virtually at a
standstill in the forward areas. The High Command, despite
the Somme and Vimy, still persisted in these methods. That was
the last lesson of Vimy. So it became of a piece with Loos, the
Somme, Passchendaele, senseless actions whose aftermath ruined
Britain so that to this day she had never recovered. You cannot
kill 700,000 stallions of the best breed, out of a small country,

and then expect the nation to hold up. If we are honest, that is what really caused the French failure in 1940. Napoleon killed or incapacitated the prime stallions. Joffre, Foch and a few others finished the job in 1914-1918. They have been breeding to their scrubs ever since. What does one expect? Haig and his commanders dissipated and destroyed the finest army Great Britain ever did, or ever will, put into the field. The army of 1918 was not a shadow of the army of 1916. I believe this deterioration was shown in the mass surrenders of Burma, Singapore, Tobruk, etc. I think our people of 1914-1918 would not have quit so easily. It seems to represent lack of faith in leadership—or maybe the young men of 1940 were smarter than we were; they would not die needlessly."

George Alliston echoed him: " Just a big loss to us; the people who are the backbone of the country in peace or war. As regards the value of the Battle of Vimy, I am sending you a photograph, showing the type of prisoner we took in the next scrap, Hill 70, on 15 August, 1917; I am the one with the rifle. The flower of the German army, too, fell during 1915-16-17, and Vimy was proof that their strongest point could be taken." That old photograph was indeed eloquent, and helps to explain much that followed in Germany after the war, with the best and the bravest wiped out.

There is nothing very surprising in this. It was the standard view of the 1920s and 1930s; the story told by the men who came back, to their families and friends. It was rooted in the common experience of millions all over Europe, on both sides of the trench lines. And as the twenties gave way to the thirties, it was increasingly felt that the political and governmental scene was noticeably the poorer for the men who ought to have been there, but were not there, were mouldering instead in the soil of Flanders and the Somme. There was a sense of decay in society, of outright decadence; and to this widespread feeling the rise of the dictators, promising a brave new world, was mainly due. That was not the mood of 1914, and there were deeper reasons for slaughter than merely generals baffled by a task mentally beyond them. Europe was very fat and prosperous in 1914, glowing with energy and wealth; like a well-fed horse that needs exercise; they chose this way of working it off. They went to war, cheering. Haig was not unrepresentative; a poor representative, certainly; but a representative all the same, of a secure and special society, bent on suicide.

The Admiral would be a more attractive, a fairer, representative of that society. Brave, just, and—within limits—professionally efficient. Liking war perhaps rather too much for the good of his men; and treating it too much as an interesting hobby —a series of unique, unexpected experiences. Not a business. Like some of the officers—like some of the wagon-drivers, even —treating the clash of mighty industrial juggernauts as simply a slightly scaled-up Zulu campaign. Because some representatives of the society which committed suicide still remain, retaining the old, comfortable attitudes, but without the ferocious determination which underlay the real thing, there still linger here and there defenders of the attrition policy who see these battles as glorious feats of arms. But this is a sentimental, weakly comfortable point of view; an emotion rather than a thought. Recalling the long-ago era of, " I'm sure dear Mr. Baldwin knows best," only too rapidly followed by, " I'm sure ' Tiger ' Gort is only just waiting to strike " (as Rommel's panzers poured past Vimy Ridge), and lately trying to cite Montgomery's Normandy plans as an example of a policy of bull-headed, Haig-like attrition.

The official historians who published between the wars were limited to considering the immediate details rather than the background implications, and their verdict on Vimy was unanimous. It was a limited success. The British historian (1940) criticised the inflexibility of the time-table, which prevented a much greater exploitation of the victory; he saw an opportunity wasted. The German historian (1939) was slightly more impressed; the British had achieved " a purely tactical, but nevertheless quite remarkable, success "; but pointed out that the artillery tactics used positively guaranteed that such a victory could never be more than local.

For Canada, however, Vimy Ridge was something special. Already, in 1922, France had ceded to Canada " in perpetuity " 250 acres of the Ridge, on Hill 145; and in 1925 the construction of the great Canadian Memorial began. It took some ten years to build, and was made of stone from a Roman quarry on the Dalmatian coast; the base was 200 feet square, the twin pylons rose 125 feet above the Ridge. The design was by a Toronto sculptor, Walter S. Allward, who wrote of it: "At the base of the strong impregnable walls of defence are the defenders, one group showing the breaking of the sword, the other the sympathy of the Canadians for the helpless. Above these are the mouths of the guns covered with olives and laurels. On the wall stands the heroic figure of Canada brooding over the graves of her valiant dead; below is suggested a grave with a helmet, laurels, etc. Behind her stand two pylons symbolising the two forces—Canadian and French—while between, at the base of these, is the Spirit of Sacrifice who, giving all, throws the torch to his comrades. Looking up, they see the figures of Peace, Justice, Truth and Knowledge, etc., for which they fought, chanting the hymn of peace. Around these figures are the shields of Britain, Canada and France. On the outside of the pylons is the Cross." And on 26 July, 1936, the monument was unveiled by King Edward the Eighth with the words, "It is a memorial to no man but a memorial for a nation."

This was literally true, in two ways; both political. Firstly, by linking Britain and France, it helped towards the unity of a nation made up of elements from both countries. Secondly, and more important, it symbolised the point at which Canada, from a colony, had become a nation. Field-Marshal Haig had grumbled that the Canadians appeared to be regarding themselves as Allies rather than as members of the Empire; and Canada had had to fight to keep her divisions together in one Canadian Corps. The crest of Vimy Ridge represented the exact place where the young nation had proved her fitness by taking on a hitherto impregnable fortress held by soldiers of the foremost military nation in Europe, and capturing it in a matter of hours.[1] After Vimy, the Canadian Corps was to be commanded

[1] In the present state of the British Empire, this sense of hard-earned achievement, of having come of age through trial by ordeal, may be hard to understand, when superficial respect, such as a seat at the United Nations, is automatically accorded to any two men and a goat in a mud hut, following the ceremonial presentation of a chromium-plated Cadillac and a golden bed (debited to the American taxpayer) plus an honorary airline (paid for by the British taxpayer); and when nations which could not repel an assault by a platoon of South African mercenaries threaten war on all and sundry and demand that their human dignity be respected. But it is superficial; the Empire has been so weakened by two wars that the take-over bids by greater powers are in progress, and this is merely the more ludicrous aspect of that process.

by a Canadian, General Sir Arthur Currie; and in the Second World War there was to be a Canadian army, commanded in the decisive Normandy campaign by General Crerar, who had been present at Vimy as a Major. That was appropriate, for his army was born there.

The first Vimy Day of the Second World War called forth some anxious comment in Canada. Under the headline, WHAT OF THE MONUMENT? one newspaper commented: " Three years ago Edward VIII, in the presence of a great crowd of Canadian pilgrims, dedicated the Canadian Memorial on Vimy Ridge, that spot of Canada in France. Now again war has come and more Canadians have answered the call. One wonders what fate has in store for this Canadian monument. Will it survive this new conflict? Only time can tell!" It survived, in fact, to be strikingly represented on the 1944 Christmas Card printed by General Crerar's First Canadian Army Headquarters, which had just advanced some 300 miles in a matter of months. The lessons had been learned. " The sudden and rapid eruption " of a front had been achieved, by the Germans in 1940 and the Western Allies in 1944; and all Vimy saw of the fighting was the dust of the armoured divisions as they poured through. And the doctrines used stemmed from the ideas of an officer of the Tank Corps, J. F. C. Fuller, and dated back to 1917. One wonders what the old Canadian Corps could have achieved, if it had been saved for Cambrai instead of Vimy Ridge; and if the implications had been realised early at GHQ level.

After the Second World War, some British writers said openly what has been only thought about before. Writing of 3 May, 1917, the " blackest day of the war," where only the Canadians had succeeded, one of them commented: " To some witnesses it seemed that there was an extra ounce of verve in a Canadian assault, carrying with it an abundance of new ideas: not least was the sensation of 'sharing' displayed by all ranks. It has never been clearly explained why Canadian troops could sustain heavy casualties and retain their efficiency, whereas British troops suffered a debilitation from heavy losses, particularly if they lost heavily in officers. One reason for this disparity could be the difference in the basic education given by the two countries. For a more general educational establishment in Canada drew the classes closer together, welding a closer relationship between all ranks and prompting a genuine competition for the lead based on merit: the educational system in Great Britain, by designing a more rigid system of leaders and led, held the two apart and inhibited the sharing of knowledge and even the passage of information . . . Certainly as the war progressed the superior training and performance of the Canadians (and for that matter of the Australians, who were not dissimilar in many ways) became increasingly obvious, noticed as forcibly by friend as by foe."[2] In fact, the English class system, dating probably from the Norman conquest, showed a two-way weakness. Up, by placing too heavy a premium on birth and marriage (Haig only kept his job because he married in the right direction), with far too little regard for ability. Down, by actually convincing people that this or that subject—say, common map-reading, which any child can do—was too ' deep ' for them; and, far more seriously, causing them to combine in conscious opposition, so that any initiative came to be looked on as treason—currying favour with the ' boss class '. In effect, there was one General Soldiers Trade Union, which encouraged restrictive practices, as a matter of self-defence. The number of officers who cottoned on to this, in the Second World War at any rate, must be as near Nil as makes no matter; but it was so.

It was perhaps less so in Scottish units, where all round educational standards were much higher. Here, Sergeant David Layton, M.M., a very professional English soldier indeed, may be quoted: " How strange but true it is that certain characteristics of peoples always show up clearly in war. The Canadians, Australians and New Zealanders bubbled over with confidence—they were fearless but sadly lacking in discipline. The French—volatile—but so undisciplined and always dirty. The Italians—a complete washout. The Germans—disciplined to a degree—but like the Curate's Egg, good and bad in parts. The English—phlegmatic but never know when they are beaten. The Scotch—dour and determined—the only troops who loved using the bayonet. The best fighting troops in the world and the most feared at close quarters." No one can be quite unbiased in this

[2] *The Shadow Of Vimy Ridge*, by Major Kenneth Macksey, M.C. (Kimber, 1965).

matter, rightly so. Perhaps the condemnation of the Italians is too sweeping; possibly the amount of initiative allowed in the German army (to junior officers and senior NCOs) rather discounted; certainly the Canadians could, and did, give an outsider the *appearance* of being lacking in discipline, but to an insider, it was clearly not so. For going on the rampage with drink inside them, the Scottish units were by far the worst— English, Germans, Belgians, they would take them all on.

And yet, with the Canadians, the most marked characteristic seemed to be that they did not really care if they had an officer along or not; they did not have to be told. If there was an opportunity, they would take it; with no shadow of a trace of feeling that they were either acting 'above their station' or 'trying to keep in with the bosses'. If it needed doing, they did it, whether the officer was dead or not, and without bothering to find out if perchance the General approved. The affair of Kelly's Blocks is a nagging case in point. Because they did not like the trench that had been given to them, Kelly and his three companions went and took the German strong-point, which offered better housing, and without so much as asking 'by your leave' either of the Germans or their own superiors. Kelly was a rum-lover and a thief of other people's rum, before he died on the Douai Plain before the Vimy height. Which makes more than appropriate the marble plaque in the Memorial Chamber of the Peace Tower in Ottawa, on which the inscription reads:

> *They are too near*
> *To be great*
> *But our children*
> *Shall understand*
> *Where and how our*
> *Fate was changed*
> *And by whose hand*

SOURCES

The foundations of this book consist of about 80,000 words of eye-witness testimony, supplied by more than 100 people; plus many official and unofficial histories, acknowledged in the text. Help not so acknowledged, and for which the author is especially grateful, came from a number of organisations. The Canadian Broadcasting Corporation kindly made available the script of "The Battle of Vimy Ridge," the ninth programme in their series "Flanders' Fields", for which they recorded in all some 600 veterans (57 for Vimy), with the ultimate intention of placing these recordings in the Public Archives at Ottawa. The series was produced by Mr. J. Frank Willis, originated by Mr. A. E. Powley, and researched by Mr. Frank Lalor. Another half-a-hundred witnesses came through the helpful co-operation of the editors of *The Legionary*, national magazine of the Royal Canadian Legion, *The British Legion Journal*, and the *C.V.A.U.K. Quarterly News Magazine.* In addition, the Canadian Veterans' Association of the United Kingdom were most helpful in arranging for the author to attend the 1965 Vimy Ridge Memorial Parade in Whitehall and the 1965 Battlefield Tour, which enabled him to visit the Ridge in company with some of those who had fought there.

The number of people who went to considerable trouble to assist the author is too great for individual mention; but some were particularly important. Lieutenant-Colonel Harwood Steele gave invaluable help in recreating the atmosphere and characters of the Canadian Corps. And among those who were able to produce diaries or other contemporary and near-contemporary evidence were Major J. A. Iveson, Major Harvey Crowell, Wing Commander E. J. D. Routh, Captain H. U. S. Nisbet, Walter Bapty, M.D., Mr. E. B. Elgood, Mr. M. W. Bracewell, and Mr. W. I. Fawcett. Many others were obviously in possession of notes and Regimental Histories. It was clear also that the great majority of those who offered to help did so because they took a keen professional interest in the matter and research had not proceeded very far before the author became aware that he was in good hands; recollections were very much more detailed and precise than might be expected after such a lapse of time. The reason was, that the events under review were regarded as important by the witnesses, at the time and after, and therefore they were retained in the memory. Gus Sivertz, for instance, was unlikely to forget what happened to him that day, and his narrative is still horrifyingly vivid. There was also the possibility, on several occasions, of checking one man's memory against another man's diary, when both were describing the same incident, and the case of Captain Routh's last fight witnessed by ex-Sergeant-Major W. G. Smith, is illustrative of the comparative accuracy attained.

Absolute accuracy in describing any very rapid sequence of exciting events is, of course, impossible—even five seconds afterwards. The exact order of events sometimes becomes confused, and the limitations of the restricted field of vision of the human eye, plus the fact that it focusses, just like a camera, and like a camera, blurs and ' suppresses ' both foreground and background, must be remembered. This latter is not merely the cause of much conflicting evidence in the Courts during traffic accident cases, but is also responsible for causing many of the accidents in the first place. There is, further, the fact that the human brain cannot concentrate at full efficiency for much more than twenty minutes, even in favourable conditions; weariness, cold, and hunger all detract from efficiency. Eye-witness evidence is therefore fallible in this respect: not in the accuracy of what was actually noticed, but in the fact that what was seen was part only of the picture. Hence the need for many witnesses, rather than a few. These limitations accepted, the author believes that the present reconstruction of the battle is tolerably accurate, although for the final judgment on that, the verdict of the veterans will have to be awaited. For the author's own comments, of course, he bears sole responsibility. Few striking disagreements with official histories were revealed; but, in any case official ' documentation ' is also based on the testimony of human beings, not computers, and with some extra hazards built in (as some of the present witnesses rather pointedly remarked).

A final word of thanks must go to my wife, who translated for me reams and reams of ' General Staff German ' from the two German official histories; and in Gothic print, what's more! With her, it now ranks as a translation task to equal the putting into German of a Transatlantic treatise on " D.D.T. Dusting in Rat Infestation," the previous all-time brain-cracker.

The witnesses whose testimony has been either quoted, or used as background information, are listed below. C.B.C. recordings are marked *; and where I have contacted an original C.B.C. witness for a very much fuller account, they are marked **. My thanks to them all.

1st Canadian Division

Col. H. S. Cooper*	3 Bn	1 Bde
A. E. Wright*	4 Bn	1 Bde
F. C. Bagshaw*	5 Bn	1 Bde
Jack Pinson*	7 Bn	2 Bde
George R. Alliston	7 Bn	2 Bde
Dr. T. G. Caunt*	8 Bn	2 Bde
Major-General D. M. Ormond*	10 Bn	2 Bde
Vic Armstrong*	10 Bn	2 Bde
Col. W. S. M. MacTier*	13 Bn	3 Bde
J. Gordon MacArthur, M.M.	13 Bn	3 Bde
H. Campbell*	14 Bn	3 Bde
Arthur Bonner*	16 Bn	3 Bde
Lt.-Col. R. S. Robertson*	16 Bn	3 Bde

2nd Canadian Division

Harry Secord*	18 Bn	4 Bde
Wilfrid Derbyshire	19 Bn	4 Bde
W. M. Nickle*	21 Bn	4 Bde
Capt. Royden Barbour*	25 Bn	5 Bde
F. MacGregor*	25 Bn	5 Bde
Cecil R. Macleod	25 Bn	5 Bde
Albert C. Woodward	27 Bn	6 Bde
L. R. Fennel*	27 Bn	6 Bde
Brig. Alex Ross*	28 Bn	6 Bde
Major H. R. H. Clyne*	29 Bn	6 Bde
G. Scott*	29 Bn	6 Bde
Elmore Philpott*	Div Arty	
W. G. Smith	Div Arty	
George Stebbing	4 Fd Coy, Can Engrs	

3rd Canadian Division

E. B. Elgood	Sigs	HQ 7	Bde
Brig. W. J. Home*	R.C.R.	7	Bde
N. G. Dean*	R.C.R.	7	Bde
Major Eric B. Finley*	42 Bn	7	Bde
Col. Rev. Dr. G. Kilpatrick*	42 Bn	7	Bde
Lt.-Col. A. G. Pearson*	PPCLI	7	Bde
R. G. Barclay*	PPCLI	7	Bde
George T. Hancox*	PPCLI	7	Bde
Percy Boxall, M.M.	49 Bn	7	Bde
Donald Patrick, M.M.	Sigs	HQ 8	Bde
Roland Irwin, D.C.M.	1 C.M.R.	8	Bde
M. E. Parsons, M.M.**	2 C.M.R.	8	Bde
Gus Sivertz**	2 C.M.R.	8	Bde
G. Dorman*	2 C.M.R.	8	Bde
Col. H. C. McKendrick*	4 C.M.R.	8	Bde
A. E. Barker	4 C.M.R.	8	Bde
Thomas Wildridge	4 C.M.R.	8	Bde
Fred Walker	Div Arty		
Arthur W. Frost	8 Coy, Can Engrs		
Charles W. Evans	Div Ammo Column		

4th Canadian Division

Col. W. S. Wilson*	38 Bn	10	Bde
Col. E. S. Russenholt*	44 Bn	10	Bde
D. M. Marshall*	44 Bn	10	Bde
Allen W. Hart*	44 Bn	10	Bde
A. A. Galbraith*	44 Bn	10	Bde
Tom Goodall*	44 Bn	10	Bde
T. H. Hewitt*	46 Bn	10	Bde
Bob Brown*	46 Bn	10	Bde
C. K. McDonald*	50 Bn	10	Bde
Major-General V. W. Odlum*	Sigs	HQ 11	Bde
H. J. Ayris	Brigadier	HQ 11	Bde
Alex W. Jack*	54 Bn	11	Bde
Stanley Baker*	54 Bn	11	Bde
Maj. Harvey E. Crowell**	85 Bn	11	Bde
Tommy G. Adams*	85 Bn	11	Bde
M. W. Bracewell	102 Bn	11	Bde
Walter Bapty, M.D.	M.O. 102 Bn	12	Bde
Col. Arthur Farmer, O.B.E., M.M., E.D.**	M.G. Coy attd 102 Bn	12	Bde
W. Nicholl	72 Bn	12	Bde
R. Crowe*	72 Bn	12	Bde
John Cornish	3 Can M.G. Coy attd 72 Bn	12	Bde
Lt.-Col. S. Scott*	78 Bn	12	Bde
Archie Brown*	78 Bn	12	Bde
Gordon A. Mitchell	78 Bn	11	Bde
W. I. Fawcett	78 Bn	11	Bde
D. C. Higgins*	Div Arty		
H. L. Smith	11 Fd Coy, Can Engrs		

5th Imperial Division

Capt. H. U. S. Nisbet	1 R. West Kents	13 Bde
David Layton, M.M.	15 R. Warwicks	13 Bde
Arthur Baguley	1 Cheshires	15 Bde

Canadian Light Horse

S. J. Duffield	4 Tp ' B ' Squadron
D. H. Keay	3 Tp ' C ' Squadron
F. M. Morton	3 Tp ' C ' Squadron
Thomas Smith, D.C.M.	4 Tp ' C ' Squadron
Rev. G. H. Hambley, M.A.	M.G. Support (dismounted)

Canadian Corps Artillery

Brig. R. J. Leach*	
W. L. Jenkins*	2 Siege Battery
Major J. A. Iveson, O.B.E., M.C.	145 East Cheshire Heavy Battery
G. P. Roberts	No. 9 Gun, Royal Marine Artillery Howitzer Brigade
General Raymond Brutinel*	Canadian M.G. Corps

Miscellaneous Canadian

Lt.-Col. Harwood Steele, M.C.
Brig. J. S. Stewart*
Brig. The Hon. G. R. Pearkes*
Maj.-Gen. H. S. Worthington*

51st Highland Division

Major H. Smithson	' C ' Bty, 64 Army Brigade RFA

Royal Flying Corps

W/Cdr E. J. D. Routh	Flight Cdr No. 16 Squadron
Frank Millard	Photo Section, Nos. 11 & 23 Squadrons
W. T. Gibbs	No. 59 Squadron

Observation Balloons

Lieutenant W. G. Dreschfield	No. 36 Balloon Section

C.Y.M.C.A.

Mrs. Daisy M. Barnard	Bramshott & Witley

British, 1916

F. B. Raisin	5 Bn Sherwood Foresters
Frank R. Crossland	Yorkshire Hussars Yeomanry attd R.E.

1st Bavarian Reserve Division

Michael Volkheimer	Bavarian Reserve Infantry Regt No. 3.

INDEX

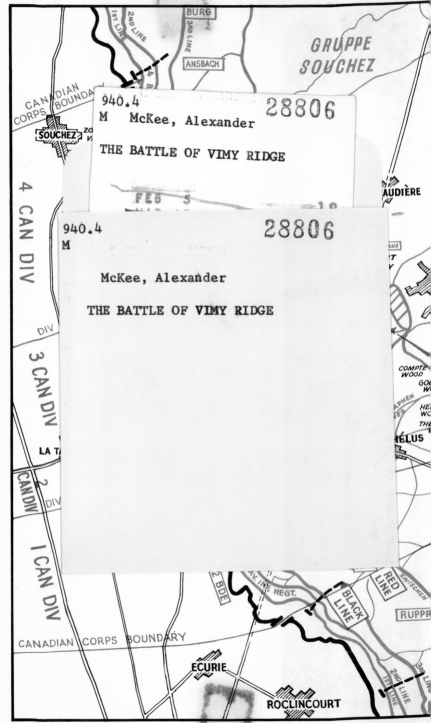